The Washington Pay-Off

AN INSIDER'S VIEW OF CORRUPTION IN GOVERNMENT

Robert N. Winter-Berger

A DELL BOOK

Published by
DELL PUBLISHING CO., INC.
750 Third Avenue
New York, New York 10017
Copyright © 1972 by Robert N. Winter-Berger
Reprinted by arrangement with
Lyle Stuart, Inc., Secaucus, New Jersey 07094
Printed in the United States of America
First Dell printing—October 1972

To my dearest Mother,
and to Toni Strassman,
without whose inspiration and moral support
I could never have written this book.

Contents

George Meany of the AFL-CIO is fawned over in Washington . . . , but not entirely for his intellectual brilliance. And not because he can deliver labor's votes. He can't. What he can deliver and does deliver is political money.

The present U.S. Ambassador to Great Britain was not appointed for his contributions to creative foreign policy and diplomacy . . . but for his contributions of political money.

This is not new. Back in the fifties, the President appointed one of his big contributors—ambassador to a country—when it was found he didn't even know where the country was.

So, jobs like that, and Washington influence, are in effect for sale. All it takes is money, . . . political contributions in election years. If you give enough, Washington's favors can be yours—influence, flattery, social success, invitations to swell affairs . . . and even ambassadorships to countries with nice climates and cheap servants. Perhaps more important—influence on domestic policy, such as taxes, affecting your own business and income.

Running for office has become incredibly expensive, and candidates have to get money somewhere. The Democrats get a lot of it from the unions, and the Republicans a lot of it from rich individuals and corporations.

No doubt there are some rich unions and people of charitable soul who will give money expecting nothing in return, but they are scarce. A big political contribution usually is seen as an investment. It's a scandal everyone admits. . . . But it's worse now because running for office costs more.

Public cynicism about politics and politicians already runs high. If this is not cleaned up, the political system will come apart . . . with influence, dominance, and even control put up for sale to the highest bidder.

David Brinkley
NBC Nightly News

November 16, 1971

The first time I met John W. McCormack, the then Speaker of the House of Representatives, he took me on a tour of his elegant offices in the Sam Rayburn Wing of the Capitol. McCormack didn't use these offices much, spending most of his time in his office directly across the corridor from the House chamber. But this was the end of the day, we had business to discuss, and he wanted me to see the layout. As the tour ended and we were standing near the double doors of the main entrance, Speaker McCormack put a hand on my shoulder and pointed to the paneling above the doors.

"And there is the motto of this place," he said. I looked at the paneling and saw nothing. I glanced at McCormack, waiting for the punch line. Still pointing, and in a monotone as though he were reading, he said: "Nothing for Nothing."

I got the message, which was as direct as it was witty.

This happened in January 1964. I had just been hired as a public-relations consultant to get McCormack some national publicity that might win him the

Democratic nomination for Vice-President at his party's convention that summer. The job lasted only a few weeks, but it led me into a new career that lasted five years, during which time I was frequently in both of McCormack's offices. In both of them, the motto was the same.

In 1966, as a Washington lobbyist, I paid a friend $500 in cash for a personal introduction to House Minority Leader Gerald R. Ford, Republican from Michigan, and it was a good investment. Because it was good, it subsequently cost me another $500 in cash, plus a number of favors. Jerry Ford knew about this, and it did not faze him. In one of our early conversations, Ford had occasion to say: "In Washington, money's the name of the game. Without it, you're dead." He was telling me something I already knew.

I also knew that it was "dirty" money, paid out by the millions each year by individuals, groups, organizations, and businesses who wanted to get something done in Washington—or not done or undone. Technically, such money is supposed to be a campaign contribution for the Senator or Representative who pulls the strings that produce the magic, and much of it is. But there is also a heavy spillover into the pockets of the Congressman or someone on his staff, or the contact in whatever government agency may be involved. The favor, to label it euphemistically, may not be in itself illegal; but trying to get it done legally, through the labyrinthine channels which now exist, would take much longer, and cost much more; and even then it might still not get done. Money overcomes these obstacles; and, as a result, the most politically favored people in the country are the monied people.

Standing in the midst of all the financial transactions,

collecting the money from the vested interests, taking his cut and then doling out the rest to his contacts in government, is the lobbyist, the key figure in all the wheeler-dealing that permeates every level of the federal government. Without the lobbyist, corruption in government would be minimal, simply because the efforts to corrupt would be so disorganized, so diffuse. On the other hand, a lobbyist who has two or three good connections in high places in Washington can represent an unlimited number of clients, achieving more for them in five minutes than they could achieve for themselves in five months. In Washington, it is the quality, not the quantity, of one's connections that counts, and, as with anything, quality costs more.

The political cesspool produced by Washington lobbying is nothing new. In 1788, James Madison wrote, in the *Federalist Papers:*

> A landed interest, a manufacturing interest, a mercantile interest, a monied interest and many lesser interests grow up of necessity in civilized nations and divide them into different classes, actuated by different sentiments and views. The regulation of these various and interfering interests forms the principal task of modern legislation and involves the spirit of party and faction in the necessary and ordinary operations of government.

Today, almost 200 years later, the need for controls on the front men for the vested interests is so much greater because, very simply, the abuses are so much worse.

In 1946, Congress made a half-hearted effort to put some controls on lobbyists by passing the Legislative

Reorganization Act. The act defines a lobbyist as one who indirectly or directly attempts to influence passage or defeat of any legislation before the Congress, and it provides some ineffective regulatory machinery to supervise and govern the activities of the lobbyists themselves. The law was all right as far as it went, but it did not go far enough. It left open many areas where a lobbyist could "operate" without any regulation whatsoever. The law merely requires registered lobbyists to report their contacts with members of Congress, their expenses, and the political contributions they make directly to the campaign funds of Congressmen. But a lobbyist does much more than try to influence legislation. What happens on the floor of the House or the Senate is only a small part of his job, unless one of his clients' interests are affected by some legislation before either House. Actually, the main part of a lobbyist's job in practice is to circumvent the legislation that already exists, to cut through red tape, to get priorities and preferences for clients who have no legal rights to them. To achieve this, he needs the cooperation of one or more members of Congress—the more influential they are, the fewer he needs—who will write the letter or make the telephone call to the government department or agency handling the matter. He gets this cooperation by paying for it—preferably in cash. It is in this expanded area of operation that the work of a lobbyist can become sinister because he can operate without any regulation whatsoever, without any record of what he has done, and without any evidence of how he bought his way through.

The 1946 act requires a lobbyist to register as such with the Secretary of the Senate and the Clerk of the House of Representatives and to submit to both a quarterly report of his expenses and fees. In most reports, the expenses listed are comparatively low and the fees listed are rarely accurate. In the first place, a lobbyist doesn't operate on his own money. The campaign donations a lobbyist makes are most often his clients' money, and the 1946 act does not require him to report these. The lobbyist can, of course, make his own donation or buy a certain number of tickets to his pet Congressman's fund-raising dinner. But when he does, either he is trying to make a good impression on the Congressman or he doesn't want his quarterly report to make him look suspiciously inactive. In regard to fees, a lobbyist usually puts a price on each request a client asks of him, the price depending on how many government employees will have to be paid off. Because the lobbyist alone knows the number and amount of the pay-offs, the amount of the fee he keeps for himself is strictly his own business. Thus the fees in his quarterly reports scarcely need reflect the actual amount of money involved. There are some 1,400 registered lobbyists in Washington, and they are only the tiny part of the iceberg that shows. Washington is so infested with nonregistered lobbyists that lobbying can be defined as the fourth—and invisible—branch of the United States government. But in spite of the advantages offered by nonregistration, being registered gives a lobbyist a certain respectability, which enables him to go ahead and use the 1946 act as a license to corrupt public officials.

I became a lobbyist out of a chance meeting with Nathan Voloshen. Some of the stationery in Voloshen's New York office identified him as an attorney. In fact, he had been admitted to the practice of law in Maryland, but he was not a member of the New York bar and could not practice in New York. However, Voloshen shared an office with a lawyer named Stanley Singer at 6 East Forty-fifth Street in Manhattan, and over the years, when I had occasion to visit the office, I often heard Voloshen and Singer discussing legal technicalities of matters Singer was handling. Euphemistically, Nathan Voloshen could be described as an "internuncio" between all departments of the federal government and anybody who wanted something done— or undone—by one of these departments. Actually, he was a Washington lobbyist, although one of the nonregistered variety, and therefore he did not submit the required quarterly reports on earnings and expenditures. He operated out of the office of House Speaker John W. McCormack, his close friend for over twenty years.

I was first introduced to Nathan Voloshen in November 1963, but I really met him two months later, in January 1964, through mutual friends. Voloshen was then in his mid-sixties, a short, compact man, expensively dressed, outgoing, affable, likable. When he learned that I was in public relations, he turned to me and asked:

"What can you do for John McCormack?"

"What does he need?" I asked.

"A youthful and virile national image," Voloshen said, and his expression showed that he knew this would be difficult. He went on: * "With Kennedy dead and

* Here, as elsewhere throughout the manuscript, I have relied on my memory, which is excellent, as well as on notes I had made, to register conversations of which I have first-hand knowledge. In many cases the conversations are verbatim as they occurred. Even when they are not, the sense and substance are strictly accurate.

shen back on the phone, McCormack took me for the tour of his office. It was then that he showed me the invisible motto over the door.

I immediately went to work. I managed to persuade *The Saturday Evening Post* to do a series of articles on little-known but powerful members of the House, which obviously would have to include the Speaker. Voloshen asked me to make sure that the series also included Adam Clayton Powell, a close friend of his, and I did. I was also able to place features about McCormack with the Hearst and Scripps Howard newspaper chains. For these services, Nathan Voloshen initially paid me $1,500.

During the few weeks of legwork the job required, I had free access to Speaker McCormack's "hot line" office. Usually Voloshen was there, either phoning or conferring with somebody. Afterward, Voloshen would comment to me that a certain deal was going well or that another had been successfully completed. Voloshen lunched at McCormack's table* in the House dining hall every day he was in Washington, and when I was in town I often joined him. Generally Martin Sweig was there. McCormack himself was present on an average of twice a week. Occasional other guests included people for whom Voloshen was doing a favor, and Voloshen had no compunction about discussing the favor—and the price for it—no matter who happened to be present. When McCormack was there, he would frequently nod in assent to whatever Voloshen was saying. It soon began to dawn on me that Nathan Voloshen would be a

* The Speaker had no regular, prearranged table in the House dining room. Whichever table the first members of his staff or clique chose upon arriving there automatically became the Speaker's table.

good man to know better. How often in the past had I gone to Washington on behalf of my public-relations clients and made the mistake of trying to get something done by walking through the front door of some department or agency and starting to fill out the proper forms. Inevitably, I encountered the frustration of delays and red tape, of misdirection and double-tracking and broken appointments. It occurred to me now that Voloshen might be extremely helpful in opening a few side doors for me around Washington. It also occurred to me that it might be beneficial for my clients if I actually became a lobbyist for them. I talked this over with some of them, reminding them that they might have to make a campaign contribution to some Congressman from time to time, but they all agreed.

This move seemed to me to be a natural progression for me. In college I had studied law, but I did not really feel drawn to law. My father had been in the garment industry in New York. During my summer vacations, I had done public-relations and advertising work for companies in this business, and I had found that I enjoyed it.

During the summer of 1945, I went to work for A. Davis & Sons, Inc., one of the country's biggest manufacturers of women's suits and coats. I was at that time in college with Al Davis, the son of Milton Davis, the president of the company, and thus had more than just a business relationship with the management. While working there, I had an experience that should have given me an insight into the world of lobbying and steered me from it. But I was young then, perhaps naïve, and so I was convinced that it had to be an isolated incident.

During World War II, the Coat Corporation of

America, a division of A. Davis & Sons, had a government contract to make uniforms for the military, obtaining the material on government approval from manufacturers. Quite a bit of the material was siphoned off to the black market. The company did not report these earnings nor did it pay any taxes on them. The Internal Revenue Service discovered the fraud by checking tax reports of other companies, then hit A. Davis & Sons with an action for $200,000 plus penalties. The owners, Milton and Charles Davis, also faced a prison sentence. The company got a lot of publicity it didn't want.

President Franklin D. Roosevelt was then still alive, and he was making a personal crusade of prosecuting industrialists who were profiting from the war illegally. Francis Biddle, the U.S. Attorney General at that time, was known to be absolutely unapproachable for any deals. The Davises took on as attorneys the New York firm of Simpson, Brady, Noonan, and Kaufman. Irving Kaufman* was a friend of Tom Clark, then an Assistant U.S. Attorney General, who headed the Criminal Division of the Department of Justice. All the law firm could do at the moment for the Davises was create legal roadblocks to give the company time to figure a way out of its trouble.

President Roosevelt died on April 12, 1945, and Harry Truman succeeded him. Truman asked Roosevelt's cabinet to stay on; but most of them wanted to resign and gradually began doing so, among them Francis Biddle. Rumor spread through Washington that Truman would appoint Tom Clark as the U.S. Attorney

* Kaufman later became famous—or infamous—as the federal judge who sentenced Julius and Ethel Rosenberg to the electric chair.

General. As these rumors reached New York, Charles Davis told me that Clark himself had telephoned Irving Kaufman and said: "You can stop worrying now." There was great jubilation when this news reached the Davis household.

Tom Clark was in fact appointed U.S. Attorney General on May 24, 1945, and was sworn in on July 1. Meanwhile, Lamar Caudle, a Clark protegé, was appointed to Clark's old job, heading the Criminal Division of the Department of Justice. On July 31, 1945, Milton Davis and Charlie Davis, the latter of whom was powerful in Democratic circles, pleaded guilty by prearrangement through their attorney Irving R. Kaufman before Federal Judge Gaston L. Poterie to an indictment charging conspiracy to file a false statement with the Renegotiation Board of the Army Quartermaster Corps. Isaiah Natlack, chief of the local Office of War Frauds of the Department of Justice, said the defendants filed a statement in 1942 saying their profits were $73,000 instead of about $200,000. The Davises were fined $30,000. Nothing was said about the rest of the money. Nothing was said about further prosecution, and there was none.

About two weeks later, on a stifling August day, Al Davis and I saw Tom Clark himself enter the large showroom of A. Davis & Sons, on the seventeenth floor at 225 W. Thirty-seventh Street in New York. What struck me about him was that, despite the heat, he was wearing a fedora. I watched him cross the room and accept a suitcase that was given to him by Charlie Davis, and he walked out with it. After he left, Charlie told me, in a bragging fashion, that the suitcase contained $250,000 in cash. I was stunned. Years later, as a lobbyist, I learned on my own that, in Washington, big favors cost big money. Not long ago, in talking to me, Al Davis indicated that his uncle might have been exaggerating, but he confirmed that the sum had been substantial.

Tom Clark went on to become a member of the United States Supreme Court, resigning in 1967 when his son Ramsey Clark, a man of the highest integrity, became United States Attorney General, so that the father would not be called upon to sit on any cases the son might bring before the court. In 1968 the Republicans won the Presidential election, and so Ramsey Clark lost his job on January 20, 1969— and the country lost one of its finest public servants.

When I finished college and decided to go into public relations, I concentrated on the garment industry because I knew so many people in it. I organized the British Menswear Guild and promoted it internationally. I handled the world promotion, and sometimes managed the business affairs, of such Paris designers as Balmain, Chanel, Castillo, and Cardin. Representing the Australian government, I worked in world capitals for the Australian Wool Growers, the Australian Shell Industry, and the Australian Cultured Pearl Industry. Other clients came to me through friends, friends who were themselves in public relations or who were lawyers or newspapermen. I represented individuals who were leaders in industry, government, show business, and society. Often my first meetings with new clients were at dinner parties. In New York and Washington, dinner parties are often business events, with people being brought together in the expectation of working out some kind of deal. Dinner parties are less conspicuous and less committing than meetings in offices or restaurants or bars. At a dinner party, you can step to one side with someone and look as if you are discussing baseball while actually you are wheeling and dealing. There are, in fact, people who make a living out of giving dinner parties for people who want to get something done and people who can get it done, taking a cut from both sides. My life in public relations in New York had followed this pattern for years. I expected my social life as a lobbyist in Washington to follow much the same pattern—but it did not.

Though I realized I probably would be spending more time now in Washington than in New York, I decided at the outset not to live in Washington. The town is too small, and there is no privacy in it. Gossip is the very lifeblood of Washington, and the most popular dinner guests are blabbermouths who either have a lot of gossip or can be relied upon to spread some. Even when I stayed in town for dinner with some Congressional contact, I always took the air shuttle back to New York no matter how late the hour. I did this to escape the complete lack of privacy which is typical of Washington and to avoid the intrusion of business into my private life. In the morning, I usually took the train back down to Washington, which allowed me to nap if the previous night had been a late one, and to map out my day.

From the beginning, I kept detailed diaries, listing everyone I had had contact with during the day, what we had discussed, and what had resulted. I kept all the mail I received, business or personal, which had anything at all to do with my work as a lobbyist; I kept the envelopes as well. I made carbon copies of anything I put into writing; and, when it was necessary, I had the carbons notarized as being true copies. I also wrote long memos to myself, so that I would not have to rely on my memory alone for the details of conversations or events. And I accumulated considerable memorabilia. If, for example, I popped into a side-street New York bar for a nightcap and saw there any person in government or in any business related to government, I would tell the waiter or the bartender that I wanted a dated copy of my check, even if it were just for one drink. On leaving, I'd take along a packet of the bar's matches. At home, I'd staple the matches to the front of the check. On the back, I'd note the time I first noticed the person, who he was, who was with him, whether he saw me, whether we talked—and, if so, about what—and which of us left first and with whom.

Call it an idiosyncrasy, or an obsession, but I was concerned about more than my income tax, about more than my lobbyist quarterly reports. I was above all concerned about keeping my nose clean. I knew I was in the favors business. I was playing the you-scratch-my-back-and-I'll-scratch-yours game. I wanted to make certain that I would know whenever the hand approaching my back had a knife in it. I had to be able to prove, whether in a courtroom or in a back alley, where I had been and what I had been doing, in case this information affected my life or limb or anybody else's. I didn't enjoy keeping such close tabs; but as long as I knew my record was clean, I wasn't afraid.

To show the precariousness of doing business in Washington, as Clark Clifford has said, "A lawyer in Washington is like a soldier walking through a minefield. You only have to make one mistake and you are through." The same would apply to a lobbyist.

Nevertheless, it was always somewhat terrifying to realize that the Washington lobbyists constituted the single most potent political pressure group in the history of the world. Huge sums of money were being spent every year to protect the vested interests not only of corporations, railroads, trade associations, labor unions, public utilities, medical interests, educational groups, and farm groups, but also of individuals of every economic size, shape, and form. Congressmen are approached by lobbyists not only in their Washington offices but wherever they go—in their offices, in their home districts, at their country clubs, in their churches and even in their own homes. Congressmen are approached not only by lobbyists, registered or not, but by other Congressmen, by the Pentagon, by executive departments, by the White House, by politicians at the state and local levels, by agents of foreign interests, foreign governments, and—last but not least—the interests of organized crime. No man can long resist such pressures; he may yield at first because of his need for support in order to survive politically, but the longer he survives, the lower his resistance becomes. When anybody knowingly moves in such circles, it becomes essential to his own survival that he be able to prove exactly where he has been, what he has done, and with whom he has associated.

No matter how close a Congressman and a lobbyist become over the years, if any of their deals should backfire it is the lobbyist who becomes the sacrificial lamb. This is basically why a lobbyist operates underground, burrowing like a weasel—which, incidentally, was the underworld's nickname for Nathan Voloshen. Because Voloshen did his burrowing at the top of Capitol Hill, he became undoubtedly the most powerful of the Washington lobbyists operating on an individual basis, or sometimes in concert with other loners. But when events brought Nathan Voloshen out into the open and into the spotlight, House Speaker McCormack, who had had personal contact with him practically every day for almost twenty years, tried to pass off the relationship as casual and give the impression he really didn't know Voloshen had been using his Washington office for countless deals. Similarly, when events brought me into the spotlight, Jerry Ford's office, where I had been on a first-name basis with everybody for three years, told the press that all they knew about me was that I was some kind of lobbyist who came around once in a while. So I experienced firsthand what I had already observed frequently in situations involving others: in Washington, there is no loyalty, no friendship, no sense of responsibility for anyone except yourself. This was why I had conducted my own business with such care and attention to detail.

Until there is a backfire, a lobbyist enjoys unique privileges on Capitol Hill. As long as he remains underground, he can procure unlimited favors for his clients from legislators with whom he has built a close relationship. Moreover, an effective lobbyist becomes an unofficial liaison between various members of Congress on both sides of the aisle. He circulates Congressional gossip, usually as a means of getting information for his favorite members; for the same reason, he airs the individual positions of various Congressmen on pending legislation. Very often votes will be unofficially traded before a Congressional vote through the good offices of an influential and trusted lobbyist. It is in this unregistered role that a lobbyist becomes most dangerous. A member of Congress often comes to rely on the judgments and intelligence he receives from his pet lobbyist. In this sense, a lobbyist may appear to be working for the Congressman; but he is first of all working for himself and his clients, and so the judgments and intelligence he passes on to the Congressman can be diluted or altered in a way to serve his purposes more than the Congressman's. It is in this area that the lobbyist poses his greatest threat to the inalienable right of the electorate, for it is in this area that it is impossible to apply controls as long as lobbying is allowed to continue as it is currently being practiced. Congressman Wright Patman of Texas has said: "There is no effective legal control over the lobbying activities of individuals and groups, and the time is fast approaching, I am convinced, when Congress must decide just how far it is willing to allow these lobbyists to go on influencing national legislation."

Now lobbying allows for specific dishonesties. When a lobbyist sits down to ask another favor of his understanding Congressman, there is no discussion as to whether the request is against the public interest or against the law itself. In fact, the Congressman doesn't want too much information in the first place. Once he knows what the lobbyist wants, the Congressman comes up with a list of the documentation he will have to have before he can make his move. He doesn't suggest that perhaps existing documentation might have to be doctored to meet the specifications, and he doesn't want to know if it has been. This gives him the protection of the 1925 Corrupt Practices Act, which makes his ignorance of any illegality his best defense. What he is not ignorant of is the fact that once he makes his move, the lobbyist will come along with the little envelope of green stuff. Then the Congressman can go into his act of: "You didn't have to do this. I'm grateful to you for it, though. I'm glad I was able to help." And the lobbyist knows full well that without that little envelope the

Congressman wouldn't have made a move at all.

I went into lobbying without any expectation of making a fortune at it. Years in public relations had taught me that know-how and know-who were effective ways of getting things done, and things got done faster in Washington when there were gratuities involved. In lobbying, campaign contributions were legally permissible, and I made it clear to my clients that this was the only gratuity that would be expected of them. I also made it clear that they were not to expect any miracles from me. To assure that, I had new clients sign the following type of form:

> Receipt is hereby acknowledged for your check dated_____for the sum of_____, in return for which I have agreed to look into the problem of_____.
>
> I will do my best to expedite the solution to the above-mentioned problem. However, I do not claim to guarantee anything and/or fix anything.
>
> You have asked me to use my best efforts and have offered to pay me.
>
> If the foregoing meets with your complete understanding and approval, would you please sign the enclosed copy and return it to me.
>
> Very truly yours,
> Robert N. Winter-Berger

I wasn't being a boy scout. I just didn't want to become a convict. Even so, it was a sad commentary on the state of affairs in Washington that such a blunt and graphic letter should have to be written and countersigned in the first place. People knew there could be fixes or they wouldn't have expected them, and clarifying my stand with that letter cost me a lot of clients. Because of the curbs I put on my efforts, I didn't expect—and I didn't get—any really big clients. But I have always preferred to work on my own and to work on behalf of individuals rather than organizations or corporations.

During my five years as a lobbyist, my clients provided me with ample money to use for campaign contributions and gratuities. Not all the money went to Congressmen. For example, Edith Pargament, Speaker McCormack's secretary, complained to me early in 1964 that John Pappas,* a Boston businessman and once part owner of the Suffolk Downs race track, had given her only $250 in cash the previous Christmas. She was insulted—and she was a secretary. The following Christmas I gave her $500 in cash. All Congressmen have secretaries and aides, and often these are the people who determine which visitors and which mail the Congress-

---

* The Pappas brothers—Thomas and John—of Boston split the major parties between them, Tom going Republican and John going Democrat, each heavily supporting his own candidates. John was a frequent visitor to Speaker McCormack's office. Tom endeared himself to the Republicans by raising millions for the GOP coffers from scores of wealthy Greek-Americans. He was an early supporter of the candidacy of Spiro Agnew for the Vice-Presidency. A close personal friend of the Vice-President's, he has been to the White House on several occasions, for both dinner and luncheon. He accompanied the Vice-President to Greece in 1971, and in May of 1971 he donated a $50,000 box in perpetuity in the Eisenhower Theatre in Washington in the name of Tricia Nixon and her husband Edward Finch Cox. The Pappases, who made their fortune in oil, steel, and soft drinks, got into a little trouble in Greece in July 1971, when Tom, there developing a $200-million chemical and steel complex, was accused of seeking to bankrupt an Athens steel company his agents were said to have bought on his behalf. He was acquitted after a two-day court hearing.

man sees every day, so they must be included in a lobbyist's budget. Jerry Ford was the only Congressman
who told me outright not to give presents of any kind to
him or to his staff—and he wasn't being a boy scout
either. When he gave me these instructions, he specified:
"Just don't hand out anything *in the office*. And I don't
want to know about anything you hand out to my people on the outside."

I was willing to pay to meet Jerry Ford for a number
of reasons. I had always been a Republican, and there
were times during my two years of lobbying mostly
among Democrats when I felt like Sammy Davis, Jr.
trying to "pass" at a Ku Klux Klan rally. There were
also times when I felt a bit disgusted by the speed with
which a McCormack Democrat was willing to go miles
out of his way to get a favor done in return for some
contribution. I wasn't so naïve as to believe that Republicans were all saints, but at least I expected a little
style. Furthermore, I had learned that in Washington, as
in life, it was a mistake to put all one's eggs in one
basket—or, in this case, on one side of the aisle. There
were 435 members of the House; every two years there
was a turnover; and though the Democrats were in
power in 1966, I did not expect this to go on forever. I
needed some friends on the Republican side. I chose
Jerry Ford because it looked as if he would be around
for awhile. He had entered Congress in 1949, and not
only had he survived, he had risen. After some fierce in-
fighting, mostly against Melvin Laird, the then Wisconsin Representative, he recently had become Minority
Leader. Lobbyists learn early to operate as close to the
top as they can: that's where the action is, that's where
you get things done. A junior member does not have
much influence, is generally not on any important com-

mittees, and has yet to prove his durability. As his durability increases through re-election, his power increases proportionately, but the more durable he becomes, the more indebted he becomes, both politically and financially. So he does favors, in order to keep his head above water.

I suppose I could simply have tried to walk into Ford's office and introduce myself, but politicians learn early to beware of strange lobbyists bearing gifts. A proper introduction, however, is enough for a politician to make a lobbyist his friend for life—provided the lobbyist keeps his nose clean and his wallet handy. I knew a woman in New York whose Michigan family was close to the Fords. Known professionally as Alice Weston, she at various times had had her own television and radio shows in the Midwest, and in between had done public-relations work. Alice Weston's father was one of the wealthiest men in western Michigan and had helped Jerry Ford financially as a young man. At the time, Alice was with the Jean Loach Agency, a New York public-relations firm. We already knew each other, as I had also done some free-lance work for Jean Loach. I telephoned Alice, made an appointment, and when we met I told her what I wanted.

As I recall the conversation, Alice said, "I don't think I can do much for you, Bob. I've never been very close to the Fords myself. My brother is, though. Pete and Jerry went to school together."

"Can your brother do anything for me?" I asked.

She thought about it. "I could ask," she said. "But I don't think we should handle this on a social level. Let's make it business. I'll tell my brother you're a client of mine. That way, you can pay me."

I wasn't surprised. "All right. How much?"

"Five hundred dollars."

"All right."

She thought some more. Then she said: "Of course, if this works out well for you, I think you should pay me another $500."

I again agreed to her terms.

She smiled. "Good. I'll see what I can do. By the way, if you get to know the Fords, see what you can do about them. They're such hayseeds. They don't even know how to dress."

A couple of weeks later, Alice Weston sent me a photocopy of a letter written by her brother to Jerry Ford. Dated April 19, 1966, it was on the stationery of Lokker, Boter, and Dalman, Attorneys, Holland, Michigan, and went as follows:

Dear Jerry,

My sister, Alice Weston, is at the present time engaged in public relations work in New York City. She has a client, Robert N. Winter-Berger, who has expressed a desire to meet you and discuss some matters with you. I have suggested to her that she call you and identify herself as my sister, and indicated that if it were at all possible I was sure that you would give her such time as you might have available. I know that with your added duties as the Minority Leader, you must have an extremely busy schedule. However, I would appreciate anything which you could do to be of assistance to her.

We are all most interested in the developing Senatorial contest. While I hope that Bob

Griffin makes it, I am also hopeful that his opponent will be one other than G. Mennen Williams.

With kindest personal regards, I remain

Very truly yours,
Peter S. Boter

That didn't sound so buddy-buddy to me, but I knew, given the past relations between the Boters and Ford, that Jerry would get the message and would probably see me. We gave him a few days. Then Alice made the call and the two of us went to Washington together for that first visit. I had already decided to level with him, so I told Ford that I was a lobbyist, that I had been working out of McCormack's office for two years, that I now wanted to work with him, and that I had felt the best way to make contact with him was through the letter of introduction from a personal friend.

I remember saying: "Frankly, I'm a little disgusted by some of the things I've seen and heard so far and I'd like to find out if the atmosphere is more wholesome on the Republican side of the aisle. But I want to make it clear that I'm not interested in carrying any tales to you that I might pick up around the Speaker's office."

"I admire that," Ford said. "I respect you for it. I think we can work together. But now I want to make something clear. My only interest in money is raising money for the Republican Party. I prefer not to see your wallet. When you think a contribution is legitimate, send me the check. I also think we shouldn't lunch together, the way Nat Voloshen does with the Speaker."

"Voloshen will never see me with you."

"Just don't let me be seen with Voloshen."

"I understand."

"One more thing," he said. "The first time you make

a mistake, no matter how close we may be by that time, we're through. I'll tell people I don't even know you."

"I understand that, too," I said.

He nodded. He asked: "Is there anything I can do for you now?"

"No," I said, "but I would like to feel free to come and see you whenever I need some advice."

He nodded again. "No problem. Any time."

I felt good. By then, I was fed up with the bulldozing techniques for getting things done that I had witnessed in McCormack's office, the shouts on the telephone, the threats that this or that had to be done immediately for some friend of the Speaker or some important constituent of the Speaker. I knew that the same brutal attack was the technique for getting things done out of the White House. I was concerned about more than good manners. The brutal attack always carried with it the threat of some illegality that might one day backfire. The Republicans, as I discovered, were subtler and more discreet. If a certain favor required the filling out of forms, Republicans filled them out. If a waiver under some law was involved, a man like Jerry Ford would go to the members of the review board and discuss the case; and when the matter came before them, they would know how Jerry felt about it. If they decided in his favor for personal reasons as well as on the merits of the case, well and good. Perhaps favoritism was being displayed, but at least the proceedings were legal. To me, this seemed a safer way to stay afloat on the uncertain seas of Washington than the gunpoint method that seemed to be operative in McCormack's office.

Thus I became, I expect, the only lone-operating registered lobbyist in Washington with direct access to the

House leadership of both parties. The prescribed manner of getting anything done by any federal department
or agency invariably involves filling out numerous
forms. In Ford's office, I would discuss my client's
problems with either Jerry or his administrative assistant Frank Meyer, and then one of them would call the
proper department or agency and present the matter.
Forms would be sent over; usually I filled them out
then Ford or Meyer would go over them and they
would be submitted. We would wait a few days, and
then Ford or Meyer would start making the phone calls
that would create the pressure to break through the red
tape to get the desired results. In McCormack's office
the process was different. There, I would tell Martin
Sweig or Nathan Voloshen what I wanted done. One of
them would make the pertinent phone call and present
the matter. He would end by saying that I was on my
way over to resolve the situation. The subject of forms
would come up. Sweig or Voloshen usually would tell
the functionary what he could do with the forms, and
then make a point of saying how vitally important the
matter was to Speaker McCormack personally. I'd go
over to whatever office was involved and, more often
than not, the matter would be resolved then and there,
but in an atmosphere of hostile resentment. Gradually I
started going to McCormack's office only when Jerry
Ford said he couldn't help me on a certain matter, or
would prefer not to. As I got to know the various department and agency people better and they began to
associate me more with Ford than with McCormack,
they told me that the most arrogant and high-handed
pressure they had to take came out of McCormack's
office. They said they would be happy to see the day
McCormack's reign came to an end. Little did they sus-

pect that the Speaker, who seemed ensconced for life, was living the last, precarious days of his long reign.

Early in 1969, I found out that Manhattan's U. S. Attorney Robert M. Morgenthau was investigating the activities of Nathan Voloshen and Martin Sweig on charges of fraud and conspiracy involving government matters, government agencies, and government personnel. When I passed this information on to Jerry Ford, he gave me another surprise. I expected him to be pleased. Instead, he became angry. "Morgenthau is attacking the Establishment," he said. "This is something I can't condone. I'll never forgive Morgenthau for this."

Later that year, on October 17, Speaker McCormack suspended his recently promoted administrative assistant Sweig indefinitely and without pay, pending the outcome of a trial. Nathan Voloshen lost his latchkey to the Speaker's offices. At the time, McCormack told the press that he had known Voloshen about ten years and that their relationship had not been personal but strictly professional.

In May of 1970, Speaker McCormack announced that he would not run for re-election and would retire from politics. He explained that his wife was ill and he wanted to spend more time with her. Anybody who has known John McCormack is well aware that he loved his job so much that he hoped and expected to stay with it until the day he was carried out of his office feet first. There was, then, much more to McCormack's resignation than the public imagined. The legal action against Voloshen and Sweig could not be stopped—it was coming up on June 17, 1970—and obviously it was important to get as many of the Establishment's sitting ducks out of the crossfire as soon as possible.

The problem, basically, was—and is—in the system. In its purest form, lobbying can be creative and constructive. In fact, it was originally intended to be both. When an expert on any given subject, representing a vested interest, appears at a public session of a Congressional committee to express his opinions on a piece of pending legislation, he can achieve a great good. He can give the committee members a broader view of the subject than they might get on their own. He can show the sore spots in the legislation. Because of his professional standing, his appearance can become news and thereby stimulate public discussion. And, because of his professional experience, he can even forecast how the legislation will work out in actual practice, whether he is for the bill or against it. Representative Charles E. Bennett, Democrat from Florida, once said to me: "Members of Congress depend on lobbyists for their information." He was right, when the lobbying is out in the open and aboveboard. But, like the proverbial iceberg, only a fraction of it is.

Most lobbying is underground, because more than opinions are exchanged. Money is exchanged: money for favors, money for deals, money for government contracts, money for government jobs. The members of Congress need the money primarily to pay for their campaigns, and campaigns are becoming more expensive all the time. Not all the winners in the last Congressional election were liberals, nor were all of them conservatives, but they all had money behind them or they couldn't have run. Accepting the money puts the candidate into political debt to the contributors, and that is the whole idea. From time to time, Congress tries to put a lid on campaign costs. The latest serious effort occurred in 1971. When President Nixon vetoed the bill, the reaction in Washington was that Nixon knew that Republicans never have any great trouble raising money for a campaign, so why should the President sign a bill that would give the Democrats a break? The truth is that money is on the minds of Republicans just as much as it is on the minds of Democrats, though the stress may not be as great.

According to the federal Corrupt Practices Act of 1925, which deals with campaign spending, candidates need only account for the campaign spending of which they have personal knowledge. This is a loophole as big as the Lincoln Tunnel. As soon as a man announces his candidacy for office or for re-election to office, committees of private citizens are formed to campaign for him and raise money for him. The candidate appoints VIP's to head the important committees that will move out into the top echelons of business, industry, and finance to garner the big donations, but there may be dozens, or even hundreds, of other committees operating lower down the money ladder—committees with which the candidate may have no personal contact other than speaking at their mass rallies. Some states require all these committees to report on both the money they have raised and the way in which they have spent it, but most states do not. Thus when the time comes for candidates to submit campaign costs to the Comptroller General of the United States or the Clerk of the House, most of them don't make anything resembling an accurate report: they can always say they weren't informed of the financial activities of the lower-echelon committees.

The 1925 act tries to apply some controls on campaign giving, but again, there are many loopholes. For example, the law puts a $5,000 limit on an individual's contribution to a campaign committee, but the law fails to state that an individual can't contribute to more than one of a candidate's many committees. Corporations aren't supposed to make campaign contributions; but in 1968 thirteen executives of Litton Industries gave at least $149,000 to various Nixon-Agnew committees. Unions can't contribute, but they can form committees which can—and do. Whether from labor or management, the donation is not actually the money of the individual who makes it but comes from unofficial coffers earmarked for precisely such purposes. Another donation dodge is a loan that is supposed to be paid back, win or lose. It is a matter of public record that, in 1968, John Factor, a wealthy California real estate man better known in the underworld as Jake the Barber, an exconvict, loaned $240,000 to forty-eight Humphrey-Muskie committees. When a candidate wins, the people who loaned the money don't worry very much about being repaid. They know they'll get their money back, one way or another. When the candidate loses, however, things can get a little sticky: that is when the defeated candidate, together with any prominent friends he has in the party, starts traveling around, speaking at fund-raising dinners back home.

In 1946 and in 1970, reformers in the Congress tried to do something about the mystery of missing money, but their efforts were shot full of holes and their results left much to be desired. The goal of the reformers was to bring to the surface any private interests a member might have which could influence his decision on public matters before the Congress; but to achieve this, the reformers had to have the cooperation of many peers who were opposed to airing their interests. Their alternative was compromise, with a view toward laying the basis for more rigorous legislation in the future.

Today, a member of the House must submit an annual report to the Clerk disclosing any commercial affiliation which brings him an income of $1,000 a year or more—but he does not have to disclose how much more. A House member must also disclose stockholdings worth $5,000 or more—but again he does not have to disclose how much more. These reports are available to the public, but you have to go to the Capitol, fill out forms, and wait a long time; then when you finally see your Congressman's report you really don't find out much about him anyway. Senators submit a similar annual report to the Comptroller General but it is a sealed report and its contents are never publicly disclosed.

All Congressmen must disclose the source of any honorarium of $300 or more. These usually are fees they receive for lectures, writings, speeches to special-interest groups, seminars, and appearances on radio and television. In addition, Senators must report any gifts worth more than $50. An effort was made to require Representatives to report gifts worth more than $100, but it never got off the ground. They are nonetheless required to publicly disclose any commercial interests from which they derive more than $1,000 income or in which they hold more than $5,000 worth of stock. Representatives are also required to report any unsecured loans of $10,000 or more that have been outstanding for ninety days or more. But they have a way around this. On the eighty-ninth day, they can have the loan refinanced and thus do not have to report it. For all practical purposes, the loan becomes a gift, the Representative merely paying the interest as long as he remains in office.

The various forms of outside income go mostly to Congressmen of influence. That is precisely the point. In Washington, either a man goes up the ladder or he gets off it. Lobbyists watch the changing scene intently: their success depends upon riding with the winners. Nathan Voloshen and Carl Albert, for example, had been friends for years. As a member of the Rayburn-Johnson-McCormack team, Albert had a promising future in Washington. Like McCormack, Carl Albert was not well-known nationally, but he was well-known in Washington, where it counted. Though McCormack was Voloshen's ace in the hole, I was frequently present during my five years in Washington while Voloshen and Albert discussed ways to win McCormack's support for some appointment or contract that would be to their advantage. Rumors about McCormack's retirement began to circulate early in 1969, although only a few people knew it would be a forced retirement, and Voloshen began to adjust his aim accordingly. On May 9 that year, House Majority Leader Carl Albert, practically a nonentity outside political circles, gave a talk at the Americana Hotel in New York to the Teamsters and Allied Educational Alliance, a Voloshen client. Another speaker on the program was Adam Clayton Powell, a Voloshen friend. For speaking half an hour to the Teamsters and their allies, both Albert and Powell received honorariums of $1,500 each, plus all expenses. The appearance of both Congressmen was arranged by Nathan Voloshen through Teamsters official Abe Weiss. After Carl Albert spoke, he and his wife had dinner with Voloshen at Broadway Joe's. Then, as Voloshen's guests, the Alberts went to a performance of *Promises,*

Promises, then the biggest hit in town, with underground tickets going at $100 a pair. Voloshen was merely feathering a nest from which he never got a chance to hatch any eggs.

I don't know where Adam Clayton Powell had dinner; maybe he just spent a quiet evening at home. Congressmen don't have much time to themselves. The minute a new Senator or a new Representative shows that he is a comer, he is besieged with invitations from the wheeler-dealers who will do everything they can to get him to use his time to their advantage. No matter where he comes from, no matter what a dullard he may be himself, no matter what a frump his wife may be, when a Congressman reaches the point where he can pick up a telephone and tell a government agency, "Do this!" he is suddenly a celebrity. And generally he likes it. It is nice to be popular. It is nice to be powerful. It is nice to have some extra money in your pocket.

Only precedence suggests that the House Majority Leader should become Speaker of the House when that office is vacated, and it was in this way that Carl Albert moved up the ladder when John McCormack retired at the close of the Ninety-first Congress in 1970. On April 8, 1971, William V. Shannon, writing in *The New York Times,* favorably appraised Albert's performance and potential during his first three months in office. As Shannon pointed out, the Speaker of the House is often described as the second most powerful man in the government, although "power" no longer carries the meaning it once did. The last truly powerful House Speaker was Joseph G. (Uncle Joe) Cannon, Republican of Illinois, who reigned over the House from 1903 through 1911. Cannon had assumed such authority that he alone was making appointments to House committees, including assigning the chairmanships. The most important House committee is the House Rules Committee through which all new legislation must be channeled before it can go before the Congress. Controlling the House Rules Committee, the arch-conservative Cannon alone determined which legislation would reach the House floor. In 1910, liberal Republicans and Democrats forced through a procedural change which made appointments to committees and chairmanships matters of party caucus and seniority.

Shannon wrote:

> Since that time, Speakers have had to make do with the next best thing to power, which is influence. The successful exercise of influence involves obtaining reliable, timely information on what members are thinking, having friends and contacts in every faction, and being skillful in persuasion, cajolery, and pressure. To exercise what the public thinks of as leadership—and make it stick—depends upon performing onstage an endless mediating or brokerage function. Speaker Albert is probably as good as the best of his predecessors in this kind of work.

Trained by McCormack and Rayburn, Albert should indeed be as good in his job as any of his predecessors, for he was taught how to respect influence and how to use it. "Influence" has, in fact, supplanted "power" in the Washington vocabulary, and everybody is aware of this. The lowest functionary in Washington, his first day on the job, will discover that although there is not much he can do, there are many ways in which he can get things done. If, for example, he works at the Immigration and Naturalization Service, he will find on his desk every morning a stack of applications for readjustment of visas from aliens who want to stay in this country for any number of reasons. Ordinarily, he works his way through the pile, judging each application in terms of the law and the circumstances. Suddenly he gets a telephone call from a ranking Congressman, who has just been visited by a lobbyist, and the Congressman—or his administrative aide—says: "I believe you have an application for a visa extension from Professor So-and-So of X-land. The professor is doing some important scientific research in this country and his visa is about to expire. If he has to leave the country, he won't be able to get back in for two years, and I think that would be a great blow to our national welfare. I have looked over a copy of the professor's application and it seems to be in order. Can you have the application approved and expedited?" To any government employee, a call from an important Congressman—or even from his aide—is virtually a subpoena. So the man digs through the applications, finds the professor's, and glances over it. If he has any questions, he knows this is not the time to ask them. He says yes, he can have it ready. He goes to work. Ten minutes later, he gets another call from the Congressman—or the aide—who says: "A representative of the professor's was here when I called the last time, so I couldn't be as emphatic as I wanted to be. The professor is working with a good friend of mine, one of my leading constituents, and I know how important their work is. I just don't want anything to go wrong with the application." The government employee quickly learns that this second call is the important one, because it says don't-goof-this, and because it says there is a lobbyist involved. Ten minutes later, the professor's representative—a lobbyist—walks in and picks up the approved application. The government man has the satisfaction of knowing that he has gotten something done; his sphere of influence, limited for the moment to his desk, has been used, and he can be confident that his horizons will grow as he continues to cooperate, enabling him to ascend the ladder to where the money is.

I know these things happen because I have handled numerous such immigration matters, and the procedure is always the same. And now I realize that this all too common practice of favoritism was the crux of what was wrong with the government's immigration procedures overall. As worthy as my client may have been, I was aware that in the same stack of applications were urgent pleas from other worthy aliens who didn't stand a chance because they did not know—or could not afford—somebody with the know-how and the know-who to make their applications rise magically to the top of the pile. Time often ran out for them because the time due them was being given to others more privileged in terms of connections and money. And yet these immigration problems were small potatoes compared to the wheeler-dealing I witnessed increasingly over the years—with connections and money always the keys to the influence that could bring about a deal. And the deals were becoming increasingly shady.

The day came when I realized I had to get away from it all. I was well aware of the things going on around me. I had seen too much, learned too much, and I had reached the point where I either had to get out or go ahead. The greatest temptation for going ahead was the money. There was so much money to be made. But I had observed that each exchange of money entangled the parties involved more deeply in their own web, until, like drug addicts, they were really enslaved. I did not want to become a rich slave. I faced the hard fact that returning to the life of a New York public-relations man would not be as exciting as circulating in the loftier spheres of Washington politics, where the laws of the land were created, interpreted, and broken. On the other hand, I knew that, on too many occasions, the laws were not passed—they were purchased—and this soured my outlook on the processes of government.

In 1969, after watching a fruitless effort by Nathan Voloshen to work out a deal for a confessed, convicted, and imprisoned swindler, I got out of lobbying. I had a lot of memories, some of them exciting, some of them terrifying, but I was sure they would fade. As far as I was concerned, the experience was over and done with. But I was wrong. As I was easing myself out of the Washington picture, Robert M. Morgenthau, U. S. Attorney for the Southern District of New York, was moving in to investigate the very practices that had most disturbed me. I found myself being drawn back, this time on the side of the government.

Every time I entered Speaker McCormack's offices, either his suite across the hall from the House chamber or his more elegant office in the Sam Rayburn Wing, I felt that I was walking into a bookie joint. Whether McCormack was present or not, there was always an air of pandemonium about the place. People scurried in and out. Telephones rang incessantly. The outer rooms were packed with noisy people. If somebody had shouted, "They're off!" I would have reached instinctively for my binoculars.

When I got to know John W. McCormack early in 1964, he was the second most important man in the United States government. John Kennedy was dead. Lyndon Johnson had ascended to the Presidency. At the time, the Constitution stipulated that, when there was no Vice-President, the Speaker of the House of Representatives filled that office. Early in 1964, then, the legal Vice-President of the United States was a man who was a ward heeler at heart. I had been hired to try to improve that image.

John McCormack had first been elected to the House

in 1928, representing the Ninth Massachusetts District in South Boston. He quickly became a protegé of Sam Rayburn of Texas, who ruled the Democratic side of the House from 1937 to 1961, most of the time as the Speaker. Another Rayburn protegé was Lyndon Johnson. Rayburn was always referred to as "lovable Sam," because, beneath his gruff exterior, he was supposed to have, like all prostitutes, a heart of gold. Sam Rayburn was a freewheeling politician, a prototype of the brutal, grabby, underhanded species of politician that, hopefully, is becoming extinct. But in that far-off era, Rayburn spawned protegés in his own image.

Succeeding Rayburn in 1962, John McCormack ran his office as if he himself were the Godfather and men like Eugene Kinnaly, Martin Sweig, Nathan Voloshen, John Donato, and Eddie Adams were his henchmen. There was little that was dignified, respectable, or honest about the operation of this office. Sweig, Voloshen, and Adams, all were subsequently indicted for criminal conduct. Sweig was convicted on one count of perjury; Voloshen pleaded guilty to charges of influence peddling and conspiracy; Adams pleaded guilty to bribery and was given a suspended sentence; Donato turned state's evidence. At Sweig's trial, McCormack pleaded ignorance, which, according to the 1925 House Code of Ethics Act, made him innocent. Rather ludicrously, on the stand, McCormack said: "I am not an inquiring fellow." To be ignorant of what was going on around him, McCormack would also have had to be deaf, dumb, and blind. Actually, if ever a man always knew precisely what was going on around him, it was John McCormack.

John McCormack and Nathan Voloshen became close around 1950. By the time I got to know both men, their relationship was so close that Voloshen had complete access to McCormack's private office in the Rayburn Wing, using the Speaker's personal desk and his personal phone. McCormack's secretaries—Edith Pargament and Bertha Drotos—took telephone messages for Voloshen when he was out of the office. Voloshen held meetings with his clients in McCormack's office, and he enjoyed introducing his clients to McCormack as part of his big-shot act.

I was present at a number of these introductions over the years. Usually Voloshen would make some oblique reference to what he was trying to do for his client, and McCormack would say: "Nat can take care of that for you. Nat's my dear friend and I will do anything I can for him. Any friend of Nat's is a friend of mine." I had heard those phrases once, I had heard them a hundred times. To anyone who had experienced the frustration and futility of trying to get something done legally in Washington, such words were sweet music, no matter how much they might cost. It was precisely this kind of talk by a man as important as John McCormack that made Nathan Voloshen the important man he eventually became.

McCormack and Voloshen met in 1945, at which point Voloshen began making contributions to McCormack's campaigns. Voloshen was small potatoes in those days, with only a few not very important clients; but as McCormack went up the ladder, so did Voloshen. It was in 1962, when McCormack became the House Speaker, that Voloshen started getting important clients with big money. Although McCormack and Voloshen were friends, they were also business partners, Voloshen providing the financing. A couple of weeks after I started doing public-relations work for John Mc-

Cormack, I had lunch one day in the House dining room with Martin Sweig and Nathan Voloshen. At one point, I recall Sweig saying:

"Say, Nat, you're running a little late on the rent again."

"I know it," Voloshen answered.

Sweig said: "The boss mentioned it this morning."

Voloshen frowned and said: "Tell him I'll have the twenty-five hundred for him tomorrow."

That was how I found out that Nathan Voloshen was paying McCormack a rental of $2,500 a month for the use of the office which was provided free to the Speaker, as part of his job, and which was actually the property of the citizens of the United States. I was amazed that Sweig and Voloshen would bring up a subject like that in front of someone who was still practically a stranger to them. Then I realized they were trying to impress me, to make me feel as if I were a member of the team. I realized, too, that they wanted me to know the financial level at which they operated, just in case I ever wanted them to do anything for me.

I also found out that there was a steady stream of gratuities flowing from New York to Washington. Every week Voloshen brought McCormack and Sweig a supply of Havana cigars; to Mrs. McCormack he brought a supply of Scandia face cream or lotion from Saks Fifth Avenue. Since Mrs. McCormack was then in her seventies, the thought struck me that she must have little use for so many cosmetics. But I was wrong. Every week she asked for, and received, six or seven jars of the creams. Voloshen's New York secretary, Margaret Stafford, used to joke about it often. She called the creams "Voloshen's Lotions."

It was about this same time that Nathan Voloshen

once tried to impress me with his influence on McCormack by boasting about a deal he had recently made. The deal involved John Donato, then by title a marketing vice-president for the Belock Instrument Corporation, but actually, like Voloshen, an influence peddler. The relationship between Voloshen and Donato was something akin to father and son. Donato was a flashy, dapper man, but around McCormack's offices he had the reputation of not being particularly bright. I often heard Martin Sweig say that he didn't like doing business with Donato because of Johnny's ineptness. Voloshen told me that Donato was frequently indiscreet in making his payoffs to politicans or to their administrative assistants, and so Voloshen usually handled this aspect of their dealings. Even so, Voloshen liked Donato and seemed to regard him as a protegé. Donato had many good contacts in the Pentagon, especially the Navy Department, and Voloshen once said to me: "With the contacts Johnny has at the Pentagon and the contacts I have on the Hill, we make a good team."

They worked as a team on a problem the Belock Instrument Corporation had while Donato was with the company. Belock had opened a facility at Huntsville, Alabama, in order to be near the Huntsville Arsenal where Dr. Werner Von Braun was heading the research on America's missile-building program. Like other companies, Belock started raiding Von Braun's project by tempting scientists with bigger salaries. The raiding got so bad that Dr. Von Braun finally warned that any company hiring away his staff would not receive any further government contracts. This put Belock in a bad spot. A fortune had gone into the Huntsville operation; the company was banking on government contracts, and Belock's raids on the arsenal staff were so well-known that the company's reputation in the industry was now threatened.

Johnny Donato took the problem to Nathan Voloshen and Voloshen took it to Speaker McCormack. McCormack wrote Dr. Von Braun a letter, asking him to receive Voloshen in his office to discuss a matter in which the Speaker was personally interested. Voloshen flew to Huntsville and met with Von Braun. Voloshen came out of the meeting with a press release, signed by Von Braun, which contained favorable references to the Belock Corporation. Belock released the statement to technical journals in the electronics field, and its reputation was saved.

When Nathan Voloshen boasted to me about this, he told me that, for his efforts, he had received 1,000 shares of Belock stock, then worth $15 a share, plus $10,000 in cash. Whether he kept it all, or just his usual third, he didn't say. He did say, however, that Dr. Von Braun had not received anything. On the other hand, Von Braun's operating funds came from the Congress, and the intervention of the Speaker of the House in a matter involving a company doing business with the government certainly must have made an impression on the man.

It was shortly after Voloshen told me this that I was able to get an impression of my own of John McCormack's powerful role in Washington politics. At the time, in early 1964, the most popular topic of conversation at Washington parties was Bobby Baker. Everybody knew about the vicious in-fighting going on in the Senate to bring Baker's business machinations out into the open, and everybody knew that, if this happened, heads could roll all the way up to the White House. After all, it had been Lyndon Baines Johnson who had

put Bobby Baker into the job that had made him a multimillionaire.

When Robert Gene (Bobby) Baker was hired as the
secretary to the Senate Majority Leader in 1955, his
salary was $9,000 a year and his net worth was put at
$11,000. A scant eight years later, in 1963, his salary
had increased to $19,600 a year and his personal for-
tune was placed at over $2 million. He was involved in
nine different corporations, including his own vending
company, a travel agency, and a motel. As secretary,
Baker's job was to coordinate the Democratic votes on
matters before the Senate. But he spent most of his
time traveling around the country, picking up donations
from industrialists to support the campaigns of Democratic candidates at all political levels and then oversee-
ing the allocations. He was a powerful man—and he
was also greedy.

Born in Pickens, South Carolina, Bobby Baker went
to Washington at fourteen to become a Senate page. He
completed his law studies in Washington and gained a
reputation as an effective legislative strategist, which led
Johnson to choose him as secretary to the Senate Majority Leader while Johnson held that post. The day was
to come when President Johnson would say that Baker
had been "just an employee around here," but Baker
was more than that. Johnson treated him like a son. If
there was any political know-how that Bobby Baker
lacked, he soon learned it from his mentor and boss.
Without question, Lyndon Johnson was the most effective strategist ever to be the Senate Majority Leader.
His strategy hinged on finding out where all the skele-
tons were and never hesitating to rattle the bones whenever anybody stepped out of line, and Johnson had
many allies. No one will dispute that Lyndon Baines

Johnson was one of the best Senate Majority Leaders this country has ever had; he had an uncanny ability to garner votes at crucial times, for bills that were important to him or to the administration he favored. This ability was not based so much on his persuasiveness as it was on his voluminous personal files, which kept track of the intimate, private indiscretions of his colleagues in the Senate. When he wanted a vote, all he had to do was to recall privately an incident to a particular Senator, which that Senator would rather not have revealed; naturally he got that Senator's vote. During this period Johnson enjoyed a close personal relationship with FBI head J. Edgar Hoover. It was Hoover who kept Johnson's "intelligence" files up to date by constantly supplying Johnson with new and titillating information on the foibles of famous Americans. Always the loyal friend, it was Hoover who sent flowers to Walter Jenkins, Johnson's trusted aid, when Jenkins went into a hospital during the 1964 campaign, after being arrested on a morals charge. When Johnson became the Vice-President in 1961, Baker went to work for Senator Mike Mansfield of Montana, the new Majority Leader, but maintained his close ties with Johnson.

Baker's troubles began on September 9, 1963. Earlier, he had been approached by Ralph L. Hill, owner of the Capitol Vending Company, who, seeking to improve his business, wanted a connection through which he could get his vending machines into factories doing business with the government. Baker had his own vending company, called Serv-U Corporation, and his machines were in many such factories. For a fee of $5,600, Baker got Hill a contract to put his machines into Melpar, Inc., a subsidiary of North American Aviation.

Later, when Hill's contract was up for renewal, Baker wanted another payment of $5,600. According to accounts Hill subsequently gave the press, when he complained to Baker that the fee was too high, Baker offered to buy his company. Hill refused to sell. Baker then threatened to break off Hill's arrangement with Melpar.

The threat infuriated Ralph Hill, and the conversation broke into a fierce argument. A Democrat and an acquaintance of Speaker McCormack, Hill went to the Speaker several times, asking him to use his influence on his close friend Vice-President Johnson to get Bobby Baker off his back. At a few of these urgent visits, Nathan Voloshen was present, and he gave me the details later. Evidently, nothing was done to settle the Hill-Baker controversy, however, because Hill then went to John J. Williams, former Republican senator of Delaware. On September 9, the Capitol Vending Company, which Hill owned, filed suit in a Washington court, accusing Bobby Baker of using political influence to obtain contracts with defense plants for the vending machines of the company he owned, Serv-U.

For the next three days, the high-level machinations —and that is not too strong a word—to kill the suit before it could become public knowledge would have made Machiavelli look like a cub scout. But this time Johnson's famous cajoling and arm twisting didn't work. Several months later, when the Administration tried to apply pressure on Senator Hugh Scott, a Republican leader in the Senate, to muzzle Senator Williams, their schemes, for the first time, misfired. Having nothing to hide, Scott called their bluff at a news conference. The Establishment itself was being threatened, not just the Democratic side of it. The cardinal sin, by

Washington standards, had been committed: somebody
was rocking the boat. Despite Senator Williams's disclosures to the press, no real battle could ensue as long as
no arena was provided. As long as the thunder was
confined to the corridors of the Capitol, there would be
no real storm because the members on both sides of the
aisles in both Houses could be depended upon to cooperate to the extent of preventing the issue from ever
reaching a committee hearing. After all, legislation specifically giving Bobby Baker tax breaks on some of his
personal business ventures had been passed in both
Houses, passed by members who were willing to do a
favor for the bright young man who had been Lyndon
Johnson's protegé for so many years. Also, it was well-
known that the young man—an illustration of his
shrewdness, perhaps—kept "intelligence files" on
members of Congress who had visited a nightclub and a
motel he owned, where the entertainment included
party girls. But what really was at stake was the inviola-
bility enjoyed by men who could say anything they
wanted in front of television cameras in order to preserve their statesmanlike public images but return to
their offices to engage in conduct anything but statesmanlike. Ralph Hill had gone into court. A court was a
public place. Hill's deal with Baker would become
known. In turn, Baker's deals with others could become
known. There could be a landslide fatal to a great many
members of the Establishment.

Having been filed in the court records, information
about the suit should have been available immediately
to any newspaper reporter, but it took *The Washington
Post* three days to find out about it and break the story.
Meanwhile, tremendous pressures to drop the suit were
put on Ralph Hill by leaders of both parties. The risk

was great that the suit might snowball into investigations of any dealings Bobby Baker had had with any members of the Congress, and nobody wanted that—except Senator Williams, for reasons known only to himself. Senator Everett Dirksen, then the Senate Minority Leader, had been close to Johnson during the years they were both in the Senate, and he was now called into the front lines. It was discovered that Senator Williams had advised Hill to file suit, and now not even Everett Dirksen could call Williams off. Rumors that Williams was conducting his own investigation into Baker's affairs sent tremors through the Capitol.

Then, on September 12, the *Post* broke the story,* and all Washington had something new to talk about. Indeed it was all anybody talked about. Everybody knew how close Baker and Johnson were, and those who knew the extent of Baker's dealings wondered how Johnson could have been ignorant of them either while he was the Majority Leader or after he became Vice-President. It seemed clear that a lot of important people were in trouble. A Washington politician can be involved in a scandal back home and may never feel the repercussions in Washington; but to be involved, in any way at all, in a scandal in Washington itself is his major dread. Because Washington, D.C., is a company town, engaged in the business of politics, such a scandal within the federal structure and concerning someone with the highest connections caused a complete panic. Out-of-town papers did not pay much attention to what be-

* Although *The Washington Post* broke the Bobby Baker story on September 12, *The New York Times* made no mention of it until October 5, almost a month later, and then saw fit to bury its article on page 19. Bobby Baker did not make the front page of the *Times* until October 8, the day after his resignation.

came known as the Bobby Baker case, but the Washington papers banned it. This was, after all, local news for the many thousands of outlanders whose jobs made Washington their home for as long as they could hold their jobs, and a local boy was in serious trouble.

That same day, September 12, Senator Williams called a press conference and announced that his investigation had uncovered certain indiscretions and improprieties in Baker's conduct as secretary to the Majority Leader. He said he was going to ask for a meeting of the Senate Rules and Administration Committee at which he would present his findings for action. When this news reached Senator B. Everett Jordan, then chairman of the committee, he said that his committee's calendar was too heavy to grant Williams an immediate hearing. As a compromise, the Democratic leadership suggested that the committee hire as counsel some qualified and unbiased person to investigate the charges. They recommended Lennox P. McLendon, a North Carolina lawyer. McLendon, then in his seventies, was perhaps qualified, but he had been identified with the Democratic Party in North Carolina for many years— which, coincidentally, was also Senator Jordan's state— and hardly could be considered unbiased.

Williams pressed for a date. Finally, Mike Mansfield gave him a date for a closed meeting for Senate leaders on October 8, a month off. This was a stall. In a month, anything could happen—perhaps, with any luck, something that would push Bobby Baker off the Washington front pages. Hopefully, there would be time, too, for the kind of cloakroom deals that could produce enough procrastination for the affair to die from overextension. Voloshen told me that Speaker McCormack and Sweig, plus Johnson's people, were confident that the suit would be killed and there would be no hearing.

But Senator Williams would not be denied. Though he had his date for a hearing, he called a news conference every few days and announced whatever further evidence he had obtained on how Baker used his job while involving himself in various insurance, real estate, and stock transactions. One charge involved Representative John W. Byrnes, Republican of Wisconsin, and the Mortgage Guaranty Insurance Corporation of Milwaukee. Byrnes was on the House Ways and Means Committee that had granted the company a tax relief which saved it millions. Both Byrnes and Bobby Baker had thereupon become stockholders in the company, just before the stock had soared. Williams also accused Baker of conspiring to channel an illegal payment of $25,000, allegedly from former Democratic National Committee Treasurer Matthew McCloskey, into the 1960 Kennedy-Johnson campaign fund. He also charged that certain funds recorded as contributed to the campaign of the late Senator Robert S. Kerr of Oklahoma had in fact not been received at all.

On October 7, Bobby Baker resigned his position as secretary to the Senate Majority Leader. The meeting of the Senate leaders, scheduled for the next day, was dropped. In Williams's opinion, this did not relieve the Senate of the responsibility of holding a hearing to determine whether Baker had done anything illegal. Williams told the press: "Bobby Baker has run out. He should have stayed and faced the music. I'm not going to let him get away with this."

At a news conference on October 31, with Lyndon Johnson present, President Kennedy was asked about the Bobby Baker case, and he said he felt the Administration ought not to comment on the case before the

Senate had acted. Even so, there were rumors around town that, because of Bobby Baker, Kennedy planned to drop Lyndon Johnson and find another running mate for the 1964 election.

In November, Kennedy and Johnson and their wives went on a political trip to Texas. On Friday, November 22, John F. Kennedy was assassinated. Lyndon Baines Johnson became the thirty-sixth President of the United States. Constitutionally, House Speaker John W. Mc-Cormack became the Vice-President. This line of suc- cession has since been changed by the Twenty-fifth Amendment to the U. S. Constitution, which allows a President succeeding through a death to appoint his Vice-President, subject to the majority approval of the Congress.

Because of the national shock, terror, and sorrow caused by Kennedy's death, Senator Williams agreed to let the Bobby Baker case ride over to January, but neither the assassination's aftermath nor the case's postponement in any way diminished the back-room maneuvers to kill the case. Early in January, Williams publicly took up his cause again, in the Senate and in the press. The majority—Democrats—of the Senate Rules Committee suggested a closed session at which Williams and Baker could confront each other. Williams agreed to this so readily that the idea was dropped. Finally, late on the afternoon of Tuesday, February 4, the commit- tee voted to summon Baker for an inquiry on February 19, and Williams was able to add a rider to the vote to the effect that if Baker failed to appear he would be charged with contempt of the Congress. This news flashed through Washington like lightning.

At four o'clock on that Tuesday afternoon of Febru- ary 4, I had an appointment with Speaker McCormack to discuss the publicity which he hoped would get him the nomination for the Vice-Presidency. The meeting began right on time. Normally, Voloshen was always present at all meetings with McCormack, but that day he had a conflicting appointment in New York, and he suggested that I "go ahead and meet with the Speaker anyway." We were in his office opposite the House chamber. McCormack was seated at his desk. I was in a chair opposite him, a short distance away, near the fireplace. To my left was the door to the reception room. Behind me was the private door the Speaker used on his frequent trips back and forth to the House chamber across the corridor.

We had talked about five minutes when I heard the private door open, and I turned to see who it was. I immediately recognized the rather tall, broadshouldered man in the dark suit. I had never seen such anguish on a man's face before. It was Lyndon Baines Johnson, the President of the United States. A Secret Service man hovered behind him, but he remained in the hall as the door swung shut. Stunned, I froze in my chair. I didn't know quite what to do. Did they want me to leave or to stay? Neither Johnson nor McCormack gave me any indication as to what I should do. I glanced at McCormack, and I could see that he was as amazed as I was. The question struck me: Why would the President come to the Speaker at the Capitol instead of asking the Speaker to go to him at the White House?

Johnson disregarded me, but I can never forget the sight of him, crossing the room in great strides. In a loud, hysterical voice he said: "John, that son of a bitch is going to ruin me. If that cocksucker talks, I'm gonna land in jail." By the time he had finished these words he had reached the chair at McCormack's desk, sat down, and buried his face in his hands. Then I knew why he had come here, and I realized how desperate the situation must be.

To the best of my recollection at that shocking moment, McCormack said: "Mr. President, things may not be that bad." He got up and went to Johnson and placed a hand on his shoulder.

"Jesus Christ!" Johnson exclaimed. "Things couldn't be worse, and you know it. We've talked about this shit often enough. Why wasn't it killed, John?" When Johnson looked up at McCormack, I could see he was crying. He buried his face again.

"We tried, Lyndon," McCormack said. "Everybody did."

Johnson said: "I practically raised that motherfucker, and now he's gonna make me the first President of the United States to spend the last days of his life behind bars." He was hysterical.

"You won't," McCormack said helplessly.

"How much money does the greedy bastard have to make?" Johnson said. "For a lousy five thousand bucks, he ruins his life, he ruins my life, and Christ knows who else's. Five thousand bucks, and the son of a bitch has millions."

"We all make mistakes," McCormack said, glancing at me. "How could he have known, Mr. President?"

"He should have *given* him the goddamn machines," Johnson said. "He should have known better. Now we're all up shit creek. We're all gonna rot in jail."

"We'll think of something," McCormack said. He rubbed Johnson's shoulder. "Please. Calm down. Control yourself."

In a burst, Johnson said: "It's *me* they're after. It's me they want. Who the fuck is that shit heel? But they'll get him up there in front of an open committee and all the crap will come pouring out and it'll be *my* neck. Jesus Christ, John, my whole life is at stake!"

"Listen, Lyndon," McCormack said, "remember the sign Harry had on his desk—THE BUCK STOPS HERE? Maybe we can make this buck stop at Bobby."

"You *have* to," Johnson cried out. "He's got to take this rap himself. He's the one that made the goddamn stupid mistake. Get to him. Find out how much *more* he wants, for crissake. I've got to be kept out of this."

"You will, Lyndon," said McCormack. "You will."

The President moaned. "Oh, I tell you, John, it takes just one prick to ruin a man in this town. Just one person has to rock the boat, and a man's life goes down the drain. And I'm getting fucked by two bastards—Bobby and that Williams son of a bitch. And all he wants is headlines."

"It'll pass, Lyndon," McCormack said. "This will pass."

Johnson got angry. "Not if we just sit around on our asses and think we can watch it pass. You've got to get to Bobby, John. Tell him I expect him to take the rap for this on his own. Tell him I'll make it worth his while. Remind him that I always have."

"All right, Lyndon."

During this conversation, McCormack repeatedly tried to block my view of Johnson by maneuvering himself between me and the President, especially when Johnson broke down. There were a few occasions when perhaps I could have slipped out of the room; but each time Johnson would either break down again or rear up in anger, and I'd sink back in my chair, amazed by what I was witnessing.

Finally, Johnson's bull-in-the-china-shop performance ended and he seemed to become aware of me for the first time.

He asked softly: "Is he all right?"

McCormack said: "Yes. He's a close friend of Nat's."

Johnson looked up at McCormack, his expression changing to a look of discovery. "Nat can do this," he said. "Nat can get to Bobby. They're friends. Have Nat get to Bobby."

McCormack seemed relieved. "Yes, Lyndon. I'd prefer that. I don't think this is a good time for me to get in touch with Bobby."

"Yes," said Johnson. "Get Nat. Let's talk to him. Is he around?"

"He's already gone back to New York."

"Have you got his phone number? Can you call him?"

"Yes, I can call him," said McCormack, "but I don't think this is something that should be discussed on the telephone, Lyndon."

"Will you see him tomorrow? Is he coming down tomorrow?"

"I suppose so. He didn't say."

At this point, I decided to speak up. I said: "I'm having breakfast tomorrow morning with Nat. We have a ten-fifteen appointment with Jimmy Roosevelt."

Johnson looked at me. "Can you give him a message?"

I said: "Yes, sir."

McCormack tore a couple of sheets from his personal memo pad and handed them to me. "Here, write it down." I took them; I still have them.

Johnson said: "Tell Nat that I want him to get in touch with Bobby Baker as soon as possible—tomorrow, if he can. Tell Nat to tell Bobby that I will give him a million dollars if he takes this rap. Bobby must not talk. I'll see to it that he gets a million-dollar settlement. Then have Nat get back to John here, or to Eddie Adams later tomorrow, so I can know what Bobby says."

I took notes. "Yes, sir."

"Tell Nat to tell Bobby Baker not to try to get in touch with me," McCormack said. "I don't want to have any meeting with Baker."

I took rapid notes. "Yes, sir."

Johnson said: "Tell Nat this is urgent and I want him to get on it right away."

"Yes, sir."

Johnson seemed relieved. He stood up. He said: "John, come back with me to the White House. I need your support right now."

"All right, Lyndon," McCormack said. "Let me arrange for my car." By telephone, McCormack instructed his secretary to have his car sent to the White House to wait for him. Then the President and the Speaker left the room by the private door. I put the two pieces of paper in my pocket and went out into the reception room, just as another Secret Service man went out the main door in pursuit of the President. Martin Sweig was there. Edith Pargament. Others. They all knew the President had been in the Speaker's office, and they asked me what had happened. I said: "He's upset about Bobby Baker." And I went back to New York.

As he always did when we were traveling to Washington together, Nathan Voloshen called me before leaving his apartment to let me know he was on the way to pick me up in the limousine it was his custom to rent for the drive to LaGuardia. During the call, I said I had something to talk to him about. I was downstairs waiting when the limousine arrived, and I got into the back seat with Voloshen. Because of the chauffeur, I didn't want to say anything about Johnson in the car. On the plane I said nothing because other people were near. I waited until we were at breakfast in the restaurant at the National Airport in Washington, where I felt I was free to talk. I told Voloshen the story, using McCormack's papers of the previous day. Voloshen did not express any surprise at the news or at the offer of a million-dollar pay-off. All he said was that he felt Johnson was overreacting and probably nothing would come of the Bobby Baker case. Before we left the airport, Voloshen went into a telephone booth and made some calls. Then we went to our meeting with Jimmy Roosevelt, which was over before eleven. Later, Voloshen made some more calls, but whether they related to the Johnson-Baker matter I cannot say. In fact, Voloshen never discussed this matter with me again, so I never knew whether he had contacted Bobby Baker and, if so, what transpired.

As the Bobby Baker case proceeded, I began to understand why President Johnson had been so hysterical in McCormack's office that afternoon. Regardless of the extent to which Johnson might have been involved in any of Baker's ventures, the two men had been so close for so long that it seemed unlikely Johnson would have absolutely no knowledge of them whatsoever. When, in September 1963, Ralph Hill moved against Baker, Baker's attorney was Abe Fortas, Johnson's personal legal adviser and, briefly, a U.S. Supreme Court Justice, appointed by Johnson; but the case started getting sticky,

and Fortas withdrew on December 2. Baker's next lawyer was Edward Bennett Williams, who had unsuccess-
fully defended Jimmy Hoffa but successfully defended
Frank Costello.

Bobby Baker appeared before the Senate Rules Committee on February 19 and 25, 1964, and again on
December 2, but the members got precious little information out of him. Time and again, he invoked the Fifth
Amendment. It was brought out before the committee
that Baker had acted as an intermediary on behalf of a
prominent Las Vegas gambler who had extensive associations with notorious underworld figures. John Gates,
of Intercontinental Hotels, Inc., a subsidiary of Pan
American World Airways, complained to the Rules
Committee that Baker had involved both him and the
company with these Nevada gamblers. Gates said that
in June 1963, Baker and Edward Levinson had met
with him to discuss bidding on the gambling concessions
at two of the company's hotels in the West Indies. Levinson held large interests in two Las Vegas casinos and
was also a major stockholder in Baker's Serv-U Corporation. Two other casino owners who later came into
the picture were Jacob Kozloff and Clifford Jones, the
latter an associate of George Sadlo, a business partner
in several ventures of Meyer Lansky, the underworld
banker.

Don Reynolds, a Silver Spring, Maryland, insurance
broker, told the committee that he had acted in 1960 as
a "bag man" in the transfer of an illegal campaign contribution of $25,000 from Matthew H. McCloskey to
Bobby Baker. Reynolds' testimony was supported by
copies of invoices and a canceled check. McCloskey,
builder of the $20-million District of Columbia stadi-
um, overpaid the premiums on his company's perform-

ance bond, most of the excess going to Baker for alleged political purposes. This happened when Lyndon
Johnson was the Senate Majority Leader and Baker's
boss.

Reynolds also testified that with Baker's help he had
sold Johnson substantial life insurance policies over a
ten-year period from 1951 to 1961. He claimed he was
induced by Johnson's long-time aide Walter Jenkins to
buy $1,200 worth of advertising on KTBC, in Austin,
Texas, a Johnson-family enterprise, as a kind of *quid
pro quo* arrangement. Jenkins denied the statement.
Reynolds also said Baker insisted he give Johnson a
stereophonic phonograph, which Johnson said later he
thought came from Baker, even though the original in-
voice which was in the packing case showed clearly that
the set was charged to the account of Reynolds.

Baker was involved in oil deals and bank operations
in Oklahoma, and in land deals in Florida. Through his
Washington connections, he set up the FDA approval
for the importing of meat from an American-owned
packing house in Haiti. The American owner was Clinton W. Murchison, Jr., the Texas industrialist and
financier, to whom the FDA previously had refused to
grant an approval.

In 1966, after three years of courtroom maneuvers,
Bobby Baker was indicted on seven counts of tax evasion, one count of theft, and one count of conspiracy to
defraud the government. It was Senator Williams who
brought the pressure that finally put the case before the
grand jury. After his conviction, Baker began a series of
appeals in 1967 which finally ended in failure. In January 1971, Baker presented himself at the federal prison at Lewisburg, Pennsylvania, to begin serving a one-
to-three-year sentence. By that time, however, both

Johnson and McCormack were out of office. The case was over. I never knew whether Voloshen had in fact gotten to Baker, as I'd heard Johnson demand. For that matter, I never knew that Johnson really had done anything illegal which would have made him try to muzzle Baker. But I do know what I saw and heard that day in McCormack's office, and I'll never forget it.

In the course of Martin Sweig's trial in New York during the summer of 1970, Speaker McCormack admitted to having known Nathan Voloshen for twenty years but said that he had not known Voloshen was using his office in the Rayburn Wing to carry on his illegal lobbying—a charge to which Voloshen had already pleaded guilty. During the trial, Bertha Drotos, one of McCormack's secretaries, admitted under cross-examination, on June 22, that she had taken countless business messages for Voloshen on McCormack's telephone and that both McCormack and Sweig had told her to do so. Yet nothing came of this conflicting testimony. McCormack had already announced his premature retirement. In the courtroom and in the press, McCormack was treated as the Grand Old Man of politics—which he was—and the general attitude seemed to be to let him depart from the political arena as gracefully as possible. However, as noble as that sentiment might have been, it also brought about a miscarriage of justice. The Sweig trial barely skimmed the surface of the improprieties that had taken place in McCormack's office for years, with the Speaker's knowledge and consent.

I can't count the number of times I had heard Martin Sweig actually imitate McCormack's voice and pass himself off as Speaker McCormack as he called this or that agency to check on the progress of one of Voloshen's projects. The ruse was necessary because a department head might not move fast enough on a mere call from a Congressman's administrative assistant. But a call directly from a Congressman—especially when that Congressman happened to be the Speaker of the House—would make anybody move, and move fast. I was often present when Sweig later told McCormack about the call and the use of his name. McCormack had to know about these matters, in case a return call reached him or he was approached outside his office. When given such information, McCormack usually nodded and said "all right" or "okay." When a return call did come, it was channeled from Edith Pargament to Martin Sweig, who would carry through on the matter.

Similarly, in both New York and Washington, I was present when Nathan Voloshen tried to imitate Martin Sweig's voice on the phone, identifying himself as Sweig, as he put the pressure on some government agency. Voloshen made these calls when Sweig was too busy to make them himself; sometimes Voloshen told Sweig beforehand, other times he told him afterward— in the same way and for the same reasons that Sweig kept McCormack fully informed. Everybody had to be kept apprised of the others' activities to avoid any embarrassing slip-ups.

Neither Sweig nor Voloshen ever made any effort to get me out of the room while he made this kind of call. The naïveté with which I was accepted by them as one of them was typical of Washington wheeler-dealers: if you came through the door with a friend you were automatically a friend yourself. I had met Voloshen through friends and Voloshen had brought me into McCormack's office, so I was automatically a member of the team. More than once, Sweig and Voloshen urged me to

expand my horizons as a lobbyist, to move up the ladder where the money was bigger. Sweig assured me of
his cooperation, which meant the cooperation of Speaker McCormack. All I had to be sure of was that my fee
on each project was large enough to provide for cuts to
Sweig and Voloshen. I always told them that as soon as
I felt experienced enough to move up the ladder, I'd let
them know. I never made it.

Both Martin Sweig and Nathan Voloshen knew I was
working with Jerry Ford and had no objection to the arrangement. However, they did criticize me for the *way* I
was working with Jerry Ford. They encouraged me to
imitate his voice on the telephone, but I told them I
wasn't that good an actor. Then they suggested I should
tell people that I was acting on Ford's behalf whenever
I needed something done in any government department. Actually, they wanted me to become as blunt,
bold, and arrogant in using my association with Ford as
they were in using theirs with McCormack. At this
point of my friendship with Ford, he was still too
straightlaced, too sincere, too honest, to allow any such
shenanigans, and I knew better than to try. Sweig and
Voloshen were also critical of my system of using
checks when making campaign contributions to Ford or
through Ford. Cash was better, they insisted. I preferred checks; I wanted to have a record. Moreover,
Ford himself had issued strict orders that there were to
be no transactions in his office or with his staff. An important difference in my relationship with Ford and Voloshen's relationship with McCormack and Sweig was
that Voloshen was paying them for the use of their
names, positions, and power, whereas each favor Ford
did for me involved a contribution by my client, but

nothing directly to Ford.* I was well aware that Voloshen was trying to turn me into one of his "salesmen"—
people who got clients for him. Voloshen had many such
"salesmen" working for him across the country, including his satisfied customers who recommended him to
other people who needed his Washington connections.

One of the points the defense tried to make at Martin
Sweig's trial was that Sweig had done nothing wrong in
trying to help out McCormack's constituents. As long as
these favors fell within legal bounds, there was indeed
nothing wrong, obviously, assuming the people involved
were constituents. Among the defense witnesses supporting Sweig on this point was Representative Robert
L. Leggett, Democrat of California, who expressed the
broad view that he regarded the whole United States as
his constituency. He said he never had any hesitation
about letting constituents use his office, his telephone,
or his services, whether on behalf of commercial clients
or not. He said that they could make long-distance calls,
too, as long as his $10,000-a-year telephone allowance
lasted. Sweig's trial ended with a conviction for perjury.
After he was released on bail, while appealing his conviction, he didn't have to look far for a job. He became
an assistant to Congressman Leggett and went back on
the government payroll. Leggett said he hired Sweig because of Sweig's valuable experience. Actually, he had
taken on Sweig because Sweig needed only a few more
months of government employment to qualify for a
higher pension. On June 21, 1971, Sweig lost his appeal

* In contemporary Washington, it is customary to accept
campaign contributions by check, as opposed to John McCormack's "cash on the barrelhead." It may be legal, but the question is, is it more honest?

and on July 22 he was remanded to the federal penitentiary at Lewisburg and assigned to the Allenwood Prison Camp, a minimum security facility.

Another Congressman who backed Sweig's favors for constituents was Thomas P. O'Neill, Jr., Democrat of Massachusetts, whose district abuts McCormack's old district. During his testimony, it was brought out that O'Neill himself had gone to McCormack's office for a favor. He wanted to get the son of a friend into the Citadel, the South Carolina military school. He went to the Speaker because he knew McCormack was a good friend of General Mark Clark, head of the Citadel, and O'Neill felt there was nothing improper in using this approach. After McCormack's retirement, the Democratic leadership in the House each moved a rung up the ladder, and the bottom rung—Majority Whip—became vacant. Congressman O'Neill got the job.

Also testifying for Sweig was Peter J. Cloherty; although identified as a Boston salesman, Cloherty was in reality a Boston influence peddler and a friend of Nathan Voloshen. To show how commonplace it was for constituents to use their Congressman's office for their own purposes, Cloherty said that often he had Martin Sweig make appointments with government agencies for his engineering and architectural firm—Maguire Associates, one of the biggest construction companies in Boston. Cloherty admitted that he used the Speaker's office while he was in Washington on business trips. He said it wasn't at all unusual for him to give McCormack's office telephone number to two or three people in Boston and tell them that if they needed him they could reach him "at my Congressman's office." As it turned out, Cloherty's Congressman was not John Mc-

Cormack, as he implied, but Tom O'Neill from the district next door.

Nathan Voloshen told me that Peter Cloherty had some good connections with the Bureau of Customs in Boston, and Nathan Voloshen took advantage of them. Voloshen and a convicted racketeer friend by the name of Pasquale Giordano, alias Pat Martin, were having pornographic movies smuggled into the United States from foreign countries. In order to be exhibited, the movies had to have a Bureau of Customs seal, indicating that they had been screened by the bureau and approved for release in this country. Whenever new movies arrived, they were delivered to the offices of Maguire Associates, then on Tremont Street in Boston, and handed over to a girl named Esther who worked on the fifth floor. From there, Peter Cloherty took the movies to the Boston Bureau of Customs office, and the films somehow got the bureau's seal of approval. One movie was so bad that even Cloherty's high contacts couldn't get the approval and the authorities wanted to know how the picture ever got into the country. Nobody knew.

Nobody in the general public could have known these backstage aspects of the Sweig trial, and so a trial which should have blown the lid off the Capitol did not even come to a boil. This was no accident, nor was it a matter of bad management. The investigation into the intrigues of Martin Sweig and Nathan Voloshen was begun by U.S. Attorney Robert Morgenthau in the Southern District of New York and later continued by his successor, Whitney North Seymour. At the same time, Morgenthau was trying to find a way to force Swiss banks to identify the holders of numbered bank accounts, the convenient tax dodge for the rich and the crooked for so many years. In both these efforts, Morgenthau was surrounded by powder kegs. But Morgenthau, a Democrat and a liberal reformer, was an honest and a courageous man, and he was determined to carry through, regardless of the damage he might do to his own party. He didn't get the chance. Before he could go to court, tremendous pressures were put on him by the office of U.S. Attorney General John Mitchell. When news of the pressure hit the papers, the impression given was that Mitchell was just trying to get a Democrat out of the New York job in order to give it to a Republican. Although this may be politically objectionable, it is a fairly common practice. But in this instance, the reason given was simply not the real one. Without questioning Mitchell's honesty, I came to the firm conclusion that he was merely trying to preserve the Establishment by protecting high-ranking public figures from public exposure. Mitchell's attitude, it seemed to me, was that if people become disillusioned with public officials and the way they operate, then people also might become disillusioned with the entire system and the way it operates. After all, J. Edgar Hoover had on occasion suggested that the very thought of an unworkable Establishment as it now exists was subversive—a dangerous idea to have loose in a democracy. Had Mitchell been able to get rid of Robert Morgenthau in October 1969, or earlier, as he wanted, I strongly suspect there would have been no indictment of Martin Sweig and Nathan Voloshen, and John McCormack would have remained the Speaker of the House of Representatives until his death.

When Morgenthau finally did agree to resign, it was with the proviso that he be allowed to hand down the

indictments of Sweig and Voloshen. It was also agreed
that Morgenthau's successor would continue to investigate the corruption in McCormack's office. On the day
the Sweig-Voloshen trial began, Voloshen pleaded
guilty. Subsequently, because of his age—seventy-two
—and his willingness to cooperate, he was given a suspended sentence and a small fine. Sweig was willing to
stand trial, and a tepid trial it was, highlighted by the
Santa Claus performance of John McCormack, and the
testimony of a parade of witnesses whose own private lives could not survive public scrutiny. Had Sweig
not perjured himself on an insignificant point, he might
have walked out of court scot-free. The Establishment
was saved. The cast was changed a little, but the scenery
was the same, and the show would go on.

It would be the same show that I had watched so
often in John McCormack's office. In May 1969, for example, Nathan Voloshen felt he had good cause to be
proud of himself. Previously, he had acted as the Washington agent for Chicago attorney Sidney Korshak when
two of the lawyer's clients—Dinah Shore and Jill St.
John—were having tax problems with the Internal Revenue Service. In 1969, Korshak sent Voloshen another
client—the Parvin-Dohrmann Company. On May 5,
Parvin-Dohrmann was suspended from trading by the
Securities and Exchange Commission on grounds of
having underworld connections. With amazing speed,
Speaker John McCormack set up a meeting for eleven
o'clock the next morning, May 6, in the office of Hamer
Budge, head of the SEC. At the meeting were Delbert
W. Coleman of Parvin-Dohrmann, the company lawyer
Elmer Johnson, Martin Sweig, and Nathan Voloshen.

Another meeting of these same people was held the following afternoon. On May 12, the suspension against Parvin-Dohrmann was lifted.

Two weeks later, on Tuesday, May 20, I went down to Washington for my usual eleven-o'clock meeting with Jerry Ford. Afterward, I sauntered over to McCormack's office in the Rayburn Wing to pick up Voloshen for lunch. As I entered the reception room, Edith Pargament was on the telephone, but she paused in her conversation long enough to say to me: "Nat's inside," and motioned me to go in. I passed through Martin Sweig's office; he wasn't there, nor was anyone else. I entered McCormack's office. My first surprise was to see McCormack himself there. He rarely came to this office during the day. McCormack had his back to me, and I saw a white envelope in his left hand. He was shaking hands with Voloshen, who was standing in front of him. McCormack was saying: "Many thanks for this, Nat. I appreciate it. I will salt it away. Glad you succeeded with Hamer Budge. Let me know if Martin can be of any further help to you."

Then Voloshen saw me. For a moment, he seemed flustered and embarrassed, but he composed himself quickly, smiled at me, and said: "Hello, Bob. Mr. Speaker, you know Bob Winter-Berger, don't you?" McCormack turned, the envelope still in his hand. He nodded. Of course he knew me. I had been in his presence hundreds of times by now; we had lunched together about twice a week for almost five years. But Voloshen's device broke the tension and gave McCormack time to put the envelope in his pocket. We went to lunch.

The next day, I had an afternoon meeting with Voloshen at his office. He was in good spirits. He told me that his fee for the Parvin-Dohrmann case had been $50,000. He said that in the envelope which McCormack had been holding was $15,000, adding that he had given Martin Sweig $10,000. It was Sweig who had turned the trick for Voloshen with the SEC. The only man more important in McCormack's office was McCormack himself, and by his presence at the two meetings Sweig was indicating how important the Parvin-Dohrmann matter was to McCormack and how far McCormack was ready to go to get the suspension lifted.

On the heels of this success, Voloshen was ready to take on the SEC again. This time the client was Michael C. Hellerman, president of Trimatrix, Inc. The electronics firm claimed to have developed a credit verification system so infallible that every American could be given a permanent number which would even supplant Social Security digits. Hellerman applied to the SEC for a permit to sell stock but was denied it because of his previous stock violations. Hellerman prevailed on John Donato, whom he knew, and Donato turned to Nathan Voloshen. Hellerman was invited down to Washington and given the House dining-room treatment. Donato, Voloshen, Sweig, and I were seated with McCormack at the Speaker's table. During lunch, McCormack nodded to everything Voloshen said. Hellerman agreed to pay a $10,000 fee for Voloshen's efforts. But this time Voloshen's efforts were in vain. Hellerman's record was so bad that the SEC could not be pressured into changing its position—not even by the Speaker of the House. This time Voloshen failed. But he nonetheless saw fit to keep the fee.

On Thursday morning, May 29, 1969, history repeated itself, in a way. I again had my meeting with Jerry Ford. Again I sauntered over to the Speaker's office to pick up Voloshen for lunch. This time as I entered the room, Martin Sweig was standing there with Voloshen. As I stood in the doorway, I heard Sweig ask Voloshen if he could get his promised money on the Hellerman case. Sweig said he was taking a little vacation over the Memorial Day weekend and needed the cash. Voloshen said he happened to have it with him, promptly pulled an envelope from his breast pocket, and handed it to Sweig. At this point, they both saw me, and Sweig looked very annoyed. We went to lunch.

About a week later, I was having lunch alone with Voloshen and he told me that he had made a mistake in handing Martin Sweig the money in front of me. Sweig had become very angry with him when I had left them after lunch, Voloshen said, and he had assured Sweig that I had forgotten about it. I assured Voloshen that I indeed had.

But I remembered it over a year later, during Martin Sweig's trial, as he repeatedly said he felt he had done nothing wrong in his position as administrative assistant to the Speaker of the House, that he had done nothing that anybody else wouldn't do in the same position. That may be true—and it may be precisely why the kind of corruption that typified McCormack's Parlor keeps going on and on.

On June 17, 1970, *The New York Times* published an article on the Sweig-Voloshen trial, which was to begin in New York that day and which involved charges of perjury and conspiracy to defraud. According to the article, House Minority Leader Gerald R. Ford and two Senators had been asked by Sweig to appear as his defense witnesses. The Senators were Jacob K. Javits, Republican of New York, and Claiborne Pell, Democrat of Rhode Island. As I continued to read the article, I discovered to my surprise that I was the villain of the piece. Ford and Pell, according to Sweig, "would be able to testify about the relations between a man named Robert Winterberger [*sic*] and Mr. Voloshen." The article went on to say: "One of Mr. Ford's staff members said Mr. Winterberger, 'a lobbyist of some kind,' had met the Michigan Republican in his Capitol Hill office." That was true as far as it went, but it hardly went far enough. The fact was that I had been in Ford's office not once but many times. I had gone out to Michigan to help him campaign for re-election. I had arranged a vacation for him at the home of some friends of mine in

Kentucky. We had talked on the telephone for hours, and his letters to me fill a file drawer. Although the member of Ford's staff who gave that quote to the *Times* may not have known of my closer relationship with Ford, I couldn't help remembering Jerry's warning to me when we first met—if I ever made a mistake, he would simply say he never knew me.

But the real surprise came from Claiborne Pell. The article went on to say: "Senator Pell, who was in Washington, said in a telephone interview yesterday that Mr. Winterberger had come into his office about eight years ago. 'He was rather bad news, but he said he had close connections with the Speaker's office,' Senator Pell said."

I hadn't realized that Clay Pell considered me "bad news." I also hadn't realized he had such a bad memory.

I had first met Senator Pell in June 1964, around two o'clock in the morning in a New York police station. He had evidently decided to have a night on the town and he happened to be in a Greenwich Village bar when it was raided. He was arrested with the other customers and taken to the old Charles Street precinct. At the station, Pell didn't have any identification on him, or, in view of the circumstances, didn't want his identity to become known. He was allowed one phone call, as all arrested people are, and he telephoned Gustavus Ober, his one-time Princeton roommate and close friend since then. Gus called me.

I had met Gus Ober late in May 1964. After World War II, Ober, whose family is "top drawer" in Maryland, hadn't done much with his life. Finally he had settled down, taking a job in public relations in the office of Marianne (Mimi) Van Rensselaer Strong, the leading press agent for New York socialites.

Before Ober's call that night regarding Claiborne Pell, I had already come to know the Senator's wife through various social events. As time went on, I had begun to notice that Nuala Pell wasn't being escorted by the Senator to these events but by other men, most frequently by Donald Davies, the Irish textile tycoon and famous horse breeder. One evening I commented to her jokingly that Pell must be getting antisocial.

"Not really," she said, "but after giving me four children Clay lost interest in everything except his career."

Gus Ober's call that night in June awoke me from a deep sleep and, because we knew each other only superficially, I remember that it took me a few moments to place him as he said:

"I wonder if you can do anything to help a friend of mine?"

"At this hour?" I asked.

"Well, yes," Gus said. "He's an important man and he's in some trouble. I'm sure that anything you can do will be appreciated."

"Who is it?"

"Pell. Clay Pell."

"The Senator?"

"Yes."

"What kind of trouble is he in?"

Gus told me, and I realized this was going to be a rough one. I thought of the people who would have to be paid off.

"I can't do anything like this for nothing," I said.

"He'll pay you," Gus answered. "Maybe he'll become one of your clients."

"Clients like this I don't need," I said. "Let me see what I can do." I was willing to try because of my friendship with Nuala.

"Thanks," Gus said. "I'm very concerned."

He had a right to be. If Senator Pell had had any identification with him, the police would have entered his name in their record of the raid on the gay bar and it would have become a matter of public information, available to anyone. In politics, the opposition will go to any lengths to obtain information that can be used to pressure, even to blackmail, a candidate, no matter how innocent the circumstances may be. I realized that only a person of influence would be able to resolve the problem without leaving any traceable evidence, and the only person I knew with such power was Carmine De-Sapio, then the Democratic leader of Manhattan's First Assembly District South. I had come to know DeSapio through Julia Skouras. DeSapio had been a good friend of Pell's father, Herbert Pell, a prominent New York socialite and Democratic Party leader. Despite the hour, I telephoned DeSapio, whom I had known slightly for several years, and after I explained the situation to him he offered to meet me at the police station in an hour. We arrived at the same time. While I waited in the main room, DeSapio went down a hall and evidently talked to whoever was in charge. He returned in a few minutes and told me: "Everything is okay." Almost immediately, Pell came out of a large room at the back of the station. The moment was not conducive to chitchat, so there were some embarrassed handshakes and thank-you's and we all went our separate ways.

About a week later, I got another call from Gus Ober, and, as I recall, our conversation went like this:

"Bob, this is Gus Ober. Clay Pell wants to see you.

Can you meet him for drinks this evening at the Racquet and Tennis Club?"

"Yes, I can," I said. "Has he got another problem?"

"He wants to discuss something with you."

"Listen, Gus," I said, "as far as I know there were no pay-offs on that other deal, so if that's what he's got on his mind, tell him he can forget it. He doesn't owe me a thing."

"I'm sure that isn't it," Gus said. "By the way, many thanks for what you did."

"Okay."

"Can I tell him you'll be there?"

"Yes."

I expected the meeting to be awkward, all apologies and explanations. Instead, Pell never mentioned the Greenwich Village incident; he was confident, charming, easy-going, speaking with that constipated nasal drawl which the very rich seem to pick up if they spend too much time around Newport, which was Pell's baili-wick. He had nothing special to say as we took a table and ordered; but, as I remember it, as soon as the waiter set down the drinks he began to study his finger-nails and frown seriously. I braced myself.

"Now, Bob," he drawled, pronouncing it Bawb, "as you know, this is an election year."

"Yes, I know," I said.

"Of course Lyndon Johnson is going to run."

I reached for the drink. "Of course."

"Well, Bob, I think I'm Vice-Presidential material."

I put the drink down. "You do?"

"Yes. But I can't do anything about it."

"Why not?"

"The Kennedys."

"The Kennedys?"

"Bobby Kennedy. He wants it. Everybody knows that."

"Johnson will have something to say about that. He and Bobby don't get along. Everybody knows that, too."

"That won't stop a Kennedy. The Kennedys get what they want."

"At least they try."

"Yes. And that's just the point. While Bobby is trying, I can't."

"Why not?"

"I don't know if you know that I didn't get the Democratic Party endorsement when I ran for the Senate in 1960."

"I know that."

"I won the primary and then I went on to win the election by the biggest majority in Rhode Island history."

"I know that, too."

"Well, the Kennedys did it," he said, and he sounded almost regretful. "The Kennedy Machine got behind me. You know how it is in Rhode Island—nobody can get elected to anything without the support of the goddamn Catholics. The Kennedys got the Catholics behind me and, although I'm Episcopalian, I broke records. So how do you think Bobby would like it if I started making noises like a Vice-Presidential candidate while he's after the same job?"

"I don't think he'd like it."

"You're damned right. And where would I be the next time I needed the Kennedy Machine in Rhode Island? Up the creek."

"Without a paddle."

"Right. That's why my hands are tied. I want that

job, damnit. I'm sure I'd be an asset on the ticket and I know I'd be a good Vice-President. Here." He reached for a piece of the club stationery, took out his pen, and began to write. I sipped my drink. When he finished, he handed me what he had written. I still have it. It says:

"An ideal Vice-Presidential candidate should be an Easterner with proven vote-getting ability, particularly in Catholic areas, and ability to communicate on television; experienced in foreign affairs, and a Kennedy reminiscent style."

He asked: "What do you think of it?"

"Fits you to a T," I said, handing it back to him.

"Keep it," he said. "You can quote it." I put the note into my pocket and waited. Pell went on: "You see, Bob, since I can't say or do a thing that would give Bobby Kennedy the impression I'm after the nomination, I'm going to have to depend on other people to advance my cause. People like you. Do you want another drink?"

I said: "Yes, I think so."

He ordered another round by nodding at the waiter. Then he asked: "Will you work with me, Bob?"

"As what?"

"I know that you're close to the Speaker," he said, "and everybody knows that McCormack is close to Johnson and hates the Kennedys. If there's anybody in Washington who knows what's on the President's mind in terms of a running mate, and if there's anybody who will be glad that it's not a Kennedy, it's John McCormack. I want you to keep sounding out McCormack so that as soon as we know that Bobby hasn't got a chance I'll be able to make my move. Can you do that?"

The man amazed me. After acknowledging that the

Kennedys had put him where he was, he then admitted to a plot to stab the leader of the clan in the back, once the coast was clear. "I can try," I said evasively.

"I'll pay you, of course," he put in quickly. When the waiter brought the drinks, Pell asked him for a blank check, and then he wrote out a check to me for $250 on the Bank of New York. That was the only money he ever gave me.

I said to him: "You know, this can turn out to be an expensive fight."

"I'm ready for that," he said. "If Johnson decides to leave the choice up to the delegates, I've already set aside $75,000 of my own money to use at the convention battle. And if Johnson turns down Bobby, earlier, I can get all the money I need to fight anybody else and be in a good position before the convention even starts. Everything depends on when Bobby drops out or gets dumped."

So he had it all figured out.

In Washington, I had had occasion to witness evidence of the split between Johnson and the Kennedys as well as the feud between McCormack and the Kennedys. Both the split and the feud had practically turned the Kennedy Machine into an independent party. On Thursday, March 19, 1964, I attended a banquet at the National Armory in Washington, a $100-a-plate dinner for the benefit of the Democratic Party. Held each year and tied in with St. Patrick's Day, the banquet traditionally was hosted by Representative Michael J. Kirwan of Ohio, who had been in the House since 1937 and had acquired a great deal of power over the years. Kirwan had a good eye; he could glance out on the acreage of diners and tell immediately which of the party faithful were missing. Because 1964 was a Presidential election year, every elected and appointed Democrat in the country well enough to get out of bed had had to be at that benefit, plus those of us who did business with these people. James A. Farley was the master of ceremonies. President Johnson was there. So was Speaker McCormack, then constitutionally the Vice-President of the United States. And there were 5,300 more of us.

I was at Nat Voloshen's table, directly in front of the rostrum, and with us was Edith Pargament, McCormack's secretary. When President Johnson entered, he received a standing ovation. This was his first public appearance since taking office, and the party wanted to show that it was solidly behind him. It was an electric moment. Compared to the aloof and reserved John Kennedy, Johnson was a tower of virility, and everybody felt it. When the ovation subsided, I asked Edith, who was sitting next to me: "Well, what do you think of Johnson?"

The Boston woman beamed and said: "Oh, he's got *bahlls!*" We laughed. Maybe it was her Boston accent that made me think of the Kennedys. Certainly, Ted a Senator from Massachusetts, and Bobby, the U.S. Attorney General, should have been at this important Democratic affair. But they were not. I didn't hear their names mentioned all evening. They were the only two leading Democrats missing.

Without question, Claiborne Pell was walking a loose wire. He knew perfectly well that the mystique of the Kennedys had produced a political machine which operated outside the party structure in Massachusetts and was equally effective throughout New England and almost as effective across the country. The Kennedys could play dirty touch-tackle when they wanted to.

They loved a good fight—and they hated losing. They tried to keep themselves free of political indebtedness, and this is a freedom that unnerves other politicians. But what made them feared even more than they were disliked was the tenacity with which they held a grudge. Maybe it was the Irish in them. Whatever it was, nobody crossed the Kennedys twice, because the disabilities following the first cross usually left people permanently maimed in one way or another. Clay Pell knew this, and I wondered how he could be so unrealistic as to let personal ambition endanger a political career which the Kennedys had won for him in the first place. He had the background to know better.

Pell's father, Herbert C. Pell, had been a member of Congress and the chairman of the New York State Democratic Party for thirty-three years. Franklin D. Roosevelt had been Clay Pell's godfather. Another close family friend and later Pell's political mentor was Averell Harriman. On both sides, Pell's family was deeply rooted in American politics, going back before the American Revolution and including Congressmen, governors, cabinet members, ambassadors, and James Polk's Vice-President, George M. Dallas. Although at the time Pell had held an elected office for only four years, he had spent most of his adult life in some phase of politics. He had been at San Francisco during the organization of the United Nations; he had spent seven years with the State Department in the Foreign Service; he had been active with the Democratic National Committee. He was a limited partner in the brokerage firm of Auchincloss, Parier, and Redpath—the Auchincloss being the stepfather of Jacqueline Kennedy Onassis. And Pell had married well. Nuala's mother is Jo Hartford Bryce, of the A&P Hartfords. With all that going for him, it would seem that Claiborne Pell should have had the patience and perspicacity to play a smarter game of politics, but evidently the man enjoyed living dangerously, like bar-hopping in Greenwich Village gay bistros.

Nevertheless, I agreed to try. The next time I was with Speaker McCormack, I said: "Everybody in New York is wondering who's going to be on the ticket with Johnson."

"There's nothing to wonder about," he said in that gruff tone that was one of his trademarks.

"Then Bobby Kennedy is all set?"

He seemed amazed at my naïveté. "Of course not!"

"Some people in New York are talking favorably about Senator Pell," I offered.

He almost laughed. "Tell 'em to forget it, then. It's Humphrey."

This was in late June, and I'm sure Hubert Humphrey himself wouldn't have made bets on his chances until President Johnson got up in front of the convention in Atlantic City in August and named him. In any event, when I reported this to Pell, he said: "I can't believe it. Not Humphrey. Anyway, it's too early for this thing to be settled. Keep asking questions and keep talking me up."

"Do you want me to say that you're interested?"

"Say that I'd accept it."

The next time I had a chance to talk to the Speaker alone, I said: "The talk I heard in New York about Pell for Vice-President is getting back to him. From what I hear, he'd be willing to make a run for it, if the door is still open."

McCormack said: "Tell Pell to save his money. Tell him that Humphrey has got it and that he is out."

Pell wouldn't give up. On July 2, he called me from Newport, and our conversation went more or less like this:

"I just left Bobby Kennedy. The bastard says he's got the nomination sewed up."

I said: "I hope he's out of earshot."

"He's still out on his boat."

"How come you two got together?"

"We're close friends, you know," Pell said. "He heard I was here so he called this morning and said there was something he wanted to talk about in confidence. He suggested that his boat would be the best place for it. I suspected what he had in mind, and it turned out I was right."

"What was it?"

"The tricky son of a gun said that his people have been working on the delegates quietly for months now, and he's sure he's got enough of them secretly pledged to him to get the nomination. Then he said: 'I know I should have talked to you about this sooner, Clay, but we're old friends and I hope I can count on your support at the convention.' "

"What did you say to that?"

"I said he could. What the hell else could I say?"

"Well, that's friendship for you."

"I hate to work with him, of course," Pell said, "but I have to. At least I have to put up the front."

"Did Humphrey's name come up?"

"Yes. I sounded Bobby out. I wasn't as definite about it as you are. I just said I heard some talk that Johnson wants Humphrey. Bobby said it wouldn't make any difference. He says that once his people start the tidal wave Johnson and Humphrey can go to hell together, hand in hand."

"Clay, now that you're going to support your old friend, do you want me to drop what I'm doing for you?" I asked.

"Absolutely not," he said, so sharply I could almost feel Bobby's boat rocking. "Don't you see what can happen? Maybe all that Bobby Kennedy will achieve is to split the convention so badly that there'll be room for me to move in."

"Maybe."

"Bob," he said, calming, "do you know Ernest Cuneo?"

"I know who he is. A big publisher and printer in Chicago." (I learned later he was a well-connected eastern lawyer who had headed a publishing group.)

Pell said: "He's in New York for a few days. I'll have him call you. I'd like the two of you to get together."

"What for?"

"To compare notes. He's got some ideas I think you should know about. Then you can tell me how you feel about them."

I asked: "Clay, can I speak my mind to this man?"

"Sure, of course," he said. "He's an old friend."

So is Bobby Kennedy, I thought. Friendship, I already knew, was a meaningless thing to these people.

A few days later, Ernest Cuneo called me and we agreed to meet for lunch on Monday, July 20, at one o'clock at the New York Athletic Club. Cuneo turned out to be a big publisher in more ways than one. He was a huge, fat man, pleasant, but quietly overpowering in the way of a man who has been the boss for so long that he has forgotten that opposition can exist. I didn't have many notes to compare with him. I told him about my conversations with the Speaker, but I could sense that he already had heard them, from Clay presumably.

I remember saying: "Frankly, I feel Clay should forget about it."

He shook his big head slowly, patiently. "Clay isn't going to give up," he said. "You know that, don't you?"

"That's up to him."

"You don't think that John McCormack is the end of the line, do you?"

"No, Johnson is."

"Well, has McCormack told you that Johnson himself says that Humphrey is definitely the man?"

"Not specifically, but he wouldn't have to. He knows what business I'm in. I'm sure he knows why I've brought up Pell's name. And if there is anybody in Washington who knows what's on Lyndon Johnson's mind, it's McCormack. If McCormack says it's Humphrey, then everybody else can forget about it."

The big head wagged. "I think you're wrong."

"Suit yourself."

"If Bobby Kennedy starts his revolt, that convention will go up for grabs."

"Clay said you had some ideas."

"Yes. I think we should get people thinking about Clay as the Vice-Presidential candidate. If we can convince the party leaders that the people at the grass roots are talking about Clay as the candidate, maybe we can get some action at the top."

"Maybe."

"I know Walter Winchell well."

"I know. Everybody knows you've been his mentor."

"I've gotten him to do some things on Clay. Did you know that Jim Farley and Clay's father were buddies years ago?"

"No."

lawyer Richard Wels, realized that Guterma could become a valuable government witness against others on
whom cases were being prepared. Wels was ready to advise his client to cooperate provided that Guterma be
released from prison at the earliest possible moment,
that pending indictments against him be dropped, and
that his fine be remitted. The office of the Attorney
General agreed to all these conditions. The day Guterma became eligible for parole, his request for the parole
was turned down by the parole board. His lawyer immediately called Kennedy in Washington; Kennedy
spoke to the head of the board; the board was promptly
reconvened, in an unusual move, and Guterma was
paroled. All other pending indictments were disposed of.
In order to dispose of the other indictments pending
against himself, apart from the one which resulted in his
original conviction, Guterma pleaded guilty to a series
of counts before Judge Herlands in the Southern District, with the approval of the Attorney General, and in
April of 1963 the Judge sentenced him on these counts
but placed him on probation for five years. Judge Herlands noted, at one point in the proceedings, that he
found Alexander Guterma "to be a man of truth, after
having an unusually long time to examine him." Guterma became a government witness. Practically every important case Kennedy won as Attorney General resulted
from Guterma's cooperation. But the fine still had not
been remitted by 1967.

My assignment was to try to get it remitted. By this
time Kennedy was a New York Senator; but since the
agreement had been made while he was the Attorney
General, I felt certain that he was still a party to it and
that he was the first person to see to get the agreement
fulfilled. I made an appointment with him at his Wash-

ington office. When I arrived, I was lucky to get inside the door. The appointment had been canceled because of other pressing matters. The Senator was out, and I could not even get to see his assistant, Joe Dolan. I did talk to Dolan's secretary, Polly Busselle, and she said that everybody was so busy she didn't know when in the near future I could get another appointment with Kennedy—or even with Dolan. I left.

I decided to talk to Jerry Ford about the problem, but he felt this was not the kind of matter he should get involved in. He said, however, that he would approve the remittance if the question ever came up. He suggested I go to Speaker McCormack, but I knew that would be a waste of time. Disliking Kennedy, McCormack wanted nothing to do with him, even though something such as this carried the potential to make Kennedy look bad for having broken a promise.

The reason that Wels asked me to intercede on his behalf, rather than choosing to be represented by an attorney—as is usually the custom—is that in the September 1967 discussions which he and Mr. Guterma had with Assistant United States Attorney Henderson of the Civil Division of the United States Attorney's office for the Southern District of New York, Mr. Henderson conceded that the promises and commitments with respect to the remission of the fine imposed on Guterma had in fact been made. But the Justice Department, Henderson went on, was afraid that if it lived up to the commitment at that time, the minority party might exploit the action, making it a political embarrassment to the department. Because of this possibility, Henderson concluded, the U. S. Attorney's office could not live up to its commitments.

Since I was close to Jerry Ford, and he was the Minority Leader of the House of Representatives, Wels wanted me to discuss the matter with him in order to get his assurance that neither would he interfere nor would the minority party make an issue out of any settlement. It worked, because Ford agreed to keep his party in line.

Remembering that Clay Pell and Bobby Kennedy were old friends, I called Pell's office. He was at a meeting in the Capitol, but I was able to make an appointment for the next day. I went back to New York for the night. During the evening, Pell telephoned me at my apartment and I recall that he began the conversation with an abrupt but friendly:

"I see that we've got an appointment here tomorrow afternoon, Bob."

"Yes, we do." I said. "Is it all right?"

"Of course. Is it something we can discuss on the phone?"

"Yes."

"Will it take more than an hour?"

"Nowhere near that."

"Well, then, Bob, why bother with the trip down here?" he said. "Let's talk about it right now."

We did. When I finished, he said: "All I can recommend, Bob, is that you put all this into a detailed letter and send it by registered mail, return receipt requested, to Ramsey Clark. Use your stationery that shows you're in public relations and lobbying and that you're not the attorney of record, and you'll frighten him to death."

Clark had by then succeeded Nicholas deB. Katzenbach as Attorney General. On November 30, 1967, I wrote a detailed letter on the matter, but nothing came of it immediately. Word reached me that people in the

Johnson Administration did not want to create the image of Democrats making deals with convicted criminals—especially since an election was coming up the following year. In fact, as it turned out, over three years passed before the matter was finally resolved, by multimillionaire industrialist Alfred A. Strelsin—and associates.

According to that same *New York Times* article of June 1970, Sweig said Senator Javits might be called to testify about a charge in the indictment that in 1968 Nathan Voloshen had helped prepare a letter to military authorities on behalf of Gary Roth, a New York soldier who had later received a hardship discharge. The *Times* said that Javits's Washington office acknowledged having a routine constituent file on the soldier, but added that it had no knowledge of intervention into the case by anyone from around Speaker McCormack's office. Since the New York grand jury had been working for months on the indictment against Sweig and Voloshen there was little about the case that could come as news to anybody involved, including Jacob Javits. Less than a month before the *Times* article appeared, I had had dinner next to the Senator with a friend of his at Trader Vic's in New York, and, as we chatted, the subject had never come up.

Javits's host at Trader Vic's that night was Alfred Strelsin. With them was the Senator's son Joshua, and his nephew, Eric. Though Strelsin's headquarters were in Chicago, he had business interests in the East and therefore spent a lot of time in New York. After finding ourselves at the same parties a number of times, Strelsin and I became friends. Although seventy-two years old in 1970, he looked much younger. He was a gentleman of the old school, always pleasant, amiable, and extremely generous.

Al Strelsin always made good money, although nobody could determine where he got the really immense capital he could always come up with for a new venture. In 1917, he had started the Reliance Advertising Company in Chicago and acquired many important clients. After World War I, he had obtained the rights to a German-devised technique for laminating road signs to make them more visible at night, and through political connections secured contracts from cities, counties, and states all over the country. In the 1930's, he organized the General Scientific Corporation, which made scientific instruments. The company later became the Cenco Instrument Company, of Chicago, which in 1971 had a volume of $110 million a year and employed 4,000 people. Also in the 1930's, Strelsin set up the Park Construction Company and got a contract to build part of the Sixth Avenue subway in New York. In addition, at Westbury, Long Island, Strelsin had founded and was the chief stockholder of the IMC Magnetic Corporation, with some 400 employees. IMC made fans and blowers for hi-fi sets, and electronic equipment used in communications systems.

It was Al Strelsin who resolved the problem of Alexander Guterma's unremitted fine for his conviction of stock swindling, which I had first tried to solve in November 1967. Since that initial effort, two years had gone by with no tangible results. Then, Guterma's lawyer—Richard Wels—helped provide some of the evidence which resulted in the indictment of Martin Sweig and Nathan Voloshen. Subsequently, the U.S. Attorney's Office in New York evinced a more cooperative attitude in trying to get Guterma's fine remitted. Toward this end, papers were filled out and filed with the Department of Justice in New York and were forwarded to Washington. To show Guterma's good faith, Wels made a partial payment to the government of $11,000 against the total fine of $140,000. But even then, Washington again turned down the application, and the remission was not granted. So now Guterma owed the government $129,000, and, until he paid it, he was still on parole, a restricted man.

About this same time, Al Strelsin was engaged in a multimillion-dollar Florida land speculation. Associated with him in the enterprise were Dave Baird, senior member of the Wall Street firm of Baird and Company; investment banker Charles Allen; and John Markesy, who headed the speculative promotion itself. Strelsin, Allen, and Baird decided they were not satisfied with the job Markesy was doing, so they went to Alexander Guterma with a written contract involving stock options and they offered him the job. Guterma wanted to accept it, but he reminded them that he still had a little problem with the government—a $129,000 problem—and until the sum was paid he would not be allowed to travel much. He had not even been allowed to go to a wedding party over in New Jersey in 1967. Strelsin, Allen, and Baird thereupon offered to advance Guterma the money to pay the fine. Guterma realized, however, that his check for that amount to the government would bring the Internal Revenue men running to try to find out where suddenly he had got so much money, thus possibly creating all sorts of new problems. For this reason, I was told, Strelsin made the payment of $129,000 directly to the government, thereby repaying Guterma's debt to society and making him a free man. Strelsin,

Allen, and Baird bought out John Markesy and Guterma went to work for his three generous friends.

At Trader Vic's that night in May 1970, Al Strelsin put many questions to Jake Javits about matters relating to his many companies and various government agencies. Each time, Javits would say: "Tell Ben," or "Get in touch with Ben about that," or "I'll see Ben about that in the morning."

Benjamin Javits, Jake's older brother, had put Jake through law school on his own earnings as a young lawyer, and later the two brothers formed a partnership, Javits and Javits, with Ben as the senior partner. Ben was very active at high levels of the Republican Party and he became Jake's political mentor when Jake was ready to go into politics in the 1940's. Besides being a lawyer, Ben was something of an economist, and he once wrote a book, *Ownerism*. When President Kennedy started antitrust suits to put pressure on big industry to keep prices down, Ben held a news conference at which he denounced Kennedy for denying stockholders the right to make money. Ben organized the United Shareholders of America and the Telephone Shareholders of America, the latter being holders of communications stocks, such as AT&T. Both were special-interest groups, and Ben appointed himself their lobbyist in Washington. At the time of the Trader Vic's dinner (May 1970), both groups were still in existence, and Ben, who wasn't practicing law anymore, at least in the usual sense of the word, was still running them.

But back in 1961 Ben Javits was still practicing law. In October of that year Lewis S. Rosenstiel, the founder of Schenley Industries, had hired Ben to obtain for him a difficult annulment from his third wife, the former Susan Lissman. Ben had said that he and his brother could help but legal fees would come to at least $175,000. Rosenstiel had put up the money. Two years and $400,000 later, the annulment still had not come through. When Rosenstiel had asked Ben Javits what was going on and what had happened to his money, Ben had replied that he and his brother were still trying and that they had used up the money in the course of doing so. Furious, Rosenstiel then had hired Roy Cohn to sue Javits and Javits for $445,000 for the improper disbursements of funds. Rosenstiel felt he had been swindled. Had he been found guilty, Ben Javits could have been disbarred.

Javits and Javits* had counter-sued Rosenstiel for $175,000 in legal fees, and Ben had insisted that he could account for the original payment. Both cases had lingered on without going to trial. Then in 1966, Rosenstiel had amended his complaint upward to $785,000, explaining the increase as additional legal costs. Javits and Javits had replied by raising their suit to $177,000. Next Rosenstiel had offered to drop his suit provided that (1) Ben Javits either got the annulment or returned the monies and (2) Ben stopped practicing law. Rosenstiel had dropped his suit on March 16, 1970, but the court records contained no details on the settlement.

Roughly seven months after the dinner at Trader Vic's, on January 5, 1971, Ben Javits was suspended from the practice of law for three years for "attempting to perpetrate a fraud upon the courts of Mexico and the United States." *The New York Times* reported: "In two

---

* Jacob Javits had left the law firm of Javits and Javits upon becoming a Senator, later associating himself with the firm of Javits, Trubin, Sillcocks, and Edelman, which he resigned from in September of 1971. The firm of Javits and Javits became Ben Javits and his son Eric.

opinions castigating the 76-year-old lawyer for professional misconduct, the Appellate Division sustained a report by the Association of the Bar of the City of New York that he had paid 'Mexican public officials and another Mexican national in order to improperly obtain and subsequently defend a nullification of a Mexican divorce decree.' "

It was the Rosenstiel case. What Ben Javits allegedly had tried to do was have Rosenstiel's wife Susan's Mexican divorce from her first husband nullified, which would have meant that she was still married to him, and on this basis Javits could have had the marriage to Rosenstiel nullified in American courts. The court decision against Javits was four-to-one, but the minority opinion, written by Justice James B. M. McNally, held that Ben Javits should be disbarred. McNally wrote: "Respondent knowingly embarked on a course of professional misconduct in compliance with the demands of his client. He was motivated solely by monetary reward and his conduct evinces professional irresponsibility." Ben Javits, who was on vacation in Florida at the time, said he would appeal.

Besides Javits and Pell, other members of Congress mentioned by *The New York Times* as possible witnesses for Sweig were the then House Majority Leader (and later House Speaker) Carl Albert of Oklahoma, and Representatives Emanuel Celler and John J. Rooney, both Democrats of New York. I knew these three men. They were all great friends of Nathan Voloshen. Rooney was particularly important to Voloshen. He was the ranking member of the House Committee on Appropriations and chairman of the Subcommittee on Appropriations for State, Justice, Commerce, the Judiciary and Related Agencies. His chairmanship of this powerful subcommittee put him in charge of the budgets of these government departments and agencies. And in Washington, the man who holds the purse strings calls the shots. Nathan Voloshen always went to Rooney whenever he needed to get something done in any of the agencies or when one of his clients was having problems in prison or with a particular parole board. During the 1968 campaign, a fund-raising party was held for John Rooney in October at the Overseas Press Club in New York. As I accompanied Voloshen to it, he said: "I've got to keep John on my side. He's important to me." At the party, Voloshen made his way to Rooney and handed him an envelope containing $2,000 in cash. I had watched him count out twenty $100 bills and slip them into the envelope beforehand in his office. Voloshen said: "John, as you know, it isn't the first and it won't be the last."

As they shook hands, Rooney threw an arm around Voloshen's shoulders and said: "Nat, anything you want is yours. You're a dear, dear friend. I'm proud to know you."

On that June morning in 1970, as I read *The New York Times* article about me, which mentioned most of these men, I was struck by the fact that all of them seemed to be such dear, dear friends. They had all been friendly with me once, but now I was the "heavy." Perhaps they would still have been friendly had they met me through Martin Sweig. As McCormack's aide for many years, Sweig was Establishment, and he had to be saved at all costs in order for these other members of the Establishment to save themselves. But they had met me through Voloshen—or socially or in a police station —and so, like Voloshen, I suddenly had become expendable. I had seen this happen before in Washington, to people who for one reason or another suddenly had become a threat, so I was not really surprised. I was, however, saddened by the thought that these were among the men who run the strongest and richest nation in the world, at perhaps the most critical hour in the world's history.

If there is a precise moment when I came to a major turning point in my life, it was on that day in June 1970. Suddenly I determined to do something about what I judged to be an impossible situation—a situation in which the very leaders of government, who should have been setting an example for the country, seemed to have sunk to a new low of conniving and corruption.

The Godfathers,
the Judges,
and the Weasel

Behind his back, Nathan Voloshen's underworld friends referred to him as the Weasel. Voloshen was aware of this and it infuriated him. His secretary, Margaret Stafford, told me how, from time to time, some crime lord would come into the office and say: "I want to see the Weasel." The name was a code word, in a sense, identifying the caller as one of the insiders. Sometimes if Voloshen's door were open he would hear the nickname. When he did he always needed a few minutes to calm himself before he could conduct the business at hand.

Nonetheless the name was apt. Voloshen was a small man, and his *modus operandi* was certainly the burrowing technique, although Voloshen did his burrowing for the underworld at the top levels of government and in the high courts of justice. It was a wonder that he got away with it for as long as he did, and yet actually it was no wonder at all. In 1967, House Minority Leader Jerry Ford told me that he had been trying to investigate Voloshen's gangland connections for some time but had got nowhere. "You can only go so far on the man," he said, "and then the walls of protection come down before you can really get at him."

A year later, Arthur Viviano of the FBI's New York office, who was investigating Voloshen on behalf of U.S. Attorney Robert Morgenthau, told me that he had been compiling a file on Voloshen for eight years and finally had been allowed to proceed on it only because Morgenthau had forced the bureau's hand. This is high protection, indeed, and it could only come from very high places.

The fact was, Voloshen moved in high places. First, he enjoyed the many privileges accorded him by Speaker McCormack. But he was also the vest-pocket lobbyist-friend of House Majority Leader Carl Albert; House Majority Whip Hale Boggs; former Representative James Roosevelt of California; and former Representative Adam Clayton Powell of New York, who at the time of his closest association with Voloshen was chairman of the powerful House Education and Labor Committee. In September 1966, when James Roosevelt was with the U.S. delegation to the United Nations, I tried to see him on behalf of a client, but had great difficulty in making any sort of contact with him. His personal secretary, Maureen Corr, said he was far too busy to see me, having just returned from a European trip. Finally, in desperation, I mentioned to her that I was a friend of Nat Voloshen's. She asked me to call back the next day. When I did, I was told that Ambassador Roosevelt would be happy to see me at my convenience. The Voloshen magic had worked.

Certainly, Voloshen's key connection for the underworld was John Rooney of Brooklyn, whose important committee posts have already been detailed.

Nathan Voloshen moved into the big time of the underworld in 1948. At the time, he was a trouble shooter for the New York law firm of Hartman, Sheridan, Tekulsky, and Donoghue. A close friend of his was a Prohibition-era racketeer named Anthony Carfano, more popularly known as little Augie Pisano, and Little Augie had made it up the ladder through his contacts with Al Capone. Voloshen and Pisano met through their girl friends. Voloshen was very close to Shirley Lewis, the then wife of Irving Allen Segal, a stockbroker friend of Pisano. Little Augie was also the confidant of such colorful figures as George Scalise, Frank Costello, Vito Genovese, Albert Anastasia, and Al Capone. Pisano was having an affair with Janice Drake, wife of comedian Allan Drake. Shirley and Janice were the best of friends.

By 1948, Little Augie Pisano ranked among the elite 400 of the Mafia. Then around fifty years old, he controlled a small army of henchmen in a wide variety of rackets. He was well-known for his refusal to relinquish any of his activities to the younger, more ambitious members of his "family," and it was probably this more than anything else that led to his sudden death a decade later. It was in 1948 that Little Augie introduced Nathan Voloshen to George Scalise, whose specialty was labor racketeering. In 1940, Scalise had been sent to prison on a 10-to-20-year sentence for rifling funds of the Building Service Employees Union, of which he was president. He had been out only a short time when he met Voloshen.

The purpose of the meeting was to bring together two men who could well use each other's connections. Voloshen was looking for clients; Scalise was looking for someone whose contacts in government and in the courts could make life easier for him and his boys. It was a happy meeting. One of the first contacts that Scalise made for Voloshen was with Mortimer Brandenberg, president of the Distillery, Rectifying, Wine, and Allied Workers International Union of America, AFL-CIO. Voloshen subsequently became the union's legislative representative in Washington for a fee of $1,200 a month plus expenses. Among other things, Voloshen had to act as an arbitrator among the various warring factions in the union, posing as a father confessor, supposedly keeping all confidences, but in fact passing everything on to Brandenberg. He and Brandenberg then took the problems to George Scalise who would tell them how to proceed. Voloshen would go back to the factions with his recommendations for settlements, which were actually Scalise's orders. When Brandenberg was brought into court by dissident union members on charges of misappropriating union funds, it was Voloshen who set up the machinery which produced endless delays, until it seemed that the case would never go to trial. Later, Scalise introduced Nathan Voloshen to Bill Bufalino of the Teamsters Union and eventually to Teamsters' president Jimmy Hoffa. Voloshen became close friends with both these men. It was Voloshen, too, who got Bill Bufalino's ex-convict brother Eugene the job of head of the Rectifying Union on the West Coast. The Bufalinos were very grateful. When I was introduced to Eugene Bufalino in February 1964, he said: "I think the world of Nat. I would do anything for him. Anything." Rather than sounding affectionate, he sounded threatening.

Scalise's contacts in the complex union networks were both thorough and effective. A word of introduction from Scalise to any union officer was all that Voloshen needed. Voloshen once told me that "Uncle

George," as he called Scalise when he wasn't around, was his most valuable contact and said he would gladly split all net fees with him. On many occasions, I saw Voloshen pass envelopes to Scalise, which, he told me later, contained cash. I also saw him give Scalise such gifts as cigars, radios, watches, toasters, and perfumes.

In the mid-1950's, Little Augie Pisano, George Scalise and Sol Cilento, secretary-treasurer of the Rectifying Union, became defendants in Manhattan District Attorney Frank S. Hogan's indictments based on testimony by Louis B. Saperstein, an insurance broker. Saperstein had told a grand jury that the three men had taken $299,000 in kickbacks from him on deals which they referred to him as investments for the union's welfare fund. Before the trial, Saperstein was in a car one night with a girl friend when unknown persons approached and shot him in the head. To everybody's surprise, he survived.*

Scalise, Cilento, and Little Augie were indicted for bribery in 1955, but the charges against them were dismissed by Judge Jonah J. Goldstein, on technical grounds. The Court of Appeals, however, while dismissing the indictment against Little Augie "on the grounds of insufficient evidence," ruled that Scalise and

---

* "Louis Saperstein died in November 1968, from arsenic poisoning," *The New York Post* reported via an AP dispatch. "His death," the dispatch went on, "was ruled a suicide. He had been scheduled as the principal witness against [Angelo] DeCarlo and [Daniel] Cecere," two reputed mob bosses. The *New York Daily News*, in reporting the same story, noted, on August 10, 1971: "Saperstein, an insurance broker from whom DeCarlo and Cecere allegedly extorted money, died in November 1968. Although an autopsy later showed that Saperstein's body contained enough arsenic to 'kill a mule,' his death was ruled a suicide."

Cilento had to stand trial. On April 8, 1957, both men, also to everyone's surprise, pleaded guilty to "conspiracy and bribery." One month later, on May 8, 1957, General Sessions Judge John A. Mullen sentenced Scalise and Cilento to a year in prison.

On September 25, 1959, Little Augie had dinner with some friends at Marino's on New York's Lexington Avenue. The friends were his girl friend Janice Drake, her good friend Shirley Lewis, Shirley's husband Irving Allen Segal, two known hoods—Tony Strollo (alias Tony Bender) and Anthony Mirra—and Nathan Voloshen. Voloshen told me later that Segal knew Voloshen was having an affair with Shirley but didn't seem to mind. The marriage was already on the rocks; there was a divorce, and some years later both remarried, Shirley marrying Harvey Axelrod, a dress manufacturer. But she continued to be a close friend of Voloshen's. "Shirley's the only one I can relax with," Voloshen once confided to me. So it was a relaxing evening.

Augie had been staying out of the limelight. He had been a prime suspect in the 1957 barber-shop murder, in New York's Park Sheraton Hotel, of Albert Anastasia, who was supposed to be his best friend; Augie had not circulated much since. As the dinner ended, Segal accompanied Augie and Janice to Augie's Cadillac. A few hours later, Augie and Janice were found shot to death in the Cadillac, parked in Elmhurst, Queens. All the people at the dinner were questioned by the police. But the double murder was never solved.

When George Scalise got out of jail, he gave the impression that he was going into retirement, but actually it was semiretirement. Nathan Voloshen bragged to me many times that he had become the "front" for Scalise and his operations. With his contacts on Capitol Hill and in the New York courts, Voloshen was the perfect front. By 1964, George Scalise was an elder statesman of the New York mob. Though not as well-known as Frank Costello, he was every bit as powerful.

Although George Scalise and Frank Costello were alike professionally in many ways, they were two very different types. Costello looked like the ordinary businessman you might meet at some Rotary Club luncheon. Twice I saw Costello with Nathan Voloshen in House Speaker McCormack's offices and Costello didn't look out of place. Scalise, on the other hand, was a typical Hollywood prototype of a hood. His skin tone was always sunlamp perfect; his hair, his mustache, and his eyebrows were always dyed the perfect brown. The combination of his heavy perfume, his dark hair, and his sun-red face creased with the age-lines of a man in his sixties, made him look like some female impersonator, rather than a man vainly trying to recapture his virility—or at least give the impression that he hadn't lost it. He favored large sunglasses, the color of which always matched his clothes. If he wore a brown suit, he would wear brown sunglasses, a brown shirt, brown tie, brown pocket handkerchief, brown socks, brown shoes, brown Homburg, brown overcoat, and, if it rained, he would have a brown umbrella and brown rubbers. He was always a perfectly coordinated symphony of the color of his choice on a particular day. All of this was topped off by his constant puffing away on a huge—and expensive—Havana cigar. To see him coming down the street was to envision a veritable blithe, but definitely dangerous, spirit.

On mornings when Nathan Voloshen did not go to Washington, he often began his day by conferring with George Scalise, usually in Voloshen's office. Wherever the conference took place, however, a radio had to be playing full blast, because of Scalise's dread that his conversations might be picked up by some listening device. On days when Voloshen moved around New York, he always carried a transistor radio in his attaché case, in case his office told him that Scalise wanted to meet him somewhere. They played the radio at top volume even while they walked down a street. Despite the fact that Voloshen knew he was moving in a dangerous milieu, he didn't seem worried about it. He once told me: "I'm sure the boys won't let anything happen to me. I'm far too valuable to them in the courts and in Washington. And if anyone gets rough with me, I can always have them taken care of."

On Tuesday, January 2, 1968, I received a phone call at home from Michael P. Direnzo, a well-known criminal lawyer with offices on New York's Lower Broadway. He and Voloshen had worked on cases together, and he told me that he had been trying to reach Nat all morning but that Margaret Stafford kept telling him Voloshen was out of town. He wanted to know if this was true or if Voloshen was avoiding him for some reason. I told him I was sure Margaret was telling the truth. He then asked me if I could do him a big favor and contact Nat for him. It was urgent. He said he had a client, Salvatore Granello, alias Sally Burns, who had a problem. Granello was part of the Mafia family headed by Vito Genovese. He had been a major operator in Cuban gambling casinos during the Batista regime and he had become increasingly powerful in gambling, loansharking, and labor racketeering in New York after Castro forced him to leave Cuba. At the moment he was serving time in Danbury Federal Prison for income tax violations. Danbury is a country-club type of prison, and Granello was enjoying his stay there, so much so that he had declared himself top man of the place, as far as the prison fraternity was concerned. His assumption of authority had gone over well with the inmates, but when he had started arrogantly countermanding the warden's orders, Granello's present troubles had begun. The warden, quite understandably, hadn't liked Granello's antics a bit and had put him in solitary confinement, arranging, meanwhile, to transfer him to the strict federal prison at Lewisburg, Pennsylvania. Granello didn't want the change, so he had asked Direnzo to try to arrange for him to stay at Danbury. After all other efforts had failed, Direnzo had decided that Nathan Voloshen was his only hope.

Direnzo asked me if I would give Nat the information and also ask Nat if he could do him a favor. He said that Granello—or Burns, as he was usually called —didn't have much money but that his son Michael had promised that he would try to raise the money necessary. I called Nat at Speaker McCormack's office in Washington and relayed the information to him. Voloshen said he could accommodate Direnzo and would happily do it as a favor, since Granello's son couldn't pay him. This was typical of Nathan Voloshen. Although he was a greedy man, he was also a generous man. If you asked him to loan you $50 to carry you through the day, he would hand you a couple hundred, just in case some emergency arose, and he would not expect to be paid back. This was within the code of "brotherhood" he felt for those with whom he did business, especially for his friends. He knew that if you had money you'd be willing to pay his price. But he was also ready to go along with you if you were temporarily down on your luck. Whatever else he was, Nathan Voloshen was not a petty man.

When new clients were introduced to him, and it was time for him to discuss his fee, he always had several pat phrases, some of which I heard hundreds of times:

"Well, you really have a problem. Without my help, you have two chances for getting out of trouble—slim and none."

"I would like a retainer, before I move, of $5,000 in cash. Of course, I can't guarantee anything. I'm not perfect. Even Ted Williams strikes out once in a while."

"With your problems, because of my connections, I'm the only one who can help you."

"My fees may sound large, but you have to remember, I have to split all along the way."

"I'm not a greedy man. I can only wear one suit and drive one car at a time."

The next morning in his New York office, Voloshen told me that he had been successful on Tuesday in Washington and said that I could reassure Michael Direnzo that Granello would stay at Danbury. Later that day, Voloshen showed me a telegram from Martin Sweig, at the time McCormack's secretary, confirming that Granello would indeed stay on in Danbury.

Several days later, Voloshen told me that he had been informed by Michael Genovese, Vito's brother, that Granello had some money and could easily afford to pay Nat $5,000 for the favor. When Granello had gone to jail, he had put his son Michael, then nineteen, under the protection of Thomas Eboli, alias Tommy Ryan, lieutenant to Girardo Catena. Catena was the overseer of the Genovese family's operations in New York, and the money would have been put up by the Genoveses had it been requested. Nat was hurt. He felt he was being played for a sucker. He thereupon asked Direnzo for the $5,000. Direnzo said he couldn't do anything about it but that he would convey Nat's request to young Michael. Michael Granello replied that he was in fact broke, that he wouldn't pay, and added that he had no idea anybody had been asked to help his father. Direnzo rather nervously passed this message back to Nat, who had a good laugh over it. I remember how amused he was as he said: "Mike Genovese has assured me that the family will pay me. I'm too valuable to them to let him disappoint me. They'll pay me. I'm not worried. I just enjoy making Mike Direnzo's life a little difficult for a while."

Later on in January of 1968, Nat told me that young Granello had been called before a family council of the Mafia, where he denied that he had made a promise to Direnzo to pay Nat if he could. The council felt that Michael could pay but wouldn't. At that time Nat told me that the council—"they" as he put it—was going to check with Direnzo. Then Nat asked me to recount what I knew about the event, and I did so to the best of my recollection. During the first week of March 1968, I stopped by unexpectedly at Nat's office one morning, and Margaret Stafford told me that Nat was busy. I was about to leave when Margaret said she would let Nat know I was there. When she did, Nat told her to send me right in. Heading for the door, I asked Margaret who was with Nat, and she said: "Mike Genovese." A little startled—and somewhat terrified—I went in.

Mike Genovese was not at all like Uncle George. He was a very conservative, mild-mannered man. He had on a light brown tweed sports coat, dark brown pants, and dark brown shoes. He wore a large brown hat which he did not remove during our discussion. His two beady eyes stared at me through dark horn-rimmed glasses. Nat introduced us and asked me to recount the circumstances of Direnzo's call to me the previous January. Still standing, I went through the account again. After I finished, Genovese looked at me for a moment and, as I recall his words, said: "You say he told you that Burns or his son would pay Nat if they got the money?"

"Yes," I said. "He said they were broke."

Genovese said: "Well, that's their story. They can afford it, but they lied. His kid said to us he never promised to pay anything to Direnzo. He didn't know nothing. Well, don't worry, Nat. I'll pay you today. We'll put an X through Sally's kid. He don't exist no more as far as I'm concerned. Don't let's talk about him no more. He don't exist. I'll put an X right through him." Then he looked at me and said: "Okay, kid."

Nat motioned me to leave. As I turned, he asked me to wait outside. I waited until Mike Genovese had left, whereupon Nat called me into the office. He let me know that he had been paid. Now it was up to the Genovese "family" to get the money back from the Granellos.

In December 1968, young Michael Granello was executed in gangland style. An X had been put through him.

When Sally Granello got out of Danbury prison in 1969, he vowed to find his son's executioners and kill them. During the year he put into the search, he could not get any specific information from the Mafia hierarchy. In April 1970, Nathan Voloshen told me that Granello still had not paid the $5,000 back to the Genoveses. Several indictments against Granello were still pending, and the Department of Justice was getting ready to go to trial. Voloshen told me that some of his Mafia friends were afraid that, frustrated by his inability to find his son's killers, Granello might talk too much to the FBI. In October 1970, Granello's bullet-pierced body was found in the trunk of a car parked on the Lower East Side: two more murders that were never solved.

Voloshen was correct in feeling that he was too important to his Mafia friends to be seriously endangered by any of their machinations. Men like George Scalise and Frank Costello had deals going all over the country, but their major base of operations was in New York, and it was in New York that Nathan Voloshen had his best contacts in the courts. Of these, the best was New York State Supreme Court Justice Mitchell D. Schweitzer. A New Yorker, Schweitzer had practiced law until elected to the Municipal Court in 1944. Ten years later, he was elected to the General Sessions Court, which was later merged into the New York State Supreme Court. At the time of this election, Justice John Murtagh, New York Chief Magistrate, said to Richard Wels, as he later recounted to me: "Jesus, what a mistake! That guy will sell everything in the courthouse that isn't nailed down."

The first time I ever saw Nathan Voloshen, he was with Justice Schweitzer. It was Thursday, November 21, 1963, at the bar of the Regency Hotel on Park Avenue in New York. I was there at the request of Marjorie Abbajay, an entrepreneur of sorts, whom I had met the previous summer through Gregg Dodge, then the wife of socialite Horace Dodge. At the time, Marjorie Abbajay, who was of Lebanese extraction and claimed to be a cousin of Danny Thomas the entertainer, wanted to work out a deal with me in my public-relations work. She said she could get me a lot of clients, provided we split the fee. The client she specifically had in mind at the time was James Lofland, the financier who had been indicted on charges of selling fraudulent oil leases and stolen securities. Involved in this matter were Marjorie herself, Kurt Keller, a senior partner in Wertheim & Company, investment counselors, and J. P. Maguire, then head of John P. Maguire & Company, Inc., important factors to the textile industry. It had already been established by New York State Attorney General Louis Lefkowitz that Lofland had paid $5,000 to an employee of Dun and Bradstreet to get himself a good rating. In view of the fact that the Lofland case, involving over $3 million, had already made the front pages, I asked Marjorie why he felt he needed a public-relations man. She explained that I would have nothing to do with Lofland but that my job would be to do everything I could to keep Keller's, Maguire's, and her name out of the papers during the trial, in which they were to be witnesses. I didn't see how their names could be completely omitted from news accounts of the trial, but I felt I would be able to have their roles minimized at least. I asked Marjorie who was going to pay the fee. She said that Keller and Maguire, through their lawyer Edwin Kyle, were putting up a total of $50,000 cash to cover the necessary pay-offs for the trial and she would get my fee out of that. She asked me how much I wanted. Knowing I would have to split the fee with her, I asked for $1,900. She said that she would be getting the money in cash during the day from Kyle, and she asked me to meet her for cocktails at the bar of the Regency Hotel to get my payment. Knowing that she was trying to talk me into a partnership with her, I realized that the speed of the payment was her way of trying to impress me. I said I'd be there.

When I arrived at the bar, Marjorie was already there, sitting at a table with James Lofland. I sat opposite him. We chatted a few minutes, and then Marjorie suggested that Lofland write the check for my fee. I knew Lofland had a notorious reputation for writing bad checks, so I said I wouldn't mind taking the cash if she had it. As I recall, this irked Marjorie, and she said: "You don't have to worry. Ed Kyle gave me the $50,000 this afternoon. I've got most of it with me, in my purse." She opened her purse to let me look. I saw a white business envelope, thick and pulpy, which I saw was full of money. "We've already banked enough to cover your fee," she said.

Before Lofland could write the check, a small, elderly man came to the table. Marjorie said: "Hello, Nat." Nathan Voloshen smiled at her and said hello. He nodded greetings to Lofland. Then Marjorie introduced me to him.

Voloshen glanced at me as I stood up, but as we shook hands he was already returning his attention to Marjorie. He went to her. "Is everything all right?"

"Yes," said Marjorie. She took the thick, pulpy envelope from her purse and gave it to Voloshen.

"The Judge will be very appreciative," he said.

Marjorie looked at the table from which Voloshen evidently had come, about fifteen feet away. She asked: "Is that the Judge?"

"Yes," Voloshen said.

Marjorie leaned over to me, a little excited. "Bob, that's Judge Schweitzer."

I looked at him. A young woman was at the table

with him. When I looked back at Marjorie and Voloshen, they apparently had finished their conversation. Voloshen had straightened up. He said goodnight to Marjorie, nodded first at Lofland and then at me, and went back to the table with Justice Schweitzer and the young woman.

I asked Marjorie: "What does Nathan Voloshen do?"

Her answer was: "He's a fixer."*

James Lofland then wrote out a check for $1,900, drawn on a bank in Scottsdale, Arizona, gave it to me, and I left. Next morning, Friday, November 22, I deposited the check in my bank. Later that same day I heard the shocking news that President Kennedy had been assassinated in Dallas. On Monday, while I was home watching the Kennedy funeral on television, Marjorie Abbajay called me and asked me to send her my check for $950—her split. I pointed out that the check had been drawn on an Arizona bank and said I preferred to wait until it cleared. She insisted that the check was good and again asked for the money. I told her that, like the rest of the country, I was in shock over the Kennedy death, that it would probably be a day or two before I returned to my business, and that I would send her the

---

* Although Justice Schweitzer did not actually sit on this case, Nathan Voloshen told me later that the money had been given to him so that he could "trade off" cases with other presiding judges. In court circles, this means that, in one way or another, judge A lets judge B know that a case before judge B is of personal interest to him, thus hopefully making judge B more sympathetic to the cause, or the side, of concern to judge A. Judge B, of course, is in the position to put judge A in his debt. Once having done the favor, judge B can go back to judge A and, to use the common expression, say: "Don't I have some credit in your bank?"

check at that time. I never did send my check, and as it turned out my intuition had been good: Lofland's check bounced.

When it did, I was furious. I knew it would be useless to complain to Marjorie Abbajay, so I telephoned Edwin Kyle, the lawyer, and complained to him as forcefully as I could by letting him know I had seen an envelope—which contained money—pass hands between Marjorie Abbajay and Nathan Voloshen. Kyle tried to calm me and suggested that he could set up a formal introduction to Nathan Voloshen, a close friend of House Speaker John McCormack, who he assured me could be very helpful to me in my business career. I knew he was trying to change the subject, but I let him go on, and from what ensued came my meeting and friendship with Nathan Voloshen.

Later, when James Lofland went on trial, I followed the case in the papers. Not once did I see the names of Marjorie Abbajay, Kurt Keller, or J. P. Maguire; so, though Lofland went to prison, the main purpose of the pay-off—to keep their names out of the papers and out of the court case—had been accomplished. Later, Edwin Kyle got in touch with me and offered to make good on Lofland's bad check provided I returned the check to him. By then I had learned to keep any evidence which would show where I was and what I was doing at any given moment, and I turned the offer down. In one of his fatherly moments, Nathan Voloshen advised me: "Bob, never part with that check. You don't know how much business you'll be doing with these people in the future. With that check, you'll be able to keep them in line." I still have it.

Nathan Voloshen was quite open with me about his relationship with Justice Schweitzer. Ordinarily, judges are supposed to rotate assignments; but in practice those with the most seniority have been allowed to pick their own spots. Schweitzer favored Part 30. This is where all motions are heard, where defendants who plead guilty are sentenced, where lawyers are assigned to indigent defendants and—most importantly—where cases are assigned to judges for trial. Voloshen told me that there were a number of judges with whom Schweitzer could trade off favorable decisions if he couldn't do the job himself. Voloshen usually took an active part in the trades.

On February 7, 1966, for example, a young man by the name of Robert Friede was sitting in his car in front of 167 East Second Street, New York. Police approached him and asked for his driver's license. When he opened his wallet two packets of heroin fell out. The police searched the car and found, in the trunk, the body of Celeste Crenshaw, nineteen, who had died from an overdose of drugs which Friede later admitted having given her. Friede, the police learned, was the stepson of William Jaffe, a prominent New York lawyer and socialite, and the grandson of the late Moses L. Annenberg, once publisher of the Philadelphia *Inquirer,* an alleged ex-Capone associate and ex-convict who died in the Lewisburg penitentiary.

An old Chicago friend of Moses Annenberg's recently recalled his beginnings to me when she said:

"Oh, I knew him well. He was connected with Al Capone, you know. If you did something he didn't like, he'd send someone around to hit you on the head. Can you imagine, today his children are getting $10,000 a month and are putting on all those airs?"

On August 11, 1939, Moses L. Annenberg was initially indicted by a federal grand jury for the income tax evasion (including penalties) of over $5 million, which was the largest income tax evasion case in the history of the Department of Justice. Indicted with him on charges of aiding and abetting the evasion were several others, among whom was his son, Walter H. Annenberg. Subsequently, after another indictment was handed down, Moses Annenberg pleaded guilty and agreed to pay the United States government $8 million to settle $9 million in tax claims, penalties, and interest against him. As part of the settlement, the government agreed to dismiss all income charges against most of the other defendants—which included Annenberg's son Walter. He had traded his own incarceration for his son's freedom. On July 1, 1940, Moses Annenberg was sentenced to three years in federal prison. Ironically, his son Walter, in 1969, was appointed by President Nixon as the United States Ambassador to the Court of St. James.

In March 1966, in court before Justice Schweitzer, Robert Friede said that he had not meant to kill the Crenshaw girl and pleaded guilty to second-degree manslaughter, possession of narcotics, and violation of probation. In New York, second-degree manslaughter is punishable by up to fifteen years in prison, but Friede had a previous felony conviction and faced a sentence of up to thirty years. The date for sentencing was set for April 15.

On April 8, a week prior to the sentencing, I saw Nathan Voloshen, Justice Schweitzer, and William Jaffe, Friede's stepfather, having a drink together at the King Cole bar in the Hotel St. Regis. Obviously, the mere fact of their meeting is in itself no proof, or even implication, of any wrongdoing on anyone's part. In fact, I might not even have made a mental note of the meeting had it not coincided so closely with Friede's impending sentence.

On April 15, Justice Schweitzer gave Robert Friede a suspended sentence of seven and a half years for the manslaughter conviction, a suspended sentence of one year for the narcotics conviction, and a prison sentence of from two and a half to five years for violation of probation.

Some time in 1967, Justice Schweitzer again met with William Jaffe to discuss Friede. At Schweitzer's invitation, Jaffe rode in a chauffeured Rolls Royce from his home in New York to Schweitzer's home in Scarsdale, and the two men spent more than an hour together. Shortly afterward, Harris Steinberg, the lawyer who represented Friede at his trial, wrote a letter to State Parole Commissioner Russell G. Oswald. In the letter he said that Justice Schweitzer felt that, all things considered, Robert Friede represented a good risk for parole as soon as he became eligible. On November 13, 1967, Friede was paroled from prison after serving nineteen months. He moved to the state of Washington.

Later, regarding another case, Schweitzer had dinner one evening in May 1969 at the Pier 52 Restaurant with Nathan Voloshen and Stanley Reiben, a lawyer who represented one Raymond Freda. While serving a five-year term at the federal prison at Lewisburg, Freda had been brought before Schweitzer in another matter involving charges of unlawful entry, third-degree assault, and possession of a dangerous weapon. Schweitzer had Freda sentenced to a year on the unlawful entry and ten months each on the other two counts. In 1968, Freda finished his federal term and was brought into New York to start serving what should have been thirty-two months. He served a year, at which time Stanley Reiben moved for a resentencing on the other two counts. On April 11, 1969, the case appeared on Schweitzer's calendar. He ordered a stay of Freda's commitment until May 12 and he released Freda on $1,200 bail. On May 21, Schweitzer ruled in court that the two sentences of ten months, to be served consecutively, had been improper, and, reversing his own decision on the matter, Schweitzer revoked the sentences, enabling Freda to walk out of the courtroom a free man. Nathan Voloshen told me later that he had had to pay Schweitzer $10,000 for that decision.

As I testified to the New York State Joint Legislative Committee on Crime, Voloshen on many occasions had discussed with me the lengthy litigation involving former Representative Adam Clayton Powell, who had been sued by a Harlem resident on the charge that Powell had called her a "bag woman." Voloshen claimed to me that he could have settled the entire Powell matter, through Schweitzer, for about $10,000, but that Powell had refused. Voloshen said that, through him, Schweitzer had asked Powell to hire a certain attorney, who happened to be Jewish, but Powell said that he didn't particularly want to be represented by a Jew. He wanted a black man. So the case dragged on and on and cost Powell not only much more than $10,000, but also his political career.

Another case of which Voloshen was particularly proud concerned Manuel Bello, of Lowell, Massachusetts. Bello, a close friend of George Scalise's and, according to the *New York Law Journal,* "a reputed member of a criminal syndicate," had been sent to prison for trying to dispose of $100,000 worth of stolen securities. When Bello's petition for a rehearing came before Justice Schweitzer, he set a date for it on his own calendar. He also chose a lawyer to represent Bello by the name of Henry Blumenthal. A week before the re-hearing, Schweitzer, Blumenthal, Nathan Voloshen, and I had dinner at La Fontaine, a restaurant on East Forty-fourth Street known for its assortment of loitering prostitutes, and it was at this meeting that the justice and the attorney planned their strategy. When the case came up, Justice Schweitzer first allowed Manuel Bello to withdraw his plea of guilty which had resulted in the original sentencing. Next, Schweitzer allowed Bello to plead guilty to the same charges. Then Schweitzer gave Bello a new sentence covering the amount of time he already had spent in prison, which meant that Bello was scot-free, and he was allowed to walk out of court. Voloshen never told me what that deal had cost him, but he did say that he had done it more for George Scalise than for Bello, so price meant nothing.

On another occasion—March 14, 1968—I tried to reach Nathan Voloshen at his office, and his secretary told me that he had instructed her to have me meet him at six-thirty that evening at La Fontaine. I got there on time and when I did not see Voloshen at the bar, where he said he would be, I headed for the dining area in the back. I saw Voloshen at a table with Justice Schweitzer. Seeing me, Voloshen beckoned to me. It seemed to me that they had not been together long. Voloshen had a habit of trying to make his New York contacts feel that House Speaker McCormack was always thinking about them, and he was indulging himself in this pursuit as I joined the two of them.

"By the way, the Speaker says to give you his regards," Voloshen was saying to Schweitzer.

Schweitzer smiled and nodded, then said to me:

"I'm impressed by Nat's friends in Washington."

I nodded and smiled. We talked a few more minutes and then, as I recall, Voloshen said to Schweitzer: "I have some things to talk over with Bob. We'll go to the bar." He started to get up. I followed suit.

Justice Schweitzer said: "All right. I think I'll order my dinner."

Voloshen took an envelope out of his breast pocket and handed it to Schweitzer, saying: "This is what I promised you." The Justice nodded, smiled, put the envelope into his pocket, and reached for the menu. As Voloshen and I were walking to the bar, Voloshen said: "You saw what I just had to do. There was money in that envelope. His friendship is very expensive." That was the first time I had ever seen such a blatant pay-off made in a public place, and I was somewhat shaken by it. That night, I made a diary note of the event.

Actually, I had often been present when Voloshen arranged gifts for Justice Schweitzer—theater tickets, whiskey. Many times I heard Voloshen telephone the Judge, as Voloshen called him, and tell him what had been arranged. Voloshen considered his generosity toward Schweitzer and Speaker McCormack a business expense, and he could well afford it. He never spoke to me about his income, but judging only from the transactions that I either witnessed or was told about, I estimated that Voloshen must have been clearing between $300,000 and $400,000 a year. He often said to me that he kept at least a third of his "fees" for himself— more when he could get away with it—which meant that he grossed about $1 million a year. It didn't put him in the *Fortune* 500, but it was still a tidy little sum.

In 1968, Voloshen told me that he had become involved in an effort to form a stock exchange in Miami,

Florida. He said he needed someone to do some research, and he offered me the assignment of obtaining charters of other stock exchanges which Stanley Singer, a lawyer who shared Voloshen's offices, could use as models for the Miami charter. I was able to obtain several without much trouble; I was paid $500 for the job, and this was all I had to do with the project. Voloshen told me that the Miami project was being backed by Meyer Lansky, the reputed financial wizard of the Mafia, and that Lansky had paid my fee. In a study of Lansky's underworld connections, *The New York Times* listed as Lansky's friends men like Frank Costello, Vito Genovese, Morris Lansburgh, Gerardo Catena, Sam Cohen, Sam Garfield, and Harry Stromberg. All these men were also friends of Nathan Voloshen's, and he was as proud of this as he was of his friendship with Speaker McCormack. Voloshen told me that he had met with Lansky at least three times to discuss the project.

At the same time, Voloshen was involved in another Miami operation, a plan masterminded by Michael Hellerman, the discredited financier for whom Voloshen had been unable to get approval from the SEC to sell stock in his Trimatrix computer company at a later date. The plan was to buy up control of a Miami investment company—the Imperial Investment Corporation, then headed by Gerald Devins—and parlay its stock to a false high before selling out.

Acting on behalf of three reputed gangland overlords —Carmine Tramunti, Vincent Aloi, and John (Johnny Dio) Diogardi—Hellerman and a Miami lawyer went to Gerald Devins and bought over 150,000 shares in his Imperial Investment Corporation. By selling the stock back and forth to each other, the promoters were able to raise the price from virtually nothing to $24 a share. When, however, the mob decided that it would be a good idea to take over the company, Devins refused to sell them any more stock. They began to threaten him. Several times in 1968 and 1969, I heard Nathan Voloshen threaten Devins on long distance calls to Miami. Voloshen enjoyed this; it made him feel like a big shot. I once heard him advise the promoters to "give Devins a little time and then go over and wreck his office."

Still Devins resisted. Then Michael Hellerman, with two New York men—James Burke and Pasquale Fusco —flew to Miami where, joined by Vincent Lombardo, Meyer Lansky's son-in-law, they got Gerald Devins into a hotel room and roughed him up brutally. When they finished with him, they helped themselves to all the blank stock certificates of Imperial. They were charged with picking up over 20,000 additional shares from individual investors by using the same strong-arm tactics, but at a subsequent trial Carmine Tramunti and Vincent Aloi, among others, were acquitted of that charge.

The SEC began to hear about the questionable stock transactions at Imperial in 1969 and started to investigate them. Voloshen became aware of the investigation, but the news did not deter the promoters. In August 1969, the SEC found out about the threats and the beatings and asked the FBI to investigate. Voloshen also knew about them, but still the project went on. In February 1970, the SEC suspended Imperial's license to do business, sending the stock back to zero, and the investigation into the company picked up speed. The problem now facing the promoters was to have the investigation squelched. Ordinarily, Nathan Voloshen might have been able to do this, but by now Voloshen himself was indicted and was under intensive investi-

gation by the Department of Justice. It was George Scalise who decided that Nathan Voloshen was too hot to
handle the problem, and, for this reason, called in Eddie
Adams.

For years, Eddie Adams had been passing himself off as a public-relations man, but it was well-
known in Washington circles that he was soliciting campaign contributions for Lyndon Johnson and Hubert
Humphrey. He was the one who went around picking
up the money for Johnson and Humphrey; he was the
man to see if anybody wanted something done in Washington that required the personal intervention of Johnson or Humphrey.

My first contact with Eddie Adams was on March
12, 1964, at a $100-a-plate fund-raising dinner in the
Federal Hall of the International Inn, a motel in Washington. The dinner was hosted by Senator Russell Long
of Louisiana, in honor of Democratic Congressman
James H. Morrison, also of Louisiana, who was facing
an election campaign that year. As he usually did for
such events, Nathan Voloshen had taken a table. It was
Number 44, right in front of the rostrum of the long
table for the ranking guests. At our table was Senator
Long's administrative assistant, R. E. Hunter. Another
table guest was Eddie Adams.

A few days before, I had visited George and Julia
Skouras at their New York apartment. I had come to
know Julia through my public-relations work and we
had become friends. At the time George was dying of
cancer. All the Skourases were heavy contributors to the
campaign funds of politicians on both sides of the aisle,
and George and Julia felt particularly close to Lyndon
Johnson. While I was with Julia that day, she told me
that she felt it would be good for George's morale if

Lyndon Johnson gave some indication that he knew that George was ill and would wish him well. When I found myself at the same banquet table with Eddie Adams that night, I wondered if he could do anything about it.

The conversation went something like this. I leaned over to him and asked:

"Do you know George Skouras?"

"Of course," he said.

I said: "George and the President are close friends."

"I know." He was cordial but cautious, waiting.

"George is very sick," I went on. "He's dying of cancer."

"I'm sorry to hear that."

"I'm sure the President would be sorry to hear it, too. The other day George's wife told me that if the President knew he would undoubtedly call George or drop him a note."

Adams just looked at me for a moment. Then he said: "I'll mention it."

Two days later, when I visited the Skouras apartment again, Julia was all smiles when she greeted me. She said: "I can't thank you enough, Bob. Let me show you what the President sent. George was so touched." Johnson had sent a picture of himself, personally inscribed to George and Julia. And there was a note, expressing the hope that George would be well soon. Evidently, Eddie Adams had followed through, and I was impressed.

Because Eddie Adams usually followed through, he seemed to be the best man to succeed Nathan Voloshen on the Miami deal, it being understood that the two of them would split the fee. Adams was a quiet man, and he operated quietly. He was almost eighty when I met him, and I soon discovered that we lived in the same neighborhood. For a man of his wealth, he lived modestly, on East Seventy-sixth Street, only a block from me, and I began to see him on his strolls to the shops. Unlike Voloshen, who operated in the grand manner at all levels, Adams was relatively unknown outside the higher circles of politics, to which he limited his activities. But the big shots knew him—Carmine DeSapio, Eddie Weisl—and he was among those who had contributed $1,000 or more to Arthur Krim's President's Club from 1963 through 1966. As a front, Adams had bought into the Champlain Advertising Company, Inc., at 60 East Forty-second Street, but he appeared to have little to do with it. The agency had four small rooms, three employees, and specialized in preparing and placing ads in foreign language newspapers.

Eddie Adams's efforts on behalf of the Miami operation proved abortive, ending with indictments of practically everybody involved, including himself. On November 19, 1970, Hellerman and fifteen others were indicted on the Imperial takeover. Adams nevertheless continued to try to get the investigation squelched. About the time of the first indictment, Adams and two other men, Joseph Bald and Harold Blond, allegedly conspired to approach Robert T. Carson, administrative assistant to Senator Hiram Fong, Republican of Hawaii. The subsequent indictment charged that Bald met with Carson in the North Senate Office Building on November 16 and offered him $100,000 to have the investigation squelched. The indictment charged that a week later, on November 24, Carson offered a $100,000 political contribution to U. S. Deputy Attorney General

Richard Kleindienst to quash the investigation. Kleindienst refused. Steps were taken that brought about the indictment of Carson, Bald, and Eddie Adams, with Blond turning government witness. Thus Eddie Adams, so long a powerful man behind the scenes, was brought out into the open, and his career in Washington was finished. Subsequently, Eddie Adams pleaded guilty to the charges and Robert Carson was found guilty after a lengthy trial. Thus, ironically, those who tried to get the indictment quashed were convicted, while those under indictment were acquitted.

Voloshen was not a well man: among other ailments, he suffered from a heart condition. Because of this, he did not like to be alone, always fearful that he might be stricken among strangers who would ignore him and not know what to do for him. For this reason, he would sometimes call me to his office and ask me to accompany him a few blocks to some appointment so that he wouldn't have to walk alone. I once accompanied Voloshen all the way to the office of Bronx District Attorney Burton Roberts, waited out in the hall while the two of them had their meetings in Roberts' office, and then traveled back to Manhattan with Voloshen. On these occasions, Voloshen would sometimes consider his future if he were exposed.

By the summer of 1969, Voloshen was beginning to see the handwriting on the wall, but he was too greedy —and in a way too naïve—to give up his Washington wheeler-dealing while there was still time. Also, he felt that Speaker McCormack and his other political friends were too powerful to let anything serious happen to him. But things had already gone too far. By fall, 1969,

Voloshen knew he was about to be indicted. He was ambivalent on the position he would take. He once told me: "If I go down, everybody else goes down." Another time he said: "If it looks like I have to go to jail, I'll kill myself. I couldn't stand jail." And another time he said: "I'll do anything necessary to avoid being cross-examined. I would never testify against the Speaker or my other friends. I'd plead guilty, if I had to." In the end, it was the third choice that he took. And this was typical of him. He lived up to the code of the underworld—the code of not copping out on your brothers.

On June 17, 1970, on the first day of the government's case against Martin Sweig and Nathan Voloshen, Voloshen pleaded guilty. He was given a year's suspended sentence and a $10,000 fine. While sentencing Voloshen, Federal District Court Judge Marvin E. Frankel noted that Voloshen was "a broken man" and made reference to Voloshen's "physical and financial ruin." Voloshen was definitely a broken man. He was finished in Washington. No public official would ever again openly come within ten feet of him. He was ill, yes, seriously ill, and he spent much of the remaining year of his life in hospitals. He was financially ruined in the sense that he would not be making any more big money because he would not be able to pull off any more big deals. But only Nathan Voloshen knew how much money he already had salted away.

It was the importance of his friends that made Nathan Voloshen an important man, and his important friends did not abandon him—privately. For example, during the three months after Voloshen's indictment in January of 1970, Justice Schweitzer met with him at least five times, according to *The New York Times,* at the home of Shirley and Harvey Axelrod. When Voloshen gave up his office in December 1969, he made his new office at Mr. Axelrod's place of business, Carlson Originals, at 512 Seventh Avenue, where he used the telephone and where the staff took messages for him. It was like old times at Speaker McCormack's office. Then, much later still, on Tuesday, February 9, 1971, at six-thirty in the evening, Roy Cohn, the attorney who won fame as an aide to Senator Joe McCarthy, threw a premature birthday party for himself, his birthday actually falling later in the month. Among his guests, I was told, were Carmine DeSapio, who at the time was fighting a losing appeal on a criminal conviction with the U.S. Attorney's office; Eddie Weisl, a top Democrat in New York; Manhattan District Attorney Frank Hogan; Justice Samuel N. Gold; Judge Samuel DiFalco; Justice Mitchell Schweitzer; and Nathan Voloshen.

The Weasel was still at it, right to the end.

On Monday, May 1, 1967, the phone rang in my apartment. It was Richard Wels. He said he had a problem with which I might be able to help, and he asked me to do him the favor of stopping by his office the next afternoon at one. I had known Wels for a few years, having met him through a mutual friend, Al Albelli, a famous reporter on New York's *Daily News*. Because of my lobbying work and public-relations background, Wels had begun hiring my services on some of his cases. We had found that we lived just around the corner from each other, and I had become a frequent guest in his sumptuous apartment.

Wels came from an established legal and political background. His father had been a famous lawyer and political figure; his maternal grandfather, a judge. In the 1930's, Wels worked in Washington with the SEC, and during World War II he served in the Navy as special counsel to the Committee on Naval Affairs, U. S. House of Representatives. When I met him, Wels was about fifty-five and had been a highly successful lawyer for about twenty-five years—Harvard Law School out of

Cornell. He was listed in *Who's Who;* he was a leader in numerous community activities; he was well connected in politics and law; and he was rich. His apartment resembled the lobby of the Metropolitan Museum—vast, and marble everywhere. He had married late. His wife Marge was a successful interior decorator, and he had two teen-age daughters. He was a brilliant lawyer, well-informed and always entertaining, and my evenings were always pleasant.

When I kept that one-o'clock appointment at his office on Tuesday, May 2, 1967, he had someone with him: E. Haring (Red) Chandor, a client and a stockbroker. As I recall the conversation, Wels began it by asking me: "Do you know Nathan Voloshen well enough to arrange an introduction for me?"

"I do," I said.

"Good," Wels said. "Now I will tell you why I want it."

It appeared that the day before, May 1, Red Chandor had visited Wels' office, bringing along Edward M. Gilbert, his close friend and client. Gilbert had achieved prominence in 1962 when, as president of the E. L. Bruce Company, manufacturers of hardwood floors, he had absconded with $2 million of the company's funds and had gone to Brazil. By choosing Brazil, a country with which the United States has no extradition agreement, Gilbert avoided government pursuit until finally he returned voluntarily on October 29, 1962. He had salted away much of his money and, according to Red Chandor, put most of the remainder into the names of his widowed mother and his second wife. He then sought legal assistance, at best to keep him out of jail, but at least to keep him out of jail as long as possible and then to get him out of jail as soon as possible.

Gilbert's lawyer was Arnold Bauman, but he also had the help of his good friend Jerry Finkelstein, New York City Democratic Chairman and publisher of the *New York Law Journal*. Eddie Gilbert pleaded guilty to both the federal and state charges against him, which meant a prison sentence. By prearrangement, however, Bauman was able to obtain delays in the sentencings, ostensibly for the purpose of giving Gilbert time to put his personal affairs in order, but actually to give Bauman time to lay out a strategy. It was hoped, first, that the New York City district attorney would ask the court to give Gilbert a suspended sentence because he had been cooperative. Failing that, it was hoped that Gilbert would be allowed to serve both sentences concurrently. This latter alternative hinged on whether the Director of Federal Prisons would allow Gilbert to serve his federal sentence while in state custody in a state facility. The sentencing judge can recommend this, as can both the federal and state prosecutors. Quite possibly, either of these arrangements could have been made. Nevertheless, Eddie Gilbert remained a free man from his voluntary return to this country on October 29, 1962, until May 8, 1967.

A week before the date, on Monday, May 1, Gilbert told Richard Wels that, over the years, he had given Arnold Bauman close to $260,000 in cash. Even so, in March and April of that year, Bauman had begun pressing Eddie Gilbert for more money, assuring him that he had been able to get Jerome B. Kidder, an assistant in the office of Manhattan District Attorney Frank Hogan and later a criminal court judge, to agree that the state would ask for a suspended sentence, in view of the federal sentence. Kidder was ready to say so in court. Kidder had even, Bauman boasted, let him set a date for sentencing, which was tantamount to picking the judge before whom the case would come up for sentencing. For his own reasons, Bauman picked Justice Gerald Culkin, a friend of Voloshen.

But somewhere along the line, there had been a leak. When news of these arrangements reached Chief District Attorney Alfred J. Scotti, he hit the ceiling. Just recently, a client of Michael Direnzo had walked out of Culkin's court scot-free. Scotti was suspicious and was already looking into it. When he heard about the Gilbert case he blew up. New York County's District Attorney Frank Hogan had long been suspicious of all cases before Judge Culkin. Kidder notified Bauman that all bets were off, that he would have to ask for a sentence, regardless of the fact that Gilbert had been cooperative. Scotti then gave the nod to the U. S. Attorney for the Southern District. On Thursday, April 27, Federal Judge Edmund T. Palmieri sentenced Eddie Gilbert to two years. Palmieri then released Gilbert on bail, pending the state sentencing which was scheduled for Monday, May 8.

Over this last April weekend preceding Gilbert's meeting with Wels, Chandor told me, Jerry Finkelstein informed Eddie Gilbert that he had tried to reach Judge Culkin but had had no luck and suggested that Eddie look for someone else with the political pull to help him. Then Arnold Bauman told Eddie there was nothing more he could do in such a short time. Gilbert gave the sad news to his friend Red Chandor, and Chandor suggested that maybe Gilbert should see his lawyer, the brilliant Richard Wels. Thus the Monday meeting came about. The three of them were in Wels' office when he called me. As I listened to this narration on Tuesday, I was pretty sure I didn't want to get mixed up in it, even to the extent of bringing Nathan Voloshen into it. I was surprised and shocked. To my knowledge, Wels had never before sought out this type of extra-legal help. He didn't have to. If he lost a case in a lower court, he could usually win it on appeal on its merits and legal points.

After Wels finished giving me and Chandor the background, the conversation went something like this.

"Now, Bob, if there is one man in New York who might be able to do something, it's Nathan Voloshen."

"Maybe."

"He is," Wels insisted. "I know what he did in the Friede case. Voloshen is the man."

I wanted no part of this. I suggested: "Dick, why don't you get someone else to introduce you to Voloshen? After all, this thing is more in their line than in mine."

"I don't know them as well as I know you. And I don't want them to know my business."

He was forcing my hand and I had to say: "Dick, I don't think I should become involved with this."

"Why not?" he asked sharply.

"Because I don't want to know what happens."

"You won't know," he said, calming. "All I want you to do is introduce Eddie Gilbert to Nathan Voloshen. You won't become involved. As a lawyer, I can tell you that you're not a part of it."

I wasn't sure. "I'll have to think about it," I said, and I left the meeting.

That same Tuesday evening, Richard Wels telephoned me at home to ask if I had made up my mind. I said I had and the answer was no. I remember the impatient tone in his voice as he said, in effect, "Now listen, Bob, I can give you a lot of business."

"Yes, I'm sure you can," I replied.

"Well, this means business for me," he said. "If I can help Eddie Gilbert out on this, I'm sure he'll turn over all his legal affairs to me. We've already talked about my handling the trouble he's having with his first wife. So if you want to keep this on a business level, I'll pay you for the introduction to Voloshen."

"I wouldn't take a penny," I said.

"Then will you do me a great favor? I'll see you get clients."

"That depends."

"Will you have breakfast tomorrow with Red Chandor?"

"What for?"

"He wants to discuss this with you."

"Why didn't he say something in your office today?"

"He didn't think he should."

"What's there to discuss?"

Wels said: "Bob, see him, as a favor to me. He's waiting for me to call him now with your answer."

"Well, all right."

"Thanks."

When at breakfast I told Red Chandor I was not going to make the Gilbert-Voloshen introduction, he became almost hysterical, begging me to meet Eddie Gilbert. I was so nonplused by Chandor's histrionics that I found myself agreeing to meet him and Gilbert at noon in the main lounge of the Princeton Club, to which Chandor belonged. I then went to Nathan Voloshen's office and discussed the matter with him. He felt he could help Gilbert; the major worry was the severe lack of time, however. At noon, at the Princeton Club, I had a very uncomfortable meeting with Eddie Gilbert. His picture had been in numerous publications throughout the country, so he was easily recognizable, which only made matters worse when he broke down and sobbed after I told him I was not going to make the introduction. He pleaded: "You've got to do it. For me, this can mean going to jail or not." I wanted to get out of there, so I told Gilbert that I would contact Voloshen and then let Wels know Voloshen's decision. I left, and I never met with Eddie Gilbert again. I went back to Voloshen's office, two blocks away, and told him what had happened. He agreed to see Eddie Gilbert the following Saturday morning, May 6, at ten o'clock, but he insisted on seeing Gilbert alone. I certainly had no intention of being there. Leaving Voloshen, I telephoned Wels and gave him the information, thinking the Gilbert case ended here, at least for me.

It didn't. Because of their personalities and methods of operation, Wels and Voloshen both kept talking to me about the case, and used me as a go-between: I was called upon a number of times to make sure that Voloshen kept his appointments by delivering him personally. Over the thirty months that the case dragged on, I found it taking up more of my time than the assignments from which I derived my income.

Voloshen told me later that, at the Voloshen-Gilbert meeting that Saturday morning on May 6, 1967, he felt he could help Gilbert but wanted a $5,000 cash retainer. He got it later in the day. Voloshen assured Gilbert that he had powerful connections in both the federal and state courts. Because the time was so short, however, he wasn't sure that he could be effective immediately. Nevertheless, he promised that, no matter what kind of prison sentence Gilbert might get, he would be out by the end of the year. Then Voloshen advised Gilbert to get in touch with Arnold Bauman and instruct him to feign illness on Monday, May 8, in order to avoid showing up in court for Gilbert's sentencing. This ruse, Voloshen felt, would cause a postponement of a week or two, giving him time to act. But Bauman didn't want to play any more games. He was in court on Monday. Kidder, who was also apparently running scared, reneged on his earlier promise and recommended a separate state sentence for Gilbert—not to run concurrently with the federal judgment. Justice Culkin complied and sentenced Gilbert to a two-to-four years' imprisonment and immediately remanded Gilbert to Sing Sing. Gilbert was stunned.

With the audacity that became typical of him over the years, Nathan Voloshen was in the courtroom that Monday. After the hearing, he went up to Bauman and introduced himself. He said Eddie was a client of his and that he would like Bauman to meet his good friend Justice Mitchell Schweitzer. The two of them went to Schweitzer's chambers where Voloshen told me he was received royally. They all discussed the Gilbert case. At one point, Voloshen related to me, Schweitzer expressed the opinion that Gilbert would have got a better break in both the federal and state courts if he had been represented by a lawyer like Michael P. Direnzo. Arnold Bauman was quite naturally infuriated by such a statement, and the visit soon ended. The incident amused Voloshen, who talked about it often. Voloshen also repeated frequently that if he had been called into the case earlier, before the federal sentence, he could have bought at least one of the judges.

A few weeks after Gilbert entered Sing Sing, Richard Wels and Nathan Voloshen met at the Men's Bar of the Biltmore Hotel to plan their strategy. Wels realized that Voloshen would need money to pay people off. In order to keep Wels out of this side of the picture as much as possible, the two of them agreed that when Voloshen needed more money he was to make his needs known to Yolande Gilbert, Eddie's widowed mother, or Turid Gilbert, Eddie's second wife. The women would, in turn, contact Wels and give him the information. When visiting Eddie Gilbert in Sing Sing, Wels or Chandor could discuss the matter with him. If Gilbert approved, Chandor would get the money. Voloshen agreed to this arrangement, but he insisted on cash payments.

By the last week of May 1967, it had been agreed between Eddie Gilbert and Richard Wels that Wels would take over as Gilbert's attorney of record from Bauman, after Bauman handled one more legal matter for Gilbert.

The last bit of legal work that Arnold Bauman did for Eddie Gilbert was to enter a motion that he be allowed to serve his federal and state sentences concurrently. The motion was made before Judge Edmond T. Palmieri and it was denied in all respects on June 16, 1967. The judge said that Gilbert was sentenced in federal court for violation of specific federal statutes, and that this ruling did not impinge upon the rulings of the state court.

After this, Wels officially replaced Bauman as Gilbert's attorney of record. At the previously mentioned Biltmore meeting in May 1967, Wels and Voloshen had agreed that Wels would not represent Gilbert in any criminal action, since Wels did not have a criminal practice. It was also agreed that although Voloshen would ask Judge Schweitzer to pick a good criminal lawyer, Wels would supervise the writing of the brief by the chosen criminal attorney, if that attorney were amenable. Wels hoped that in this criminal action it could be proved that Gilbert had been duped by Bauman into pleading guilty. Bauman, Wels alleged, had told Gilbert of a deal that he, Bauman, had worked out with Jerry Kidder, wherein Kidder had agreed to ask for a suspended sentence—or at the very worst to recommend that both sentences be served concurrently, as previously explained—because of Gilbert's voluntary plea, because of his voluntary return to the country, because of his cooperation, and because he had already been sentenced in federal court. Wels contended that Gilbert never would have pleaded guilty without this understanding.

The lawyer whom Schweitzer recommended to Wels was the famous criminal defender Maurice Edelbaum, who readily agreed to work with Wels with an assist from Schweitzer from the sidelines.

On Monday, June 12, 1967, I accompanied Nathan Voloshen and Red Chandor to Sing Sing on their visit to Eddie Gilbert. Maurice Edelbaum drove his own car. I went along only because Richard Wels had already learned that Voloshen had a habit of not keeping appointments or making phone calls, and Wels wanted to be sure that Voloshen made this trip. Chandor drove us in a pine green 1964 Lincoln which he had borrowed from a friend. Chandor's reason for going along, aside from visiting a friend and acting as chauffeur, was to discuss Gilbert's investments. The room where they met had a telephone; after Chandor had given Gilbert the latest news on the stock market, Gilbert would decide what he wanted to sell or buy and Chandor would telephone the instructions back to New York City. For allowing Gilbert these privileges, a prison official was supplied with stock market tips for his own investments. Chandor said the man was doing very well. But then so was Chandor. Voloshen told me he was paying Chandor to advise Gilbert to accede to Voloshen's demands. Between June and October, I made five or six of these trips to Sing Sing. Each time, I stayed in the car in the parking lot while the others went inside. Each time, Voloshen identified himself in the visitors' registry as one of Gilbert's attorneys. In October, Voloshen told me Justice Schweitzer had pointed out that the Gilbert case was getting close to a hearing and it might be a good idea for him to stay away from Sing Sing just in case the prosecution checked the records and found out he was visiting Gilbert in the guise of consulting legally in a state where he had no license to practice. Although a lawyer, and a member of the Maryland bar, he had no right to practice in New York. That ended my trips.

Besides the trip on June 12, Maurice Edelbaum made another to Sing Sing a few weeks later. He was scheduled to make a third trip but other matters kept him in the city, so he sent one of his assistants. Chandor told me later that Eddie Gilbert blew his stack. Gilbert announced that, in the first place, he wasn't used to dealing with underlings; in the second place, he was getting fed up with all the questioning; and, in the third place, he already had the judge fixed anyway. The assistant returned to New York in a state bordering on shock. When he reached his office and told Edelbaum what had happened, Edelbaum immediately informed Richard Wels that he was withdrawing from the case. Edelbaum had been suspended from practice for six months by the first Judicial Department of the Appellate Division of the New York State Supreme Court seven years before and apparently decided that Gilbert's case was too hot, or too tricky, for him to handle. After another discussion between Voloshen and Schweitzer—

held at Wels' request—Michael Direnzo, whom Schweitzer had originally recommended, was called in.

Michael Direnzo worked hard and long with Wels, with pointers from Schweitzer, and the case finally wound up before Justice George Postel in December of 1967. Postel's "rabbi" (the political sponsor of his judgeship nomination) was John Merli, a retired Democratic district leader and former New York City councilman. Schweitzer suggested to Voloshen that Direnzo get in touch with Merli. In that way, Direnzo would presumably have favorable access to Postel's opinion. Direnzo knew Merli, but when he tried to contact him he was told that Merli was in Florida. When Direnzo gave this news to Voloshen and Wels during a meeting in Wels' office on December 11, 1967, they all agreed that a trip to Florida was well worthwhile.

Like Scalise and Voloshen, Direnzo and Wels turned on a transistor radio full blast while discussing anything that they would not want others to hear—or to tap. This time it was Direnzo who supplied the ear-shattering entertainment as I walked with the two of them to an airline ticket office in Rockefeller Center, where Wels bought a roundtrip ticket for Direnzo and gave him a check for his expenses. At the same time, Wels arranged for his own tickets for his Christmas in Florida. Direnzo was back the following Monday morning with the news that while he was flying southward to Merli, Merli had been flying north to spend the weekend in New York on personal business. There was a rush of local telephone calls, Merli was located, and Direnzo had his meeting with Merli under the "palms" on Delancey Street.

A motion was made to set aside the state sentence on the grounds that Gilbert had been duped into making a guilty plea, Wels testified that Bauman had told him in June 1967 that Kidder had reneged on his promise. Kidder denied under oath that he had made any such promise. And Bauman, claiming a lawyer-client relation with Gilbert, refused to testify. Eddie Gilbert, who had been brought down from Sing Sing to the Tombs, the men's prison in New York City, testified at the trial as to the promise that had been made to him by Bauman. Finally Postel, after hearing all the witnesses and arguments on both sides, reserved decision, and Eddie Gilbert was sent back to Sing Sing to await Postel's decision.

A few weeks later, Postel denied Direnzo's motion —after Direnzo had assured Wels and Voloshen that he would receive a favorable judgment from Postel. To make up for his lack of success, Direnzo told Wels and Voloshen that Postel deeply regretted not being able to reach a decision in Eddie's favor but that Postel told him he would write a letter to the prison authorities and the parole board recommending an early parole for Gilbert. It was subsequently discovered in 1969, during Morgenthau's investigations, however, that this promised letter was never written.

Meanwhile, Richard Wels was himself handling a case brought against Gilbert by his first wife. Rhoda Gilbert was challenging her divorce settlement with Eddie on the grounds that he had misrepresented his true net worth to her in the original divorce proceedings. She wanted to get both Eddie's widowed mother and his second wife on the stand, under oath, because she felt Eddie had enlisted their aid in secreting funds. But his second wife threatened to leave the country with their children if there were any indication she would have to take the stand; and Eddie's mother just wasn't up to a court appearance, either physically or mentally.

When Rhoda Gilbert's brief was filed, it wound up before Justice Samuel A. Spiegel. Rhoda's lawyer made a motion to examine Turid and Yolande Gilbert. Wels opposed the motion and moved for a protective order. Spiegel denied Wels' order. Wels then made a motion for a summary judgment returnable in thirteen days, on the grounds that Rhoda did not have sufficient evidence to examine Turid and Yolande Gilbert. By this time, it was the middle of December, Spiegel was no longer sitting in the Part, and—surprise—guess who was? None other than Mitchell Schweitzer. Therefore, at this point, Justice Schweitzer also had a Gilbert case directly under advisement. He heard the case, listened to the arguments on both sides, and reserved judgment.

While this drama was unfolding, Nathan Voloshen was getting more and more money hungry. He called Eddie's wife and mother so often about money that they both complained to Wels about it. Because of their complaints, Wels revised the original plan of having Voloshen first apply for money to either of the two women, and instructed Voloshen to make future requests directly to him. This brought Voloshen and Wels into more frequent contact, mostly by telephone, and no matter how hard Voloshen pressed for more money— "for the Judge," as he put it—Wels would simply say he would have Red Chandor take the request up to Eddie. Voloshen started getting less money.

On Thursday, December 21, 1967, I was in Voloshen's office when he began harping on money again in the way that had made him so irritating to everybody lately. He said that Judge Schweitzer was pressuring him heavily, which Voloshen may have been saying only to get more for himself. He told me he had tried to reach Wels at his office that day, and was told Wels was in Florida—which he already knew anyway. Then he asked me if I could get Wels' Palm Beach number. I did. After several unsuccessful attempts, Voloshen finally reached Wels and promptly went into a tirade about the importance of immediate money "to take care of the Judge." Standing next to Voloshen during the brief conversation, I could hear some of what Wels said. Wels said the subject was nothing to discuss on the telephone and that Voloshen would have to wait until Wels returned to New York, on or about January 2, 1968. When Voloshen tried to press on, Wels hung up on him. Voloshen couldn't believe it. He kept saying: "Hello? Hello? Dick? Hello, Dick?" Then he slammed down his phone in fury. He said to me: "The Judge keeps asking for more and more money. He will get it or I will see that he renders an adverse decision."

Although by this time Yolande and Turid Gilbert had begun refusing to accept telephone calls from Nathan Voloshen, it was Yolande Gilbert's misfortune that day to answer the phone herself and find herself confronted with an enraged Voloshen. He went at her like a wild man, screaming that he had to have $15,000 for the Rhoda Gilbert case and $10,000 to give Michael Direnzo for Eddie's criminal case—immediately and in cash. He appealed to Yolande's maternal instinct, threatening her that if she didn't deliver as requested she was risking not only her son's freedom but also the pending Rhoda Gilbert case. He harangued, he cajoled, and he threatened. Apparently convinced that her son's future depended on her alone, she told Voloshen she would do whatever she could. On the morning of Wednesday, December 27, Yolande Gilbert arrived at Voloshen's office, he told me triumphantly, with $25,000 in $100 bills. Voloshen told me that she had given him a total of

$60,000 in cash, including Direnzo's fee, up to that time.

A few days later, Voloshen also told me that the plan was for Justice Schweitzer to submit to Richard Wels, for Wels' approval, a copy of the decision Schweitzer was going to hand down on Wels' petition for summary judgment. On Wednesday, January 3, 1968; Tuesday, January 9, 1968; Tuesday, January 30, 1968; Wednesday, February 14, 1968; and again on Monday, March 11, 1968, Justice Schweitzer submitted variations of his decision to Nathan Voloshen who either delivered them to Richard Wels personally or sometimes asked me to do so. To each version, Richard Wels voiced his objections both to me and to Voloshen: "This is not what we're paying for. My client is not getting his money's worth. The Judge is not doing his job." At one point, Wels said: "If the Judge can't deliver what we want, that's fine. But then let him return the money that we've paid him."

Voloshen was beginning to sweat. Repeatedly he suggested a personal confrontation between Wels and Schweitzer so that the two of them could iron out their differences. Wels, however, resisted; he knew that such a meeting between a lawyer and the judge handling one of his cases was both unethical and highly irregular. But as there seemed no other way to resolve the problem, Wels at last agreed to a meeting. It was set for seven o'clock on the evening of Monday, March 11, 1968, at the Drake Hotel on Park Avenue and Fifty-sixth Street.

Late that afternoon I was at Wels' office. He asked me to hang around and walk with him to the hotel. Although I agreed to walk to the hotel with him, I said I definitely would not attend the meeting. He just nodded. As we walked to the hotel, Wels said little, seeming nervous and preoccupied. When we reached the hotel, I accompanied Wels into the lobby. He went to the house telephone, asked for Mr. Seeman—who turned out to be Louis Seeman, a friend of Schweitzer's. Wels hung up the house phone, then turned to me and said: "They're coming down." I waited with him. In a few minutes, the elevator door opened and out came Voloshen and Schweitzer. I hung back as Wels moved toward Voloshen and Schweitzer, watching as Wels and Schweitzer met. At that point, I turned and went home.

Around nine o'clock that evening, Wels called and asked me to come over to his apartment. I did, and he told me what had happened. Schweitzer had told him there was nothing he could do but deny his motion for a summary judgment. Schweitzer said that if he did anything else, "fix" would be written all over the case. Wels said that he had then reminded Schweitzer of all the money that had been paid to him to render a favorable decision. Schweitzer had further pointed out that because the case would remain under his jurisdiction after the examination, he could then hand down a decision favorable to Eddie Gilbert on the overall matter. But this state of affairs was not what Eddie Gilbert had in mind at all. What he wanted to avoid at all costs was the court appearance of his mother and wife.

Two days later, on Wednesday, March 13, Schweitzer handed down his decision denying Wels' motion. The examination was held, the decision was filed on March 15, Yolande and Turid Gilbert in fact testified— and survived the experience. The final outcome of the case, at this writing, is still pending.

Meanwhile, Eddie Gilbert was still in prison, and there was the matter of getting him out to be dealt with. This time Nathan Voloshen delivered. In May 1968, as

Gilbert was starting his second year in jail, Voloshen got House Speaker McCormack to make a personal telephone call to Russell G. Oswald, then New York State Commissioner of Parole,* on Gilbert's behalf. This was followed up by a letter—a copy of which Voloshen showed me—in which McCormack recounted his long friendship with Eddie's father, who, according to the Speaker, had only "a few days ago asked me to intervene." Someone apparently had neglected to notify the Speaker that Eddie's father had at this point been dead for several years.

In most states, a prisoner must serve two-thirds of his minimum sentence before becoming eligible for parole; in a federal case, he must serve one-third. However, when a prisoner is a man of Eddie Gilbert's notoriety, it is rare for him to be granted a parole the first time he becomes eligible. But Eddie Gilbert got his parole on the first request—so great was the pressure of the Speaker of the House upon others in public office. Gilbert's parole was granted on July 30, and he was released from Sing Sing in September.

The state case having been dealt with, Gilbert nevertheless still faced the federal sentence. He feared he might be sent to Lewisburg, a maximum security facility compared to the country club atmosphere at Danbury. Through Wels, Gilbert asked Voloshen to do what he could to get him into Danbury. Having been able to arrange this for members of the Mafia, Voloshen had little trouble arranging it for Gilbert. McCormack's office was put into action again, and Gilbert got his wish: he

---

* And, as of this writing, State Correction Commissioner. It was Oswald who, on September 13, 1971, gave the order to storm the prison at Attica, New York, during which operation forty-two guards and inmates were killed.

was transferred from Sing Sing to Danbury to serve his sentence.

Voloshen was able to help the Gilberts in another area as well. The family nursemaid, a Swiss, had gone home, and when she tried to return she discovered that she would have to wait a couple of years to get another visa as an employed alien. The Gilberts got upset and Voloshen went to work. A telegram signed by Speaker McCormack and sent to the American ambassador in Bern was answered by a letter assuring that everything that could be done within regulations would be. The woman was given a temporary visa, which satisfied both the nurse and the Gilberts.

Each time a success was scored, Martin Sweig sent Voloshen a telegram with the good news and Voloshen showed it to Wels, who was always very impressed. This factor, more than any other it seemed to me, convinced Wels to continue going along with Voloshen on the Gilbert affair despite the many problems he was causing.

During the interminable months when Eddie Gilbert seemed to dominate everybody's life, Nathan Voloshen nevertheless found time for his other clients, some of them trying to get out of jail, others trying to stay out. One was John W. Hagenson, serving five years to life in a California prison for armed robbery. Voloshen told me that Hagenson had heard about him through Richard Horton, a fellow inmate. Horton and Voloshen were old friends. When Horton realized how desperately Hagenson wanted to get out of prison, he suggested that Voloshen might be the man to arrange it. Hagenson sent his wife all the way to Washington to meet Voloshen. (This was quite some time before Voloshen entered the Gilbert case.) To impress her, Voloshen introduced Mrs. Hagenson to House Speaker McCormack, meanwhile convincing her that he had the political connections to get her husband out of prison provided she had the cash. Somehow the woman raised it. On a trip to California, Voloshen made contact with Governor Pat Brown by using McCormack's name. Before receiving Voloshen, Brown checked with McCormack in Washington and was given the routine: "Oh, yes, Nat is a good friend of mine. Anything you do for Nat you do for me." Brown then received Voloshen and Mrs. Hagenson, and in the course of the meeting Voloshen told Brown that Mrs. Hagenson was going to make a contribution to Brown's forthcoming campaign. Voloshen extracted $10,000 from Mrs. Hagenson for Brown's campaign and $5,000 for the campaign of Edward McCormack, nephew of the Speaker, who was running in Massachusetts. He also got Mrs. Hagenson to pay him $1,000 which Voloshen said was for the campaign of James Roosevelt, who wasn't running for anything that year but was a member of the U.S. delegation to the United Nations. But Voloshen did not, however, get John Hagenson out of prison. Hagenson later announced that Nathan Voloshen had milked him for over $40,000 during this effort to get him paroled earlier. But the payments had been in cash and Hagenson had no way to get any of it back.

Another client who kept Voloshen busy was Nicholas N. Salgo, chairman of the board of the Bangor Punta Corporation, a conglomerate at 405 Park Avenue, New York. Salgo said he needed a contact with the SEC because of problems concerning mergers with companies like Piper Cub. Fortunately for Salgo, Voloshen was having very good luck with the SEC at this time; in fact, he considered himself a stock expert. Voloshen also did personal favors for Salgo. Salgo had a woman friend in

Europe whom he was trying to get into the country but who had problems getting a visa. I personally made a visit for Voloshen to Vincent Schiano, who was chief trial attorney for the legal division of the Immigration and Naturalization Service at 20 West Broadway, New York, on this matter. But what really resolved the problem was no doubt Voloshen's phone call to Schiano, telling him how important the matter was to House Speaker McCormack. In any event, the woman got into the country.

As the Gilbert case unfolded a new name got into the act: Ratnoff. While Gilbert was imprisoned in the Tombs, awaiting his appearance before Justice Postel, he had met a fellow prisoner named Ted Ratnoff. Although not an attorney, Ratnoff was known as a very good "jailhouse lawyer"; he had read law and knew a great deal about legal procedures. While both men were in the Tombs, the garrulous Gilbert told Ratnoff all about Voloshen, Wels, and Direnzo and the fortune he was paying them for legal maneuvers that weren't coming off. Ratnoff advised Gilbert that a better lawyer for him would be Stanley Reiben, the prominent Brooklyn attorney long active in Democratic politics as well as one of the founders of the Fortune Society, which aids ex-convicts. Then Gilbert went back to Sing Sing. Later on, upon his release in June 1968, Ratnoff got a job in Reiben's office as a general clerk. In light of his connection with the Fortune Society, Reiben not only was getting a good assistant in hiring Ratnoff but also he was helping to rehabilitate a crook.

Ratnoff, who now considered himself to be a buddy of Gilbert's, looked up Red Chandor. After Gilbert was transferred to Danbury, Ratnoff accompanied Chandor a number of times for the business discussions at the prison. During the drive, Ratnoff always asked Chandor a lot of questions about Nathan Voloshen's deals. At least twice, Ratnoff insisted that they make the trip in his car. Unknown to Chandor, Ratnoff had bugged his car, thus recording everything Chandor said about Voloshen and Wels. Ratnoff, in addition, had talked to Stanley Reiben about Eddie Gilbert, which led Reiben to begin telephoning Richard Wels to give him advice on how to handle the case. As the architect of the Eddie Gilbert case, Richard Wels did not like Reiben's interference at all, but he could not complain because he knew Gilbert was favorably disposed toward Reiben. Reiben and Ratnoff both became increasingly critical of Nathan Voloshen. They claimed, or pretended to claim, that Voloshen had been milking Gilbert for too much for too long. When Stephen Schaefer, Wels' assistant, visited Gilbert in jail in the fall of 1968, he was the victim of a Gilbert tirade during which Gilbert warned him that he was thinking of replacing Wels with Reiben.

In December of 1968, while sitting in Wels' office, I listened to Wels converse on the phone loudspeaker with Reiben and Ratnoff, both of whom said that Voloshen was an unprincipled crook and a thief. I was surprised at the statement's coming from Reiben because I recalled hearing Reiben's name mentioned in Voloshen's office. When I recounted this experience to Voloshen a few days later, he laughed and said that Reiben was a close friend. To prove it, he called Reiben on the spot and they made a date for drinks in an Italian restaurant called Umberto's on New York's East Fifty-third Street. After telling me that he and Reiben had worked on many projects together, Voloshen invited me to see for myself what good friends they were by joining them for drinks. We met on Monday, January 6, 1969, at 6:00 P.M. Joining the party were Voloshen's wife and Harry Maizlish, a client. Maizlish, a retired executive from Warner Brothers, owned a California radio station. He brought three problems to Voloshen: (1) he wanted to file bankruptcy papers; (2) he wanted a renewal of the license for the radio station; and (3) he wanted to get his son, a conscientious objector, out of jail. Voloshen got the license renewed, but he was unable to get the son out of jail, and Maizlish dropped dead in Voloshen's office before the bankruptcy papers could go through. In the course of his business with Voloshen, Maizlish paid him $35,000 plus an expensive fur-lined overcoat.

Nathan Voloshen and Stanley Reiben greeted each other like long lost brothers. They were obviously good friends. Another good friend of Reiben's, it came out during the meeting, was Justice Schweitzer. Reiben and Voloshen, I learned, had worked together in the Brooklyn courts on many cases concerning draft evaders. From the conversation I realized that Voloshen and Reiben both were playing Eddie Gilbert for all he was worth. While trying to give Wels the impression that Gilbert was getting fed up with Voloshen, Reiben actually was working on Gilbert to get him fed up with Wels. As far as Voloshen was concerned, he didn't care whether he got his share of Gilbert's money from Wels or from Reiben, just so long as he got it. So it was a set up, with the brilliant Richard Wels as the sucker without knowing it. Voloshen once told me that he was very lucky to have Reiben on his side.

Throughout 1968, Stanley Reiben gradually had taken over more and more of the Gilbert case, but Voloshen continued to get his payments through Wels. The total figure was around $90,000. As time passed and it became clear that Voloshen wasn't going to be able to get Gilbert out of Danbury before the eight months which would make him eligible for parole, Wels began to ask Voloshen to give the money back on the grounds that Voloshen had not done his job and therefore he had procured the money fraudulently. Voloshen ignored Wels' complaint. Angered, Wels became threatening, though certainly he recognized he could not take the matter to court.

When, in April 1969, Eddie Gilbert became eligible for parole from the federal prison at Danbury, he faced the same odds against getting it that he had at Sing Sing. But once again Nathan Voloshen put Speaker McCormack's office to work. The same pressure produced results. Once again, Voloshen got the telegram from Sweig. Even so, Eddie Gilbert was not very grateful. Gilbert felt he had overpaid for what he had got. He had ended up spending about two years in a couple of prisons. Even though he had been granted early paroles from both Sing Sing and Danbury, he had expected, for that kind of money, to have the whole mess resolved in a matter of months, if not weeks. In June 1969, Gilbert, accompanied by his new attorney, Stanley Reiben, paid a visit to Wels' office and threatened Wels with exposure unless he got the money back from Voloshen or paid the money back himself. Although Wels could have afforded to put up the money, he refused. Instead, he asked Voloshen to meet him at the Men's Bar at the Biltmore. I accompanied him to the Biltmore, where he told Voloshen about Gilbert's threat and demanded that Voloshen return as much of the money as possible. Voloshen pretended ignorance. "I don't know what you're talking about," he said, which was his way of turning a deaf ear to any subject. He further said he didn't know anything about any of Gilbert's money, and he challenged Wels to prove that he had received any. Since all the payments, with the exception of one of $5,000 to Direnzo, were in cash, there was of course no documentation. Exasperated and furious, Wels stalked out of the restaurant.

Later that day, Wels told me he telephoned his friend Robert Morgenthau, then U.S. Attorney for the Southern District of New York, and made a breakfast appointment with him for the next morning. At the breakfast, Wels said he gave Morgenthau his version of the Gilbert affair, editing out everything that might make himself look bad or culpable. Wels also related to Morgenthau many of the incidents I had recounted to Wels as taking place around the Speaker's offices in the Capitol. At the time, Morgenthau showed little interest in trying to get Nathan Voloshen indicted because he felt Voloshen was too well protected for any prosecutor to get enough evidence for an indictment.

With Gilbert out of jail and Wels and Voloshen not speaking to each other anymore, I was able to withdraw from the scene and devote more time to my own business. A couple of weeks passed, during which I did not hear from Richard Wels. Then, in July, I learned that Nathan Voloshen had been subpoenaed to appear before a federal grand jury investigating the Mitchell Lama Housing Projects. Government informer Herbert Itkin had brought Voloshen's name into the proceedings. Voloshen had met Itkin a year or so before, not realizing that the man who was soliciting his help was actually interested in bringing his downfall. The government's subpoena apparently made Morgenthau more optimistic about the chances of indicting Voloshen as well.

In early July, Wels telephoned me and asked me to have lunch with him on Tuesday, the fifteenth. After we met, exchanging polite inquiries about each other's families, Wels asked me if I knew anyone besides Voloshen who had connections in the New York State Supreme Court. I said I couldn't think of anybody else offhand, and I asked him why. Wels explained that for several months, he had been representing Richard Schine, son of the late hotel magnate Meyer Schine, in a divorce action against his wife Pat, the thorn being the alimony to be paid. Wels recalled to me that in 1968 he had represented him in this case when it came before Supreme Court Justice Harry Frank. During the course of the court proceedings concerning this case, Wels had had lunch one afternoon at Gasner's, a restaurant off Foley Square where many judges often lunched, and there he had seen Justice Schweitzer in an amicable and animated conversation with Justice Frank. It had quickly occurred to Wels to use Schweitzer to get to Frank, and he therefore had asked Voloshen to ask Schweitzer to intervene. To this end, a meeting was set up one evening early in the summer of 1968 at Kippie's Restaurant on the West Side of New York City. It was agreed beforehand that Schweitzer was to act as mediator between both sides. At one table were Richard Wels, his assistant Stephen Schaefer, Nathan Voloshen, and Jack Rapoport, Pat's lawyer and also a close friend of Schweitzer. At a nearby table were Justice Schweitzer and a close lawyer friend, Myron J. Greene. Every once in a while, Schweitzer would leave his table, go over to the two bargaining attorneys, and ask: "How are you doing, boys? Are you making any progress? Can I help?"

Evidently he couldn't because, despite his close connections to both sides, he was not able to persuade them to come to an amicable settlement out of court and/or to persuade Harry Frank to come to a favorable decision in court. Almost a year later, in July 1969, the case was still pending.

After outlining this background for me, Wels said: "I want to have some protection before I walk into that courtroom."

"I can understand that," I said, "and I'm sorry I can't help you. Even if I could, Dick, this isn't a good time to try anything. I've heard that some of the judges and their friends are going to be investigated by Bob Morgenthau's office."

He nodded. "I've heard that, too."

"Have you heard that Voloshen has been subpoenaed?" I asked.

"Yes."

I wondered how much more he heard. I said: "Why don't you just try to win your case on points?"

He shrugged. "I don't think I can. I don't think much of our Supreme Court judges."

A lot of lawyers didn't. "Then you might as well prepare your appeal," I said.

He shrugged.

He won this case in Supreme Court over a year later before Justice Myles Lane on points. With appeals going back and forth, the case is still pending.

On August 18, 1969, I went to Richard Wels' office at his request, and he greeted me with: "Bob, I've got great news. I'm finally going to nail Voloshen. I've got *Life* magazine to do an article on him. Then Morgenthau will have the 'public uproar' he needs to back up an indictment. I've got a call in to Bob now."

I didn't know how to take this. "Where did you get the information?"

He explained that Ted Ratnoff and Stanley Reiben had argued because Reiben wouldn't give Ratnoff a raise or loan him $5,000. Ratnoff had then gone to Richard Wels and had told him that Voloshen knew that Wels was putting pressure on Morgenthau's office to investigate Voloshen. This information had reached Voloshen through Martin Sweig, who had got it from a close friend of his in the Justice Department, who was reading the queries about Voloshen coming in from Morgenthau's office. Ratnoff had offered to sell Wels the tapes he had made of his conversations with Red Chandor in his bugged car. He had also volunteered to go through Reiben's office files for everything regarding Reiben and Voloshen and their deals, including everything pertinent to the Gilbert case. Wels had put Ratnoff in touch with Bill Lambert at *Life* magazine. *Life* subsequently had paid Ted Ratnoff $25,000 for his tapes, for the material from Reiben's files, and for Ratnoff's personal knowledge of the Gilbert case, Wels told me. He believed the article would give Morgenthau the ammunition he needed to overcome the lack of cooperation he was getting on his queries to Washington.

I was still with Wels when Bob Morgenthau, then vacationing at Martha's Vineyard, returned the call Wels had placed to him earlier. Wels' enthusiasm, and the involvement of *Life* magazine had its effect. Morgenthau said he would return to New York as soon as possible to get to work.

Wels was jubilant. He told me that he was cooperating with some of Morgenthau's assistants in readying

aware that there was enough power in Washington to nip the investigation in the bud, Morgenthau planned to send as few progress reports as possible to Washington until he felt he had a firm case. In the interest of caution, it was decided not to tap Voloshen's phone. Tapping a phone required a court order, and people like Voloshen have ways of finding out about court orders. Thus I became the tap. I was instructed to spend as much time as I could with Voloshen over the next three or four months while they were submitting their case to the grand jury. Not only did they want all the information I had on Voloshen's dealings over the years I had known him, but also they wanted to know what he was doing at the moment.

I started showing up at Voloshen's office early in the morning, sometimes making myself useful around the place, but usually just sitting there talking with him. When Voloshen left the office or we parted at the end of the day, I made copious notes of everything that had transpired while he had been in the office—the people who came in, the people who called, the people he called, the subjects discussed, the meetings he attended. Everything. Each evening, I would submit a report of the day's activities to Richard Wels, who would call it in to Rooney or Abramowitz. Sometimes the attorneys would ask me to look for something specific. For example, Voloshen's stationery identified him as a New York lawyer, which he wasn't, so the attorneys wanted some of the stationery. They also wanted certain documentation, which I had to locate in the files, slip out of the office, have photocopied, then put back into the files, all without being caught at it.

As the investigation progressed, more and more of Voloshen's associates were subpoenaed by the grand

jury, causing Voloshen's circle of friends to diminish in
direct proportion. John Donato, for example, made
himself scarce as soon as he heard about the investigation. One day Voloshen got a call from an old friend,
Henry Vogel, the Seventh Avenue suit manufacturer.
Vogel had heard that Voloshen was in some kind of
trouble and wanted to help him, offering to lend him
$10,000. Voloshen said he didn't need the money at the
moment but might call upon Vogel at a later date. A
week later, Vogel was subpoenaed by the grand jury
and had to testify. This time when he called Voloshen
his tune had changed completely. He told Voloshen he
could not afford this kind of publicity and that he didn't
want any further contact with Voloshen. Everybody
was running scared.

In a vindictive fervor, Richard Wels was relentless in
his pursuit of Nathan Voloshen's hide. Besides setting
up the article for *Life* magazine, Wels offered the story
to Ed Coyne of the *Wall Street Journal,* but the newspaper turned it down. In the week of October 13, 1969,
Wels got in touch with our mutual friend Al Albelli of
The New York Daily News, telling him he had a great
story but one that could not be used by the *News* until it
appeared in *Life.* Accompanied by Bill Federici, also a
prominent *News* reporter, Albelli went to Wels' office to
hear the story. I mistakenly thought it would be a good
idea for me to be there. Wels told Albelli and Federici
everything, knowing he could trust them to keep his
name and my name out of their account. He told the
story with relish. Understandably, though unfortunately
for us as it turned out, they decided to check out some
of the facts, and they asked someone in the Washington
bureau of the *News* to go to the Department of Justice
to do so. A few days later, Bill Lambert went to Washing-

ton for some last-minute checking on his *Life* article. He was told at the Department of Justice that Richard Wels and I had given the entire story to *The Daily News*. Enraged, he went back to New York and rewrote his *Life* article. Suddenly Wels and I were major characters in it, despite the fact that Lambert had promised not to mention us and despite the fact that we had given him most of his information.

Then sometime on Thursday, October 16, or Friday, October 17, 1969, the story broke that the SEC had detected certain irregularities in the resolution of the Parvin-Dohrmann case and that Nathan Voloshen was involved. Appearance of this item evidently put heavy pressure on Albelli and Federici to release their story. On Saturday, October 18, 1969, *The Daily News* published an abbreviated report of what they knew about the Eddie Gilbert case. The *Life* article came out a full week later on October 27.

Soon after I went to work as the unpaid tap on Voloshen for the Justice Department, I became aware of how efficiently his hot line to Washington was working. With everybody else deserting him and with me the only person who was spending time with him, I became his sidekick, and he confided in me more than he ever had before. Voloshen not only knew in advance who was going to be called by the grand jury, but a few days later he would also have information about the testimony. For weeks he kept telling me that I would not be called because I did not know enough. From the way I was working, without a court sanction, he was not yet aware of my clandestine role. I agreed with his conclusion, but I knew that the real reason I would not be called was that Morgenthau's office had promised not to subpoena me in return for my cooperation both in giving information and in working as the tap. The investigation was drawing to a close.

Then one day Voloshen reversed himself and told me that I would be subpoenaed. I didn't believe him. On October 23, when I went to Morgenthau's office to make a routine report, I was asked to come back the next morning for further discussion. The "further discussion" turned out to be the news that I was to appear before the grand jury immediately. I testified. When Voloshen asked me later what I had been questioned about, I told him that the jury seemed interested mostly in anything I knew about the Eddie Gilbert case.

As I've noted, during these months from August to October, there was enormous pressure on Morgenthau to drop the investigation. Pressure so great could come only from the top, from U.S. Attorney General John Mitchell. And coming from him, it came also from Richard M. Nixon. Although the influence exerted involved no effort to interfere with the course of justice, it concerned a definite effort to subvert any interference with the course of the Establishment. Men like Nathan Voloshen would come and go, but the Establishment had to be preserved. Although men like John W. McCormack would come and go, too, the issue at stake was not John W. McCormack, Democratic Representative from Massachusetts, but John W. McCormack, the Speaker of the House of Representatives of the Congress of the United States. McCormack had to be allowed to retire gracefully so that the image of his office would remain unsullied in the public mind. The connection between the Voloshen-Sweig case and the pressure on Morgenthau to resign was never emphasized in the press, and thus it appeared that a Republican administration merely was trying to get a Democrat out of the job of U. S. Attorney for the Southern District of New York in order to appoint a Republican. While not unthinkable, this happened not to be the true state of affairs. Morgenthau was a threat: through a perfectly planned publicity campaign, Morgenthau had forced Attorney General Mitchell's hand and was able to proceed with the investigation. Of a certainty, this was courageous; of an equal certainty, it was political suicide. Not only would Morgenthau face nothing but roadblocks in future dealings with the Department of Justice, but also he would face only roadblocks within his own party, simply because more Democrats than Republicans happened to be involved in the shake up. Of course, the majority of rolling heads could just as well have been Republicans, as has happened. This realization rallied both Republicans and Democrats alike to Sweig's defense, a weak pack of allies as vulnerable as he. Morgenthau refused to resign until he got his indictments and was assured Sweig and Voloshen would go to trial. Although the trial itself was a farce, it set a precedent, opening the way for other courageous men to take the same personal risks and carry out the job.

During all these events, nobody read the handwriting on the wall more clearly than Nathan Voloshen. The information fed him by Sweig let him know that too much evidence was piling up against him. He gradually became what Judge Frankel called him in passing sentence—a broken man. On December 12, 1969, Voloshen closed his office at 6 East Forty-fifth Street and went out of business. An era had ended.

Nathan Voloshen had been a powerful man, as powerful as his Washington associates; he had become powerful not because of the kind of man he was but because of the kind of men his associates were. Voloshen's name was better known on Capitol Hill than the names of many Congressmen. Giants went to him when they wanted something done in Washington, or anywhere, in the way that Voloshen could get things done—with payoffs. Alone or in tandem with John Donato or Eddie Adams, Voloshen represented such companies as General Electric, RCA, Sperry Rand, General Dynamics, IT&T, and Pepsi-Cola, as well as the Haitian government. He represented gang-operated unions, crooked managements, draft dodgers, shysters, and purchasable jurists.

Voloshen's era had to end. This conviction alone preserved my sanity during the frantic months I spied on him for the U. S. Department of Justice. Although it may seem odd, my thoughts about him were strangely ambivalent. I really liked the man. He could be kind, generous, thoughtful, considerate. He was never a bore. He worshipped his family and adored and respected his talented and beautiful second wife. It was only when he had a chance to make a buck, and to make it his way, that he could become the snarling weasel that made him intolerable. In a way, Voloshen's career ended because of his self-defeating greed.

As a result of the Voloshen-Sweig indictments, other criminal investigations were started. In the deal for the light sentence Voloshen received was his agreement to cooperate in any other investigations which might develop. One such was conducted by the New York State Joint Legislative Committee on Crime, before whom I was called to testify three times in 1970. Since I was confident that the Eddie Gilbert case would come up, I insisted on having Richard Wels present each time as my attorney. I wanted him there so he could hear for himself anything I might say about the case that could involve him. This way, I felt, there would be no repercussions if later he became involved and then tried to blame me. As it turned out, however, I was not questioned very thoroughly along these lines.

Voloshen's contacts extended not only into the federal arm of government and into cases before judges in the Supreme Court of New York. His contacts were also good in other areas. For example, when I was about to be called before the State Committee on Crime early in 1970, Voloshen called me in March and asked me to have luncheon with him at the Doral Hotel at Park Avenue and Thirty-eighth Street. At lunch, he told me that I was about to be called. "You will be called within ten days," he predicted. And I was. His pipelines were still intact.

The sessions of this investigation Voloshen knew so much about were supposed to be so secret that one session was transferred from the offices of the Waterfront Commission, where they were normally held, to an office building on Park Row so that the newspaper reporters wouldn't recognize me and thus get some idea of the direction the investigation was taking. I was astonished, therefore, when I learned, on January 14, 1971, that *The New York Times* had acquired a full transcript of the hearings of the committee. At first I thought this must have been a masterful job of journalistic detective work, but then I learned that copies had been released to the press by the committee's chairman, John H. Hughes. When I inquired why this was done, I was told by Wels: "It had to be. It was a blow for justice."

He said this even though he was not at all happy that he was mentioned in the transcript. His name had come up during the testimony of Justice Mitchell Schweitzer. According to the *Times,* Schweitzer had been questioned about any outside encounters he might have had with attorneys who had cases before him in court. He said he had had encounters with three such attorneys, one of whom was Richard Wels. The *Times* reported that, upon encountering each other, Schweitzer and Wels had talked briefly about an unfavorable decision Schweitzer had handed down against Wels. I construed this to be the Rhoda Gilbert decision. The *Times* said that when Wels started to argue, Schweitzer walked away. In preparing the story, a member of the *Times* staff had telephoned Wels, who had confirmed the meeting, but, according to the *Times,* had said there was "no prearrangement involved." This was not so. I had walked with Wels to the Drake Hotel that evening two days before Schweitzer had handed down his decision, and Wels certainly had known where he was going and why.

To the Assistant U. S. Attorney Richard Ben-Veniste, Wels later explained that his encounter with Schweitzer that night at Kippie's—while he and Rapoport, now deceased, bargained on the Schine divorce—was pure coincidence. That, also, was not true. Voloshen had set up the meeting and arranged for the judge to be present.

On Thursday, August 26, 1971, Richard Wels was questioned by William Leibovitz, who was questioning witnesses for the State of New York Court on the Judiciary, "in the matter of the proceedings pursuant to Section 22 of Article 6 of the Constitution of the State of New York in relation to Mitchell D. Schweitzer, Justice of the Supreme Court, First Judicial District."* Leibovitz was an assistant to the counsel of the court, Lawrence E. Walsh.

After the meeting, when Wels returned home that night, he phoned me. He told me he wanted to tell me what had happened but that he couldn't on the telephone, so I went to his home. He said that the questioning had taken place in a room on the ninth floor of 76 William Street, New York City, and that while he was being questioned he was under oath. Knowing that I was going to be questioned by the same court on September 1, Wels wanted me to back him up on three points that diverged from the truth. They were (1) that the meeting with Justice Schweitzer at the Drake Hotel had not been prearranged, that he thought he was going to meet only Nathan Voloshen at the hotel, and that the meeting took place after March 15, 1968; (2) that the meeting at Kippie's Restaurant was only arranged to discuss the Schine case with Rapoport and he did not know that Schweitzer would be present; and (3) the only time he met Voloshen was once when he went to Voloshen's office and learned that Eddie Gilbert had got his early parole.

Having thus been carefully briefed by Wels, it turned out, ironically, that I was never questioned on any of these three points.

---

* While still under investigation in December 1971, Justice Schweitzer resigned from the bench effective January 24, 1972, with full pension. The State Court on the Judiciary, however, sent memorandums urging that further study of the Schweitzer case be made by Presiding Justice Harold Stevens of the Appellate Division—with a view to possible disbarment proceedings or criminal action.

Capitol Hill is a beehive of lobbying. Rarely does a member of the Congress face a decision without feeling great pressures of all kinds upon him. As a lawmaker, he is continually dealing with legislation that can involve millions of dollars and affect millions of pocketbooks. The owners of the pocketbooks do not hesitate to let the member of Congress know how they want him to spend all those dollars. Although informing him is their right, the way they go about doing it is not always straightforward. Big-time lobbyists like Nathan Voloshen are a rarity compared to the hundreds—even thousands—of lower echelon wirepullers who roam the Capitol daily. Both Senators and Representatives need these people. Not only do they represent money, but they also represent votes. Because all Congressmen need money and votes to stay in office, a hidden branch of the government has come into existence: the special-interest groups. These groups use money primarily, but sometimes votes, to influence the passing of laws that benefit themselves, and they use personal contacts to get government contracts that might go to someone else otherwise. The best way for special-interest groups to get these things done is to hire the right wirepuller, the right lobbyist. In many cases, the right lobbyist is the man or woman who knows the field, who has been on the inside, who has worked for the government. The Congressman may appear to give proper consideration to a bill or a contract by paying attention during a public hearing, but the person he really listens to is the person who has private access to his ear, especially when this person's opinions are accompanied by a campaign contribution. Out of this prevailing practice evolves a certain secrecy. The public never really knows what is happening.

The problem is twofold. First, Americans have never questioned their politicians enough. We have the right to know not only how our Representative or Senator votes on a bill or contract but also why. If he votes for a bill granting favorable concessions to a bank or the banking industry, we have the right to know if he is on the board of a bank or owns bank stock. It would be extremely difficult for any individual to vote against himself, but we have the right to know when our representative in either House is voting *for* himself, regardless of what the matter is. We can't expect network television to give us this information; too many people are involved. But we can expect it from our local press, and we should demand it. We should keep a closer eye on the people we elect to run our country for us. Second, both as individual citizens and as a nation, we should take a closer look at the legion of nonregistered lobbyists who are calculatingly using their experience in government to make the government work specifically for them and their clients—and at much better salaries. Whether the lobbyist has been in the Congress or in the military, whether he was in a Presidential cabinet or held a high position in a government agency, he is of value to his clients because he has good connections and knows all the short cuts. Having been part of the Establishment, he has found out how to circumvent all the red tape to get things done. He has learned, too, that the magic word is *money*. He knows where to get it and he knows where to put it. Although what he does may not be illegal, this is often because there are no effective laws to control him. But what he does can be—and often is—definitely immoral.

These ex-office-holders-turned-lobbyists have little trouble making the transition. And it doesn't take them much time to qualify. Although the seniority rule applies in the Congress for appointments to important committees, especially the chairmanships of important committees, a member need spend only one or two terms in the House and just one in the Senate to line up enough connections for a lucrative career in lobbying when the time comes. Furthermore, he doesn't have to have all that many connections. In Washington, successful lobbying depends not on the quantity of one's friendships but on the quality of them. As a member of Congress, the future lobbyist moves in a privileged atmosphere.

For example, Andrew J. Biemiller was a Democratic Representative from Wisconsin for the two nonconsecutive terms that began in 1945 and 1949. Today he is the lobbyist—he calls himself the "director of legislation"—for the powerful AFL-CIO, and a job of this magnitude would never have been given to a man who didn't know his way around the Hill. Then there is Clyde T. Ellis, who was a Democratic Representative from Arkansas for two terms. He now represents the

National Rural Electric Cooperative Association, which is practically the farm vote. A classic example of an ambitious man is the late Scott Lucas of Illinois. After two terms in the House and two terms in the Senate, Lucas withdrew from politics in 1951 and went into lobbying. By the time of his death in 1968, he had represented twenty-five different special-interest groups, probably a record.

But a far more productive breeding ground for future lobbyists than Congress is the Pentagon. For over thirty years, defense spending has been the largest single item in the federal budget, and scores of major defense manufacturers have found out that the easiest way to get government contracts is to hire as a personal contact—that is, as a lobbyist—a retired, high-ranking military-man or ex-cabinet member whose friends and acquaintances are still running the show at the Pentagon. Not only can a man of this kind put in a good word for the manufacturer around the Pentagon, but he can also get inside information on future Pentagon projects, and he can even ascertain the approximate size of upcoming bids. Industry can always find room for a man with such contacts.

In 1969, the Congressional Quarterly Service, an organization that publishes the *CQ Report,* a weekly review of Congressional activities, reported that as of 1960—the last year for which statistics were available —"more than 1,400 retired officers of the rank of major or higher [including 261 of general or flag rank] were employed by defense contractors. The company employing the largest number [187, including 27 retired generals and admirals] was General Dynamics Corporation, then headed by former Secretary of the Army Frank Pace, which also received the largest defense orders in 1960. [Congressional Quarterly attempted to obtain more recent employment figures from the Pentagon but were told they were not available to the country.] Despite a 1966 Executive Order prohibiting a retired officer from 'selling' or negotiating contracts with his former service, one industry source told Congressional Quarterly that 'at least 90 percent of the retired officers hired for top level positions by the defense contractors ignore that regulation.' " The order was issued because so many retired high-ranking officers were flagrantly lobbying in the Pentagon. But, like "Blue Laws" and prohibition, the order has turned out to be wholly unenforceable.

These men are not only on good pensions, paid for by the American people, they are also receiving a great deal more of the people's money, in the form of the fat salaries or fees which are paid them for getting their employers, or clients, government contracts, which in turn are paid for out of taxes. Moreover, few, if any, of these men are registered lobbyists, although they are undeniably using their personal influence for the profits of vested interests.

In Washington there are also a number of associations which exist for the purpose of promoting the causes of one or more branches of the Armed Forces. There is, for example, the Association of the U. S. Army, headed by Lt. Gen. Charles G. Dodge, USAR. There is the Navy League, whose president is Maj. Gen. Charles F. Duchien, USMCR. The board of directors of the Navy League includes Dan Kimball, former Secretary of the Navy and now president of the Aerojet General Corporation. Another board member is Admiral Robert B. Carney, USNR, former Chief of Naval Operations and now chairman of the board of the Bath

Iron Works and Shipbuilding Corporation. The companies headed by both these men do considerable business with the Navy; thus each time they support the causes of the Navy via the Navy League, they are helping their own business as well.

Another such group is the Air Force Association, whose president is Peter J. Schenck. Schenck also happens to be president of the Raytheon Corporation, manufacturers of planes and guidance equipment. Yet another group is the American Ordnance Association, which crusades for military preparedness, certainly in the interest of its members, the manufacturers of weapons and munitions. The Aerospace Industries Association is primarily concerned with keeping the United States first in air travel at all altitutdes. Its chairman is E. Clinton Towl, who is also chairman of the board of Grumman Aircraft Engineering Corporation. Fifty-nine different companies each pay annual dues of $75,000 to be members of this association, a fee only the giants of the industry can afford. This perhaps explains why the giants get virtually all the contracts.

Supposedly seeking closer working relationships between industry and the national security agencies is the National Security Industrial Association, but, as usual, what is actually being sought is profits for industry at the expense of the taxpayers. The main purpose of all these associations is lobbying, ostensibly for the "noble" causes of the military, but actually for their own high profits. And yet, since both of these groups is registered as a lobbyist with the Clerk of the House and the Secretary of the Senate, as required by law—with the exception of the Aerospace Industries Association—there is no record of any campaign contributions the associations may be making to get things done for the military on the Hill, and no record of any gratuities they may dispense at the Pentagon.

During my years as a lobbyist, several small industrialists hired me to try to get them government contracts. I invariably found that there was a marked tendency on the part of all branches of the military to favor companies with which they had been doing business for years. Whenever I questioned this, I was always told that the military operated this way because these companies—invariably giants—had proved over the years that they could deliver the product they had contracted for. I was told that Pentagon experiences showed that smaller companies, however great their desire to compete, did not always have the ability to deliver. Each time, I pointed out that small companies did not seem to be getting much chance to prove their ability, but this got me nowhere. Repeated intercessions by some powerful member of the Armed Services Committee in either the House or the Senate was required to get a Pentagon contract for a small industrialist in his constituency, so strong is the grip Big Business has on the Pentagon. After all, the small industrialist can't afford to hire a retired general or admiral at a salary commensurate with his influence, so he must continue to live at the mercy of the giants, gratefully accepting the subcontracts they dole out to him.

The danger of the military-industrial complex, which President Eisenhower wisely warned us against in his final address to the nation on January 17, 1961, increases when members of the Congress get into the act. Take the late L. Mendel Rivers, for example. While he was chairman of the House Armed Services Committee, which determines appropriations for the Armed Forces, Democrat Rivers managed to acquire for his district in

Charleston, South Carolina, a naval station, a shipyard, an air base, an army depot, a missile plant, and a mine warfare center—until over 60 percent of the industry in Charleston depended on defense contracts. And when Representative Carl Vinson was chairman of this same committee, he was able to have so many military installations assigned to Georgia that, at a public hearing on a new base, an Air Force general said to him: "Sir, if you try to put one more base in Georgia, you will sink your state." Vinson and Rivers, of course, had simply been lobbying for their districts, which was in itself not improper; but having control of the purse strings they also had control of expenditures, and they used this as pressure on the Pentagon to see to it that the money was spent in their districts. Another example is Congressman John W. Byrnes, Republican of Wisconsin. In 1967, Byrnes won approval of his amendment to the defense appropriations bill, which prohibited construction in a foreign shipyard of any naval vessel funded under the bill. One of the ships funded was a new type of ocean minesweeper, and a group of British firms underbid American shipbuilders. One of the three American companies capable of building the ship was located in Byrnes' district in Milwaukee. Rather than ask the Milwaukee company to lower its bid, Byrnes simply raised the flag, got his amendment passed—and the ship was built in Milwaukee.

Not only the military is involved in this kind of influence peddling. Gary Avery, formerly the legislative assistant to Senator Walter F. Mondale of Minnesota, now lobbies for the Chase Manhattan Bank of New York. It so happens that Senator Mondale is on the Senate Banking and Commerce Committees. Ed Gadsby, former chairman of the SEC and now a partner in

the Washington law firm of Gadsby and Hannah, lobbies for the Boston Stock Exchange. John C. Bagwell, a
former Department of Agriculture general counsel, lobbies for the Hawaiian Sugar Planters Association. The
list is endless, primarily because the industrial giants
often hire several lobbyists, each to work in his specialized field.

In late October 1966, I went to Grand Rapids, Michigan, to attend a fund-raising dinner for Jerry Ford,
where the guest speaker was Richard M. Nixon, and at
one point I went to the rostrum to speak to Jerry after
the speeches were over and to talk with Nixon. At that
time, very few people in the country believed that Nixon
would be the Republican candidate in 1968, but Ford
believed it and he was talking up Nixon wherever he
went. It was for this reason that Nixon attended the dinner himself. Then a man I didn't know stepped up to
our group, touched Ford's arm, and they began to chat.
During their conversation of perhaps five minutes, I
heard the man refer to NASA, as such, several times. I
also heard him mention the name Tom Paine several
times. In two or three different ways, I heard Ford say:
"If the man is qualified, there should be no problem."
Then Ford introduced the man to Nixon, and they
talked briefly. I heard Nixon say: "Any friend of Jerry's
has my support." When the man left, Jerry turned and
commented to me: "That was one of your counterparts.
He's with General Electric." So I assumed the man was
a lobbyist.

Like all industrial giants, General Electric contrib-
utes to both parties in an election campaign, the donations usually being made through company executives,
with the bigger contributions going to the company's favorite candidate. Thus there was nothing unusual about

a lobbyist making a pitch to a politician at an affair of this kind. In fact, with so many people milling about, these fund-raising events often offer the best opportunities for getting in a good pitch without being obvious about it. Just my presence, for that matter, was a pitch in itself. During his speech, Jerry Ford referred to me by name and described me as "my good friend who has come all the way from New York for this dinner."

About a month after that fund-raising dinner, I was on my way to Jerry Ford's office in Washington one day when I saw him come out with the same man I had seen in Grand Rapids, the presumed lobbyist for G. E. Jerry nodded to me as I neared them, and he said: "I believe you two know each other from Grand Rapids." The man and I nodded to each other and I went inside. When Ford came back into the office, he didn't make any reference to the incident, nor did I. But I remembered the name Tom Paine, and I wondered who he was.

On January 31, 1968, the White House announced that President Johnson had appointed Thomas O. Paine, a General Electric executive, as deputy director of the NASA program. Paine had been with G. E. for nineteen years and, at the time of the appointment, was manager of TEMPO, the company's center for advanced studies in Santa Barbara, California. I made the connection. G. E. now had a company man at the top level of the heavily-budgeted space program. The fact that the appointment had been made by Democrats wasn't unusual. Having contributed to both parties, G. E. also lobbied both parties and, by Washington rules, had the right to expect favors from whoever was in power.

Then, in October 1968, NASA Director James E.

Webb resigned and Johnson appointed Paine the acting director of the space program. This time, there were some significant factors involved. In the first place, the Democratic Party was having trouble raising money to pay its 1968 Presidential campaign bills, and for a big enough donation the party would have even considered putting Paine on the ticket. Second, by making Paine the *acting* director, the Administration sidetracked the otherwise required Congressional hearing on Paine's qualifications, which might have moved into the area of conflict of interest in view of the fact that General Electric was already doing a lot of business with NASA. And third, by making the appointment temporary, the administration left the door open for the next President —Humphrey or Nixon—to put his own man into the job. After Nixon won the election, he appointed Paine the director of NASA on March 5, 1969, and the appointment was approved by Congress on April 3.

Sometime during the following year, NASA invited bids on a satellite program that was to cost an estimated $50 million. Among the companies submitting bids were General Electric and the Fairchild Hiller Corporation of Maryland. The bids were opened in the spring of 1970, and the contract went to General Electric. As *The New York Times* put it on July 3, 1970: "The losing competitor in the contract, the Fairchild Hiller Corporation, has charged that NASA had given General Electric preferential treatment and had allowed some of Fairchild's proprietary development to fall into the hands of General Electric." For one thing, at the time of the deadline, General Electric was given a week's extension in submitting its bid, and there was some indication that G. E. might have learned the size of the Fairchild Hiller bid. This sort of thing is difficult to keep quiet in

Washington, once the news gets out, and so pressures began to build, presumably instigated by Fairchild Hiller, and rightly so if the rumors were true.

Elmer B. Staats, U.S. Comptroller General in the General Accounting Office, which receives such bids, advised NASA that the proposed award to G. E. should be reconsidered. At the beginning of July, with the pressures building, Paine issued a statement which said: "On April 9th, I requested the General Accounting Office to conduct a review of the events leading to the selection of the General Electric Company rather than the Fairchild Hiller Corporation to build two Applications Technologies Satellites. The General Accounting Office had reported to me that the Fairchild Hiller Corporation may not have been accorded an equal opportunity to submit a winning bid because of the one-week extension granted General Electric, who turned in the lower bid. At the time the award was made, this time disparity was not known to the selecting officials. NASA will therefore reopen the bidding to Fairchild Hiller and General Electric in strict accordance with procurement regulations."

That should have been the end of it, but it wasn't. On July 10, Senator John L. McClellan, Democrat of Arkansas and chairman of the Senate Permanent Investigating Subcommittee, made a speech on the Senate floor in which he charged: "During an evaluation of cost proposals by NASA in February of 1970, NASA made a substantial adjustment to the Fairchild Hiller proposal to reflect a probable cost overrun predicted by the agency. The propriety of this cost adjustment is subject to serious question." The Senator went on to say that NASA had permitted General Electric to reduce overhead costs in its final offer so that the total was just below that of its competitor. That is, the administrator of NASA allowed General Electric to look at the bid of the Fairchild Hiller Corporation and then adjust its own bid accordingly. Such practice is, of course, illegal. At the time, NASA Administrator Thomas O. Paine declined to comment on McClellan's charges. However, a little more than a month later, on August 15, it was announced that Paine was resigning from NASA, effective September 15. According to an article in *The New York Times,* Paine had been named a vice president of G. E.; he was returning to the fold. And that was the happy end of what might have been a sticky affair—for Paine, for G.E., and perhaps for the government.

Take another case of sticky lobbying. The lobbyist this time was Thomas Hale Boggs, Jr., whose father was then Majority Whip in the House of Representatives and is now Majority Leader. Boggs, Jr. is a lawyer with the Washington firm of Patton, Blow, Verrill, Brand, and Boggs, registered lobbyists, representing the boating industry, the Geothermal Resources International Corporation, and the New Process Company. Like a great many lobbyists, Boggs, Jr. has represented a number of other clients whom he has not registered with the Clerk of the House and the Secretary of the Senate, as required by law. I know him to have worked on behalf of the Hilton Corporation, the Parvin-Dohrmann Corporation, the Baltimore Contractors, Inc., General Dynamics, General Electric, the Radio Corporation of America, Sperry Rand, and Bell Telephone, among others. Boggs, Jr. was to his father what Bobby Baker was to Lyndon Johnson. It was common knowledge around Washington that if the team of Boggs and Boggs couldn't get a bill through the House, nobody could. Besides being Majority Whip at the time,

Boggs, Sr. was the ranking member of the Ways and Means Committee, the Joint Committee on Internal Revenue Taxation, the Joint Committee on Reduction of Federal Expenditures, and the Joint Economic Committee—all powerful positions.

One lobbying effort that backfired for young Boggs involved the Baltimore Contractors, Inc., despite the fact that he probably had enough Congressional help to declare war. I first heard about this affair in the summer of 1967, when I went to visit Nathan Voloshen at his New York office. Voloshen was on the phone as I entered, and I heard him saying: "I would like to help you and I'll do the best I can. You know I've got a lot of friends down on the Hill. I've talked to the Speaker about it and he would be willing to do anything he can. I know you have been trying to get to him. But before I can do anything, I've got to have another check for $5,000." I had often heard Voloshen ask people for money, even larger amounts, so this didn't impress me. After Voloshen hung up, he said to me: "This is going to be one of the biggest things I've worked on. It involves Albert and it involves Boggs and I'm getting Senator Long in on it, too. It's a $5-million deal. This is something that I think I can do, but I may call on you, Bob, for your help with Jerry Ford."

He then told me what the "deal" was. The Baltimore Contractors, Inc., headed by Victor H. Frenkil, had obtained the contract to build a parking garage under the Rayburn House Office Building in Washington at a cost of $11.7 million. On the grounds that certain construction problems, which had not been specified or clarified in the contract, had added to the cost of the garage, Frenkil had put in a claim to the Office of the Capitol Architect for another $5 million. The late George

Stewart, then the Capitol architect, had reviewed Frenkil's claim and considered it unjustified. So Frenkil took another route to get the money. The building committee for the new Rayburn Building was comprised of House Speaker John W. McCormack of Massachusetts, Emanuel Celler, Democrat of New York, and William C. Cramer, Republican of Florida. In normal circumstances, it should have been a fairly simple matter for Frenkil to get through to the committee, persuade it to support his claim, and use its influence to overrule the Capitol architect. But this time things weren't normal.

For Frenkil, Voloshen certainly seemed the man to get the building committee on his side. By the time I learned about all this, Voloshen already had McCormack and Celler on Frenkil's side, but Cramer didn't even want to talk about it. The time came when Nathan Voloshen could hardly talk about anything else. Victor Frenkil was giving Voloshen payments of $5,000 with regularity, and he wanted some action. As months passed, the only action Voloshen could provide was an occasional meeting in McCormack's office.

On Wednesday, January 3, 1968, I accompanied Nathan Voloshen to the King's County Supreme Court Building for the swearing-in ceremonies of Supreme Court Justice Abraham J. Multer, a former Congressman, who had received a certain amount of notoriety in connection with the Bobby Baker investigation, he and Baker having been together in several business ventures in Washington. Voloshen was attending the ceremony as the personal representative of Speaker McCormack. We were among the honored guests and sat in a special section facing the audience in the courtroom. Sitting in the first row, first seat, of the audience was Emanuel Celler. After the ceremony, Voloshen went to Celler and began a conversation, Celler towering over Voloshen and bending slightly in order to hear him and keep the talk between themselves as much as possible.

"You know, Victor is having a hell of a lot of trouble down there with Stewart," I heard Voloshen say.

I remember Celler's saying: "Don't worry about a thing, Nat. I'm with you."

Voloshen said: "Do you know anybody down there who is close to the architect's office?"

Celler did not respond to this. He moved on into the crush of people waiting to shake his hand. By this time, Voloshen had asked me several times if I knew anybody close to Stewart. I was aware that Jerry Ford and George Stewart knew each other, but I refused to bring Jerry into this matter because it smelled a little bit to me. Because of Voloshen, however, I continued to watch its development. One development was Voloshen's news to me that Frenkil was a heavy contributor to Spiro Agnew's campaigns. Once again I was struck by the realization of how, in Washington, interested parties, especially where big stakes are concerned, constantly play both sides of the aisle.

In September 1968, I was again in Voloshen's New York office when a call came from Frenkil, and I gathered from the conversation that Voloshen had been trying to avoid Frenkil. Voloshen was saying: "You shouldn't worry, Victor. Of course I'm working on it. We're all working on it. But you know we can't get you into everything. Victor, can you be in McCormack's office at ten o'clock tomorrow morning? Good. I'll see you there." Then Voloshen said to me: "Now I've got to set up another meeting to impress this guy." He telephoned Hale Boggs, who agreed to be there. He phoned Carl Albert, who agreed to be there. He also tried but

couldn't reach Louisiana's Senator Russell Long. Then
Voloshen asked me: "Are you going down to Washington tomorrow?"

"Yes."

"What plane?"

"I'm taking the train."

"Fly down with me on the eight-o'clock shuttle. Attend this meeting. It'll fill up the room."

At twenty minutes to ten the next morning, Voloshen
and I entered McCormack's offices opposite the House
chamber. Frenkil was already there, and he seemed irri-
tated. Voloshen spoke to him in placating tones, assuring
him that everything would be all right. By ten, McCormack, Albert, and Boggs were in the room, McCormack at his desk, smoking a cigar. The meeting, if it
could be called that, began on time, and about five minutes later Senator Long came in. Because such meetings
had been held before, the men all knew each other and
were on a first-name basis, and this meeting lasted
about half an hour. I felt that little was being accomplished. Voloshen and the Congressmen in the room repeatedly assured Frenkil in different ways that he didn't
have a thing to worry about. Boggs' lobbyist son, Frenkil was told, was in the course of ingratiating himself
into the Office of the Capitol Architect, working his way
up to Stewart's closest advisors, in hopes of persuading
them to advise Stewart to take another look at Frenkil's
claim, maybe a sympathetic look. When the meeting
ended, Albert, Boggs, and Long hurried away, McCormack turned his attention to some papers on his desk,
and I watched Voloshen put an arm around Frenkil's
shoulders and lead him to the door. Voloshen said:
"See, Victor? Everything is moving. You've got the best
men on the Hill working for you. We just need some

more time. Now, Victor, I want to chat with you about something." I saw Frenkil cringe. They left the room. Later, Voloshen told me that Frenkil had given him another $5,000, this time in cash.

Over the following months, I attended several of these meetings, at Voloshen's request, and they were always the same. Three or four times, I was with Voloshen out in the corridor when he put the bite on Frenkil, and he usually said: "I need something for the boys inside." I never found out if anything was actually paid to the boys inside.

Although Nathan Voloshen had an amiable relationship with Hale Boggs, he was never as direct or forceful with Boggs as he was with Albert or McCormack or Martin Sweig. Whenever Voloshen wanted to put a little fire under Boggs, he would see to it that Boggs' son Tom was at McCormack's lunch table that day. Then Voloshen, or often Speaker McCormack himself, would put the pressure on young Boggs by asking him a lot of questions about what his father was doing on some project. I once heard McCormack tell Tom Boggs at lunch: "Your father knows how interested I am in this. He knows what it means for us. Frenkil is beginning to hound Nat on this project, and I don't like that. Here's what I want your father to do." Then he rattled off the names of people to be telephoned, what they were to be told, what job threats were to be insinuated.

Tom Boggs attended some of the meetings in McCormack's office and he was able to bring along some of the staff from the Office of the Capitol Architect. But these were people who couldn't do much; and, knowing that George Stewart was adamant in his rejection of the claim, they were reluctant to do anything at all. One day Voloshen telephoned George Stewart and said that

Speaker McCormack wanted Stewart to come to lunch at the House. I was present at that lunch. Stewart did not show up, but he sent his assistant, Mario Campioli, who explained that Stewart was ill. Voloshen sat at Mc-Cormack's right; I sat at Voloshen's right; Campioli sat to my right; and in order to speak to Campioli, Voloshen had to lean across in front of me. McCormack hardly said a word during the lunch, but repeatedly and in different ways Voloshen leaned toward Campioli and said: "The Speaker is very interested in this project. Mr. Frenkil is a good friend of the Speaker's. The Speaker wants something done about Mr. Frenkil's claim—and soon. This is a serious matter and something better be done soon or there may be some changes around here."

Mario Campioli's composure impressed me. As we were leaving the room together, he shook his head and said to me: "There's something very wrong about this. Mr. Stewart said that he will not go to his grave with the smell of this deal around him."

What was wrong, in Washington terms, was George Stewart's personal integrity. As things were, the budget for the garage had been raised from $9 million to $11 million, as a result of inflation during the construction. Furthermore, the contract specified that the garage was to be built in eighteen months, but Frenkil's company took three years. Even so, had Frenkil come in with a claim of a few hundred thousand dollars, Stewart might have approved it, but he considered Frenkil's claim for $5 million outlandish. Stewart was well aware that his staff was under terrific pressure from McCormack's clan. Not only were jobs being threatened, but other jobs were being offered, better paying jobs with Frenkil's company, even moonlighting jobs that paid as much as the staff members were getting in their present positions. Another point that undoubtedly irked Stewart was that, although he was the Capitol architect, he had nothing to say about which construction companies did the work. The contracts were awarded by the three-man building committee composed of McCormack, Celler, and Cramer. Nathan Voloshen could usually get McCormack and Celler to go along with him on his choice of contractors. One of his favorite clients was the Thompson-Starrett Company, for which he had helped secure a number of choice Washington Construction plums—Walter Reed Hospital, Union Station, etc. Jules Van Raalte, then president of the company, told me subsequently that he had been a long-time client of Nathan Voloshen and that "Nat always delivered" for him. I was present when, in 1964, Voloshen persuaded a State Department official to grant Thompson-Starrett the contract to refurbish American embassies around the world. Voloshen got the company a great deal of government work, and it was generally known that government architects resented having the company forced on them by pressures from the Hill. Had Frenkil's claim been valid, George Stewart would not have opposed it. In McCormack's office, the subject of validity never came up. According to the 1946 lobbyist act, a Congressman is innocent as long as he innocently believes he is handling an innocent matter. As long as a Congressman can claim ignorance of any illegality in matters involving himself or his staff, he is not responsible should any such matter backfire. And the Frenkil case backfired.

The tremendous pressures being put on Stewart's office came to the attention of Stephen H. Sachs, the U. S. Attorney in Baltimore, and he placed the matter before a grand jury to determine whether any evidence of fraud was involved. The grand jury studied the case for a year. In the summer of 1970, *The New York Times* broke the story which revealed that when Sachs was ready to go to court he was stopped in his tracks by his boss, Attorney General John N. Mitchell. The reason given by Mitchell for blocking legal action was that the indictment handed down by the grand jury contained the names of six Congressmen whose careers might be smeared by their association with the case. They were John McCormack, Hale Boggs, Daniel Brewster, Russell Long, and Representatives Samuel N. Friedel and Clarence Long, both of Maryland. Mitchell felt that, although these men weren't named as defendants, their personal prominence as members of the Congress might result in their being tried by the press.

Actually, there was a lot more to it. Although Sachs was not allowed to proceed legally—because of a lack of evidence, Mitchell's office said—he did submit to the courts a forty-page presentment, summing up the grand jury's findings. The presentment was in a sealed envelope which became the property of the court and was to remain secret. But it did not. After the *Times* broke the story, the Attorney General's office looked into the possibility of legal action against the newspaper for breaking a rule of the court, but nothing came of it.

Nathan Voloshen, who was also named in the indictment, told me that as early as September or October 1969, Tom Boggs had arranged a meeting at Sachs' office attended by Voloshen's lawyer; Will Wilson, Assistant Attorney General in charge of the criminal division; and Henry E. Petersen, Wilson's deputy. The outcome of the meeting was an agreement that the case would not be pursued, Sachs alone arguing that it should be. Mitchell's position seemed to be that Sachs could indict Frenkil and Voloshen if he wanted to, but he could not indict the Congressmen. Sachs insisted that without the Congressmen he would have no case against Frenkil and Voloshen, but he got nowhere. The following June, Sachs' term in office expired and he retired to private practice.

At the time, Voloshen said to me: "Mitchell is afraid that if any of the Congressmen are found guilty, the whole public image of the Congress would be destroyed." Voloshen also told me about the proviso which Attorney General Mitchell added to his offer to drop the case against Frenkil: House Speaker John McCormack would have to resign from Congress. Knowing how much McCormack loved his job and his life in the world of politics, I didn't think such a powerful man would go along. But in fact he did.

All else remained the same.

Part of this "sameness" that discourages any serious student of government stems from the lack of importance which so many members of the House and Senate so often attach to their vote. In 1970, for example, the American Horse Council, an association of thoroughbred breeders, tried to get a federal grant of $1 million for research into horse breeding at the University of Kentucky. Lobbying for the council were Thruston Morton, former Republican Senator from Kentucky and former chairman of the Republican Party, and George Smathers, the former Democratic Senator from Florida. The Department of Agriculture fought the effort, claiming the research was unnecessary, and the amount requested gradually dwindled down to $100,000.

Morton approached Senator John Sherman Cooper, Republican of Kentucky and a highly respected man on both sides of the aisle, and asked him to introduce a bill for the grant, but Cooper said that he didn't understand what the whole thing was about and, besides, he was too busy. Morton then turned to Senator Marlow W. Cook, Republican of Kentucky, who, although Morton's protegé, was a new man of unknown quality in the Senate. Cook said he would introduce the bill. But on the day the bill was to be introduced Cook was conveniently in Alaska on another matter. By Senate tradition, it therefore fell to John Sherman Cooper to introduce his colleague's legislation. It passed.

It passed simply because Cooper had introduced it, and in this lay the political genius of Thruston Morton. Leslie Combs, one of the nation's leading horse breeders, told me later that Morton realized the amendment might not pass if Cook himself actually introduced it. Cook was a new man, serving his first term in the Senate. Because nobody knew him or cared much about him either way, his colleagues might take a closer look at the amendment and reject it. But Cooper, a liberal Republican, had been in the Senate since 1957; he was well liked. In the melee that usually accompanies the voting on numerous bills and amendments in either House, turning the chamber into a veritable tobacco auction, Morton knew there was a better chance that the other Senators would approve the amendment just because it was "good old John" who stood up and spoke for it. And in fact that was exactly what happened.

When Senator Cooper was asked why he had proposed the amendment, he said: "I really don't know very much about it and I usually don't introduce amendments for other people; but with my colleague from Kentucky, it is a different story and I decided to do it. Besides, the horse population is a big population and deserves the same consideration as other animals."

When other Senators were asked why they voted for the amendment, many of them said they didn't know what it was all about but that $100,000 wasn't very much money, anyway. They had voted for dear old John. Senator Philip Hart of Michigan said of his positive vote: "Why not? Coop's a nice guy." Two weeks later, New York's Senator Jacob Javits, asked to explain his affirmative vote, covered his face, trying to remember, and finally shrugged. "I don't know. Could be because of Senator Cooper. Oh, sure!" said Javits, relieved that he finally remembered. When Senator Mike Mansfield was asked whether the horse amendment would have passed if Senator Cooper had not introduced it, he said no. He added: "It's quite often that because of your liking and respect for a man, if you have doubts about his legislation, you resolve them in his favor. In fact, there have been times when I didn't agree with a Senator at all but since I knew that he was going to take a terrible shellacking I voted with him to make him look a little better." But Senator J. William Fulbright of Arkansas said: "Amendments with public money shouldn't be voted upon because you like a particular member. I can't see anybody voting for an ABM just because they like John Stennis." Fulbright had voted against Cooper. Senator John Pastore of Rhode Island blasted the amendment as a waste of money. "If we had fewer race horses," he said, "we would have less betting. If we had less betting, we would have more money in the pockets of people to spend for bread. If you want to stop gambling in the country and break organized crime, stop racing. . . . With all the pressing needs that confront our society today, I think this amendment was a travesty on the American taxpayer. The moving force behind it was the thoroughbred racing industry, and they can pay for their own research." As Vermont's Senator Aiken put it: "The horse amendment became a crusade against sin, led by Senator Pastore. I voted with him but we lost, so I guess sin will continue."

Undoubtedly the most powerful group of outsiders who used to be on the inside are the former government employees who now rank at the top of Washington law firms. When a lawyer leaves the government service, he may well decide not to return to his former practice but to remain in Washington and hang out his shingle there. Thus this large and ever-growing group of former insiders has turned into a highly influential factor in Washington. In their return to private practice, these men—and sometimes women—almost always represent clients before the same agency where they once worked. These men know the regulations of a particular agency, regulations which in many cases they have helped draft and write. They also know the men administering and applying the regulations. They may have even hired the very man they are now approaching from the other side of the desk. It would be very difficult for such a man to deal unfavorably with his old boss, the man who put him where he is. This type of relationship is the general rule in Washington—a situation that hardly works for the general good of the electorate.

The list of Washington lawyers who are ex-government employees is endless. For example, Manuel F. Cohen, Lyndon Johnson's chairman of the Securities and Exchange Commission, is a partner in Wilmer, Cutler, and Pickering. Johnson's Commissioner of Internal Revenue Sheldon Cohen has his own law firm with Lester Uretz, who was his chief counsel at IRS. Joseph Califano, special assistant to President Johnson, was a partner in the prestigious law firm of Arnold and Porter. He is now with Williams and Connolly. Among other clients, they represent the National Democratic Committee. Myer Feldman and David Ginsburg, both Presidential advisors to Johnson, are Washington law partners. A Johnson speechwriter and later an assistant Secretary of State, Harry McPherson has joined the law firm of Verner, Liipfert, Bernhard, and McPherson. And there is the perennial Clark Clifford, Johnson's last Secretary of Defense, now a partner in the law firm of Clifford, Warnke, Glass, McIlwain, and Finney.*

These are only a few from the Johnson Administration who have traveled the short but oft-used road from government service to private practice before the government. The big Washington law firms are filled to the brim with former bureau chiefs, department heads, general and deputy counsels, agency chairmen, commissioners, cabinet members, subcabinet members, White House staffers, and Presidential advisors from previous administrations. And they are not there simply because they like the Washington weather.

The kingpin of Washington lawyers who once held public office is Clark Clifford. After practicing law in Missouri for sixteen years, Clifford was summoned to

* *Fortune's* cogent article, "The Small World of Big Washington Lawyers" (September, 1969), corroborates my firsthand knowledge. Much of the material included herein from pages 209 to 215 is derived from that article.

the White House in 1945 to serve as President Truman's counsel, a post he held for five years. He then went into private practice in Washington with the firm now known as Clifford, Warnke, Glass, McIlwain, and Finney. The firm has handled many important cases involving Federal agencies, but the case that is now considered a classic involved the entire United States Congress. The client was E. I. DuPont de Nemours and Company. At one time, DuPont owned a 22 percent interest in General Motors, which amounted to a staggering 63 million shares valued at about $3 billion. In 1961, the U. S. Supreme Court ordered DuPont to divest itself of its General Motors holdings, over a period of ten years. DuPont faced a problem in complying with the Court's order: if it followed the order there was the obvious risk that bringing that much stock onto the market would seriously depress its price. But DuPont saw a way to get around this problem: it could distribute its General Motors stock to its own stockholders, who could then treat the distribution as ordinary income, taxable as such under existing IRS rules. At the time the DuPont family itself, through a holding company called the Christiana Securities Company, owned 29 percent of DuPont. In view of the then existing laws, an act of Congress would be required to allow DuPont to thus divest itself of its General Motors holdings. DuPont went to Clark Clifford for help. In the course of handling the case, Clark Clifford's office actually did no legal work at all. The firm simply advised DuPont president Crawford Greenewalt on which members of the House and Senate he should visit personally to discuss the problem. After several weeks of such visits, the House easily passed a bill favorable to DuPont and, after some debate, so did the Senate. It was a real feat of political know-how.

This kind of know-how is worth money, and it is for this reason that the big Washington law firms are staffed with former bureau chiefs, department heads, general and deputy counsels, agency chairmen, cabinet members, subcabinet members, White House staffers, and Presidential advisors from previous administrations. And they have not remained in town simply because they like the Washington weather. They have the connections in government to get things done for clients quickly and, more importantly, quietly.

It is the quietness—the secrecy—in which these lawyers are able to work that is their most powerful tool. Although every government agency—and there are more than a hundred of them—operates on a set of specific laws, the lawyers know how to get around the laws, usually behind closed doors. For example, no record need be kept of any prehearing discussions on a matter: there has as yet been no public hearing, so there is no public record of what may have gone on before it. Thus at the actual public hearing an agency can decide in favor of a certain company or individual without disclosing how and why the decision was reached. For several of my own clients, I myself went to members of a commission before a hearing, explaining my client's problem with the hope of winning sympathy. At the hearing, the commissioners could find in favor of my client without disclosing where they got all the information about him or that there had been any contact between us at all. When the person seeking sympathy is a prominent Washington lawyer who used to work in the department, perhaps even running it, he is in an even better position to win invaluable cooperation for his client. The big law firms are doing this every day of the week.

Knowing how Washington operates, the big lawyers sometimes hire the services of other big lawyers who may be better connected on certain matters. In 1968, for example, the Federal Trade Commission moved against Burlington Industries on the grounds that the company had made too many acquisitions within the textile industry. Representing Burlington was the partnership of Thomas Corcoran and James Rowe, both leading Washington lawyers for many years, both with friends in high places including the White House. Rather than proceed themselves, they turned to Herbert Bergson, who had headed the Antitrust Division of the Department of Justice under Harry Truman before forming the law firm of Bergson, Borkland, Margolis, and Adler. At a hearing before the commission, Corcoran and Rowe were present but did not participate, and Bergson did the talking. He suggested a settlement by which Burlington would not acquire any more textile companies but would be allowed to keep what they already had. By a vote of four to one, the FTC voted to accept a settlement on this basis—in effect saying: "Go, and sin no more." Later, an FTC official was quoted as saying that, though neither Corcoran nor Rowe said a word throughout the hearing, one could feel their very presence in the room as some kind of signal. At the time, Johnson was still President, and Rowe was one of his closest advisors. Thus Burlington didn't have to give up a thing. Whether the public interest was served or not was another matter altogether.

Myer Feldman has said that, in terms of style, some Washington lawyers are conduits and some are personalities. The conduits are all business; they separate themselves from their cases. But when a personality walks into the room, it is the man as well as the case that people are reacting to. Tom Corcoran is often pointed to as the prototypical personality lawyer. Lloyd Cutler is more the conduit. He has represented clients whom many find it difficult to love—the Pharmaceutical Manufacturers Association, the Automobile Manufacturers Association—with a degree of detachment, calculation, and effectiveness that inspires admiration. In 1969, New York attorney Richard Wels told me that he was trying to locate a well-connected Washington lawyer to represent a client of his, Meyer Schine of the Schine Hotel chain, in a difficult government matter involving the use of urban renewal funds, and he asked me if I thought Cutler was the man. I said he was worth a try, because in Washington circles Cutler is known to be very close to Nixon. Cutler won. His effort on behalf of the auto manufacturers in the Congressional hearings that led to the National Traffic and Motor Vehicle Safety Act of 1966 is widely considered to be one of the smoothest and most effective feats of advocacy on the Hill in recent years. His achievement was that he kept out of the Auto Safety Bill any provision for criminal penalties. Cutler won with the argument that the automobile manufacturers are at last coming under regulation and they are behaving like statesmen about it. He said they should be given the benefit of the doubt and that it wasn't necessary to make criminal provisions part of the act since the bill already provided for civil penalties. He assured that it didn't in any way further the cause of safety to make the manufacturers criminally responsible for defective machinery, and he was convincing. Ralph Nader, when asked to comment on Cutler's success, said: "Mr. Cutler succeeded as a lobbyist but failed as an attorney and a keeper of the public trust."

If there are any keepers of the public trust in this country, they should be the members of the United States Congress. These men and women should truly reflect the opinions and convictions of the American people, as divergent as these attitudes may be, and they are bound by their office to carry out the wishes of the people who have elected them. Realistically, this is not easy. And it becomes even more difficult when the member of the House or Senate knowingly lets his own vested interests influence his legislative decisions.

The rules of Congress provide the Speaker of the House and the President of the Senate with the authority to deprive a member of his vote on a given matter when they know that, for him, a conflict of interest is involved. This authority, however, has rarely been used. As a result of the Bobby Baker case, newsmen interviewed many Congressmen on the subject of conflict of interest. Although most of them complained that the publicity surrounding Bobby Baker had made the public overly sensitive about the honesty of the men they had elected to represent them at all levels of government, not one of these Congressmen admitted to experiencing such moments of conflict himself. The most common conflict of interest a Congressman faces involves the juxtaposition of public interest versus private gain. The legislation before him may in itself be good for the general public, but at the same time it may be bad for the Congressman's wallet and the wallets of his friends. Since the government of the United States is not a private corporation, the people have a right to expect their Congressmen to vote in their interest. But a Congressman whose own financial interests are threatened by a piece of legislation can be easily influenced to vote accordingly.

More than one Speaker of the House has noted: "Each member must exercise his own conscience when confronted by a conflict of interest." This would seem to be the most anybody could ask, yet even a cursory study of the outside affiliations of most Congressmen gives one the impression that their consciences must be under a heavy strain most of the time. And indeed, by the rules Congress has set up for itself, a glance at the private interests of Congressmen is the most comprehensive glimpse the public is allowed. Senator Everett Dirksen once pontificated: "All members of the Congress are screened by the electorate," a statement which might be translated to read: "If the Senator or Congressman is a big enough crook, sooner or later he'll be found out." Coming from a senior Senator, that declaration is quite incredible, but it clearly reveals the mentality of too many people in Washington. Few and far between are the candidates for public office who have ever disclosed all the sources of their personal incomes. In fact, when Dirksen himself was asked if he would make such a disclosure, he said: "Never. It would turn me into a second-class citizen." It would be impossible to determine how many of the electorate who kept Dirksen in Washington for a generation knew that while serving on the Senate Banking Committee he held stock in the First Federal Savings and Loan Company of Chicago and that, through his law firm, he accepted fees from many corporations whose side he took in legislative debates.

In the summer of 1970 I had a long talk on this subject with Representative Charles E. Bennett, Democrat of Florida. "I don't see how a Congressman can go two or three weeks without running into a conflict of interest," he said as I recall. "After all, before running for public office, Congressmen were successful men in their communities, in the professions, in business, in agriculture, and most of them continue at these interests while in office. How is a Congressman to feel if he has to vote on a bill that might be good for the general public but bad for his private business? A member would have to be an idiot or come out from a vacuum or a mental institution to be absolutely free of conflict of interest."

Although an exaggeration, the statement held a good measure of truth. A point usually missed, or ignored, by most people is that such a situation need not be the case. A member can divest himself of holdings he knows will create a conflict of interest. Occasionally a Congressman has done so, but usually the underlying motivation is that his holdings have become too well-known. Or a member could instruct his broker to manage his portfolio as a discretionary account. This is sometimes done, too, but the contents of the portfolio are rarely disclosed, and this is the critical matter.

Although the Congress had some sort of code of conduct for almost fifty years, it was not until 1958 that Charles Bennett, after an eight-year struggle, managed to get something specific on the books. Although the regulations were tepid, it was amazing that they were adopted at all. The adoption was at least a concession by the members that the House needed a watchdog, even if only a Chihuahua. In 1966, in the wake of the Bobby Baker case, a Gallup poll indicated that 60 per-

cent of the people felt that the average member of the
Congress was dishonest from time to time and to some
extent. This was a serious indictment, and it shook
Washington in somewhat the same way as had the earlier public revulsion that brought about the creation of
the Senate Ethics Committee and the House Ethics
Committee in 1958. At that time, because he had
fought so long for this kind of action, Representative
Bennett was named chairman of the House Committee
for the final months of the legislative session. But Bennett had some strange ideas, and when the Congress reconvened he was not even appointed to the committee.

On the day Charles Bennett received me in his office
in Washington, I was hoping that our conversation
would turn out to be much more productive than it did.
I had told him I intended to write a book about my experiences as a lobbyist, and so he let me take notes as
we talked. Because Bennett's efforts had been greatly
responsible for the creation of the House Ethics Committee, I expected him to have firmer convictions on the
matters of lobbying and conflicts of interest. He still
held to his belief that a member of Congress should
withdraw from law practice after his first re-election. I
asked him, then, if he felt it was improper for a Congressman owning bank stock or serving as a bank officer
to serve on the Banking and Currency Committee of either house or vote on such matters when they came before him. Bennett said: "That is a gray area." I knew I
didn't have much of his time, so I did not press him on
this, but I wondered how life could be black or white
for lawyers but not for bankers.

I also asked Congressman Bennett if he felt that lobbying, as it is practiced for the most part, should be out-

lawed. He said: "Sir, you are a radical." He said: "I am for reform, but I am not a reformer." That struck me as another way of saying that he did not want to rock the boat. Bennett went on to say that he felt lobbyists had their good side, in that they provided Congressmen with important information on pending legislation, and I agreed with that. The First Amendment of the U. S. Constitution guarantees citizens the right to petition their government, which is what lobbying is supposed to be. However, Bennett knew as well as I did that this was just a fraction of the wheeling-dealing that went on in the guise of lobbying, but he gave me the impression that he had no experience with this side of it. "Bees don't go where there is no honey," he said to me sagely. He told me he had two or three thousand constituents who managed to raise the $50,000 he needed for his campaign every two years, and he said he had no other source of income except his salary. I asked him why he had never run for the Senate, and he said: "I am not willing to run for the Senate for the simple reason that I would have to sell my soul to special interests." Because he knew that and evidently was so much against it, I wondered why he wouldn't try harder to change things.

Bennett's stand against lawyer-legislators gave him a reputation around Washington as a nut, an odd-ball, and a fuddy-duddy. At the time of his appointment to the House Committee on Conduct in 1958, he made a statement which appeared in the press as: "The purpose of this committee is to look into anything Congress will allow it to look into." The statement backfired, giving the impression that Bennett was going on a witch hunt. He said to me: "I simply meant that we weren't going to sweep things under the rug, but the way it came out in the newspapers it sounded like I wanted to look into everything—sex and everything else about the lives of Congressmen." A deeply and openly religious man, Bennett made several references to what he called his "experience with Christ," and he said he considered Jesus his brother. "I'm not interested in other people's sex lives," he said. "I am against pornography and I don't discuss homosexuality."

Bennett was of the same mind as Senator Dirksen regarding financial disclosures by Congressional candidates. He didn't feel this was necessary because, he said, the people had a chance every two years to get rid of their Representative if they were dissatisfied with his performance. I seemed unable to get through to Bennett that people couldn't accurately judge a Congressman's public performance unless they knew how much his private interests were affecting it. I asked Bennett how he would feel about (1) a law which would require elected candidates to divest themselves of all private interests and (2) a new tax of perhaps a dollar a person per year to cover the costs of political campaigns and thus free office holders of the constant worry about it. He accused me of advocating some form of revolution.

So I asked him if he felt a little defeated by the fact that he had not been reappointed to the ethics committee he had once chaired, and he said: "Let me quote my wife. 'They just didn't want to do what you wanted.' I accept that." I accepted it, too. I also accepted Bennett's assurance: "Sir, I am a very persistent man and I always win. Whether I am right or whether I am wrong, I always win."

As I was returning to New York, I accepted, as well, the realization that the house cleaning needed to make the Congress an effective instrument of government for the people of the United States would never come from within. It would have to be stirred from without by concerned citizens, whether they acted as individuals or in groups. As was noted on Sunday, July 19, 1970, in a *New York Times* article by Bob Sherrill, it is almost impossible to expect reform from within. Mr. Sherrill recalled former Senator Paul Douglas's famous remark: "Men tinged with sovereignty can easily feel that the king can do no wrong."

A lawyer, Bennett had practiced for about ten years before being elected to Congress, and he quit law shortly after going to Washington. It was Bennett's conviction that any lawyer elected to either house in the Congress should stop practicing law after his first reelection. This opinion didn't go over very well. The Ninety-first Congress contained, in the House alone, seventy-six members who, as now required, reported to the Committee on Standards for Official Conduct that they were affiliated to some degree with law firms. The members were not required to disclose how much they earned from their law firms, but twelve of them saw fit to do so.

Two who reported receiving less than $1,000 from their law firms in 1969 were John O. Marsh, Jr. and David E. Satterfield, III, both Virginia Democrats. Four who reported receiving more than $5,000, though not how much more, were Democrat Nick Galifianakis of North Carolina, Republican John W. Wydler of New York, Democrat Patrick T. Caffery of Louisiana, and Democrat Emanuel Celler of New York. Celler also reported receiving more than $1,000, though not how much more, from his firm for expenses. Six who reported specific figures were Democrat Edward J. Patten of

New Jersey, $2,159; Republican Howard W. Robinson of New York, $5,140; Democrat Charles A. Vanik of Ohio, $5,367; Democrat Jerome R. Waldie of California, $4,000; Republican J. Herbert Burke of Florida, $6,000; and Democrat Edward I. Koch* of New York, $4,331. At the time these figures were released a two-year study of lawyer-legislators by the Association of the Bar of the City of New York was also released. Of twenty-four lawyers in the House interviewed by the association, six were willing to disclose their law earnings, provided they were not named, and the figures ranged from $8,000 to $20,000. All of these figures are chicken feed for any lawyer prominent enough to get himself elected to Congress and who continues to practice law while in Congress.

The bar association study was the result of scandals involving lawyers in government. Bobby Baker was a lawyer. It was disclosed during the Baker hearing that he had received a $2,500 "forwarding fee" from Emanuel Celler's law firm for referring a client to it—and the client happened to be interested in government contracts and legislation. There was, as well, the admission by former Senator Edward V. Long, Missouri Democrat, that about $48,000 in "referral fees" was paid to his law firm by Morris Shenker, a St. Louis lawyer for the Teamsters Union. However, Long denied that these payments were connected with any effort to aid the then imprisoned Jimmy Hoffa. And there was the accusation that former Senator Thomas J. Dodd, Connecticut Democrat, accepted both legal fees and loan-finders'

---

* On June 9, 1972, I received a letter from Congressman Koch in which he said: "The legal fees were for prior services, and I, in effect, ceased the practice of law upon my election to Congress."

fees from Hartford insurance companies. The bar association report said:

"We do not propose to judge the merits of the charges implicating law practices in congressional scandals. How can we measure the actual harm done to the images of the Congress and the legal profession? It is hard to escape the conclusions, however, that law practice has demonstrated a special potential for actual and alleged congressional improprieties and that law practices have played a disproportionate role in the history of congressional scandals."

Two practices in particular, which Washington takes for granted, came under criticism by the bar association. One is the Tuesday-to-Thursday Club, consisting mostly of Eastern lawyer-legislators who go home for long weekends at their law practices. Except on occasions of extreme crisis, it is impossible to get a quorum in either the Senate or the House on Mondays and Fridays because the majority of the members aren't there. The other practice is the "double-door policy." By law, the lawyer-legislators cannot be associated with a firm doing business with the government, but this rule can be circumvented by having the legislator's name on one door to the office but not on the other, creating the impression that there are two different firms in the same suite, one of them qualified to handle government-type cases. The firm handles its stationery similarly, printing two sets. Still another questionable practice is a lawyer-legislator's letting a law firm use his name for its prestige value. The Congressman doesn't do any work; but since he is part of the firm's appeal, he gets a piece of the action. The New York Bar Association urged disciplinary action against government office holders who engage in any of these dodges.

"Banks," the report also said, "have played a role perhaps equal to that of law practices in generating congressional scandal." In the Ninety-first Congress, there were ninety-five members in the House who were officers, directors, or stockholders in banks, savings and loan associations, and other financial institutions. Because banks operate on other people's money, including the government's, it is proper that they should be subject to public scrutiny and control; but when the scrutiny and control are exercised by elected representatives who are making money from banks, there is always the risk that public interest can become secondary.

An examination of House members' reports to the Committee on Standards of Official Conduct in 1970 showed that at least forty-three members served concurrently as either directors or officers of a financial institution—usually a bank or savings and loan association in their home district. Most also owned stock in the same firm. At least fifty-two other House members did not hold such offices but did own stock in financial institutions, making them by far the most popular investment among the Congressmen. Five Representatives also served as board chairmen of banks; one of them served as board chairman of two banks. Another held the title of bank president, whereas another was a bank vice-president. At least twenty-five members were bank directors, including three men who sat on two bank boards each. One sat on three. The House had two presidents and one board chairman of savings and loan associations; twelve others were directors of such associations. One director was senior vice-president of his association. Of the ninety-five members involved with the financial industry in one way or another, five were members of the House Banking and Currency Committee, which governs banking, and five others were on the House Ways and Means Committee, which controls tax relief. Both committees consider legislation directly affecting the industry.

The New York Bar Association report further said:

> Most members [of Congress] follow some self imposed rules of interest avoidance within areas of committee responsibility. It appears to be a common pattern to refrain from making particular types of investments in areas where they might profit from 'inside information' or risk suspicion that official decisions might be made for personal gain . . . The most notable exceptions to such self-limitation occur in the respective House and Senate Banking and Currency Committees . . . Needless to say, many actions of these committees affect the profitability of bank holdings . . . The only type of financial interest which can be said to be significantly over-represented in congressional portfolios is that in financial institutions, including state and national banks, savings-and-loan companies and bank holding companies . . . Here, those who seek a causal relationship between congressional business interests and congressional decision-making may have more ammunition.

Members of the House Banking and Currency Committee who fell short of the New York bar committee's proposed standards on conflict of interest were Democrat William V. Chappell, Jr. of Florida; Democrat

Leonor K. Sullivan of Missouri; Democrat William S. Moorehead of Pennsylvania; Democrat Robert G. Stephens of Georgia; Democrat Thomas M. Rees of California, all of them stockholders in banks back home. Members of the House Ways and Means Committee with similar potential conflicts were Democrat Omar Burleson of Texas; Democrat Sam Gibbons of Florida; Republican Herman T. Schneebeli of Pennsylvania; Democrat John C. Watts of Kentucky; and Republican Joel T. Broyhill of Virginia, all of them officers and stockholders in banks back home.

One bank right in Washington does a great deal of business with Congressmen—the National Bank of Washington, D. C. One of the bank's major depositors is the United Mine Workers Union.

On April 28, 1971, Federal District Judge Gerhard A. Gesell decided in favor of a group of miners and widows who had brought suit against the UMW for misuse of the union's welfare and retirement fund over a period of twenty years. Because no interest had been paid on the fund's deposits in the bank, the miners and widows felt they had not been getting the proper benefits from their dues paid into the fund. In his decision, Judge Gesell ordered UMW president W. A. Boyle to retire as a trustee of the fund by the end of June. The judge also ordered that the union's deposits in the bank—over $75 million—were to be withdrawn and deposited elsewhere for the purpose of earning interest. The figure was about 30 percent of the bank's holdings, and a withdrawal of this size from its assets could well have put the bank out of business. Because it was impossible to determine exactly how much the fund's beneficiaries had lost as a result of the self-serving manipulations of the bank and union officers, the judge was unable to set a sentence for those responsible. However, an indirect result of the judge's decision was the likelihood that the bank, the third largest in the Capitol and a powerful lobbying force in Congressional committees pertaining to banking and currency, might well go down the drain. Among the bank's directors have been UMW president W. A. Boyle; Clark Clifford, former Secretary of Defense; and retired Air Force General Elwood Quesada, formerly head of the Federal Aviation Administration.

Another important Washington bank is the District of Columbia National Bank; there, ordinary people paid an 8 percent interest on loans. Members of the Congress got loans at 6.8 percent. And they didn't have to put up any security.* Since members of the House do not have to divulge loans payable within ninety days, it is possible for a Representative to refinance his loan as each deadline arrives, thus keeping secret his own indebtedness and his indebtedness to banking. The District of Columbia National Bank, incidentally, has been one of the biggest lobbyists in Washington for legislation favorable to the banking industry. The bank has had a few scares when a Congressman in debt was not re-elected. However, a member who is obviously safe in his seat can get virtually unlimited credit. Republican Representative Seymour Halpern of New York, for example, a member of the House Committee on Banking and Currency, ran

---

* The bank's biggest depositor has been the United States government. Federal paychecks in Washington are drawn on this bank. This is also the bank that made some loans to Bobby Baker, which probably no other bank would have risked. But Baker had helped found the bank in 1962, which perhaps made the difference.

himself into debt to banks to the tune of almost $100,000.*

Banks all over the country play similar games. Banks make campaign contributions to candidates at all levels, giving the bigger donations to the men who look like winners. Here again, the man who gets re-elected every time will find it easier to get loans. He also will be offered free stock and a directorship to which he need give little time, if any at all. In a very rare instance, Democrat Henry B. Gonzalez of Texas reported to the House Ethics Committee that a bank in his district offered him $14,000 in stock and a directorship, and he rejected both.

There are other ways for legislators to make money from banking. There are, for example, countless banking associations of all types. Members get together every once in a while for seminars, conferences, and conventions, and they like to have a prominent speaker at their main event. Who better than a Senator or Representative whose committee memberships qualify him to speak on the subject—and who is friendly toward the industry? In 1969, Democratic Senator John J. Sparkman of Alabama, chairman of the Senate Committee on Banking and Currency, earned over $7,000 from speeches to the banking community. Members of the Senate banking committee who were qualified to earn money from the same sources were Republican Senator John G. Tower of Texas; Republican Senator Charles E. Goodell of New York; Democrat Ernest F.

* The breakdown: $40,000, First National City Bank of New York; $26,000, the Capitol National Bank of Miami, Florida; $17,000, Long Island Trust Company of Garden City, Long Island; $13,000, The Oneida National Bank and Trust Company, Utica, New York. All these loans were without collateral.

Hollings of South Carolina; Republican Senator Wallace F. Bennett of Utah; and Republican Senator Robert W. Packwood of Oregon.

One is finally led to the inevitable conclusion that all matters which come before Congressional committees can be instances of a conflict of interest, depending on the composition of the committee. For example, members of the House Armed Services Committee who own stock in defense plants are Republican William G. Bray of Indiana, Democrat Philip J. Philbin of Massachusetts, Republican Robert T. Stafford of Vermont, and Republican Charles W. Whalen, Jr. of Ohio. Those who, among others, consistently voted the banking industry's position in 1969 while owning bank stocks were Republican Peter H. B. Frelinghuysen of New Jersey, Republican Henry P. Smith of New York, Republican Chester L. Mize of Kansas, Republican J. William Stanton of Ohio, and Republican W. E. Brock, III of Tennessee. The last three were on the House Banking and Currency Committee. Republican Craig Hosmer of California was on the House Interior and Insular Affairs Committee while owning oil stock. Others who voted for the maintenance of high oil depletion while owning oil stocks were Republican Page Belcher of Oklahoma, Republican James M. Collins of Texas, and Democrat John Jarman of Oklahoma. Republican Clarence J. Brown, Jr. of Ohio owned a radio station at Urbana while serving on the House Commerce Committee. Republican George A. Goodling of Pennsylvania owned a big commercial fruit farm while serving on the House Agriculture Committee.

The rules of both the House and the Senate offer a member a way out when he is confronted by a vote which may present conflict in terms of a private interest.

Instead of answering the roll call affirmatively or negatively, the member can just say: "Present." Senator Robert Kerr of Oklahoma once said of his confreres: "If every member abstained on matters involving their personal interests, I doubt that you could get a quorum on any subject." That getting a quorum would be impossible may or may not be true, but at least the practice of abstaining from voting would be honest. And honesty in the Congress is a matter on which the American people still have no guarantees.

The kind of honesty Americans deserve from their government can only be achieved by a complete openness in all government matters excepting those involving the national security. Secrecy may have its place in times of war or in negotiations with other countries when the national security is involved, but secrecy is wholly out of place in the day by day operations of most of the government's departments and agencies. Secrecy creates questions. Questions create doubt. Doubt creates distrust. And when people don't trust the men who run the country, whichever political party is in power, then the government—and the people—are in deep trouble.

Philip Elman, former commissioner of the Federal Trade Commission, pointing out that the general public seems to be losing confidence in the commission, has suggested that this problem could be overcome if the secrecy enshrouding so much of the FTC work were done away with. Elman has proposed that a public file be kept on every matter coming before the FTC, starting with the first letter or phone call or approach. The public backlash which struck when the existence of the Pentagon Papers were disclosed certainly supports this stand. Commissioner Elman felt that making public all of the operations of the FTC probably wouldn't change the outcome of many cases but that it would surely give the public greater confidence in the integrity of the due process of the law by minimizing the possibility of questionable influence and bribery. It would also put many, if not most, of Washington's thousands of lobbyists out of business.

The same kind of openness should be required of everyone campaigning for any public office. If the men and women now in Congress cannot agree on ceilings for campaign costs, they should at least have the strength of character to agree that every candidate must make a full disclosure of his campaign funds, whether the money was his own or anybody else's, and he must disclose how it was spent. The present loopholes which allow vested interest groups to form fund-raising committees in a candidate's name without being accountable for how the money is raised and spent can only be eradicated by federal laws containing stiff penalties for violations. Moreover, anyone seeking public office can only prove that he has nothing to hide when he is willing to make a public disclosure of what he owns, what he owes, how he earns his money, and what other sources of revenue he may have besides his income should he be elected. Members of Congress put Presidential nominees through rugged interrogations before approving them. Members of Congress should be willing to undergo the same interrogation themselves in order to win public approval. A person in public office is no longer a private figure, and anything about his private life that affects his performance in office should be public knowledge.

The needed changes in the way our country is being run will hardly be wrought by the politicians who are now running it. But they can be brought about by an aroused public that demands them. The people's right to know what is really going on in Washington will never become part of the American way of life unless the people make it so.

How to Buy an Ambassadorship
for $125,000

If one man in the country besides Richard M. Nixon was certain that Nixon would be the Republican Presidential candidate in 1968, he was House Minority Leader Ford of Michigan. Nixon was Ford's idol, and Ford emulated Nixon well. Ford's only disappointment in Nixon's victory was that Nixon did not carry the Congress. This would have made Ford the Speaker of the House—something Ford desperately wanted. Becoming Minority Leader changed Jerry Ford greatly. Watching him was like watching a wasp being hatched. During his sixteen years in the House before becoming Minority Leader, he was known as a plodder by his peers, but he was known hardly at all by the public. A hard and almost hidden worker on the House Appropriations Committee, he was regarded as a Congressman's Congressman and was so cited by the American Political Science Association.

The fact is, he was dull. In his early days in Washington, people used to say that he was an authentic product of Grand Rapids—like that city's furniture, he was drab and predictable. An old school chum of Jerry's once told me that during his college days Ford was known as Granny Ford. A football player, he was always prying into the personal affairs of his teammates and then lecturing them for any indiscretions that might have been violations of training rules. He brought this same prissiness to Washington, which doubtless explained why, with the exception of his friendship with Richard Nixon, he could hardly be called a member of the "in" crowd.

In 1965, Ford, as a member of a group of Republican insurgents called the "Young Turks," made a surprise move and defeated veteran Charles A. Halleck of Indiana for the post of Minority Leader. Ford suddenly became a national figure; his metamorphosis had begun. Too loyal to Nixon to have any Presidential aspirations of his own, at least for the moment, Ford nevertheless wanted to do everything he could to bolster the Republican Party in the off-year elections of 1966. Copying a page from his idol's handbook, Ford was ready to go anywhere at any time to speak on behalf of a Republican candidate, not only to help the man win but also to win the man's political indebtedness. During the 1966 campaign, Ford made a speech outside Washington on the average of one every two days. He ranged over thirty-seven states and 138,400 miles—almost six times the circumference of the earth at the equator. To save time, he often flew in the dead of night, stealing what sleep he could in the cramped seat of an airliner or in the deserted waiting rooms of some airport between connecting flights. Admirable as such dedication was, it foreshadowed the changes that turned Jerry Ford from a simply dull man into a dull and greedy man. He started wearing television-blue shirts all the time, always ready to go on the air and expound on any subject. He began calling so many press conferences that, when he missed a day, the reporters would call his office and ask if he would like to comment on the weather.

Despite his new aggression, Jerry Ford remained essentially a naïve man. The day I first met him, he asked if there were anything he could do for me at the moment. I said no, but then I asked him if there were anything I could do for him. He said yes. He had a date to give a speech at Parsons College in Iowa and was having trouble with the draft. He said that neither he nor his press secretary Paul Miltich could get the bugs out of it. "Would you like to try your hand at it?" he asked.

I said I would.

He handed me the papers, and he said: "Don't tell Paul about this. It's his job, and he might not like the fact that I've turned to somebody else."

"Whatever you say."

The speech, called "Now Is the Hour," was an inspirational pep talk aimed at a bunch of college kids who would have to find out for themselves eventually that their hour would come only when they took the trouble to wind their own clocks.

During the couple of weeks I worked on the speech, I saw Jerry Ford almost every day to talk with him about it. He knew I was still frequenting the Speaker's office and that I sometimes lunched at the Speaker's table in the dining room of the House. Jerry rarely said anything about it and he never tried to get any information out of me. Once, when McCormack's name came up, Jerry shook his head and said: "When I first became Minority Leader, McCormack tried to give me some fatherly advice. He said I should keep a little black book, listing all the people I did favors for across the country. He said that every once in a while I, or my assistant, should call up these people and put the bite on them for campaign contributions. And he said that I should make a point of putting a little aside for myself. I like John, but I'm still a bit shocked by that advice."

Any man who had been in Congress for over eighteen years, as Jerry had been at the time, and who would still be shocked by such advice could only have been protected from the Washington world by his own naïveté, which was the case with Ford in many areas. On Friday, June 10, 1966, the day before the Parsons speech, I was with Ford in his office when he received a telephone call from Marvin Watson, a White House aide, informing him that Secretary of State Dean Rusk was en route home from a conference of foreign ministers in Europe and would give a briefing the next morning to President Johnson, the Cabinet, and the leaders of Congress. Jerry said he couldn't make the meeting because of his prior commitment to speak at Parsons the following afternoon. After Ford hung up, he told me of the problem.

I asked: "Who will represent you, then?"

"Melvin Laird," he said. Laird was then the House Minority Whip, having lost the party leadership to Ford in a close contest.

"Don't miss that meeting, Jerry," I said.

"I can't be in in two places at once," he said. "This speech has been scheduled for months. I've got to catch a nine-o'clock morning flight for Chicago where the school will have a jet pick me up."

"Jerry," I said, "either charter a jet from here for tomorrow or have the school's jet meet you here whenever you're able to leave. Just don't miss that meeting."

He studied me. "Do you know something I should?"

"Look, Jerry," I said, "you haven't been the Minority Leader long, less than a year. Melvin Laird is still gunning for your job. How do you think it'll look if *he* feels that tomorrow's meeting is important enough for him to change any plans he might have, and *you* don't? If you want to stay boss, you've got to act like one."

He picked up the phone and told his personal secretary, Mildred Leonard, to get Marvin Watson at the White House. He told Watson he would be at the meeting. He got a jet from Bill Lear and later he was billed $1,500 for it. Ford mentioned the billing to me several times, always emphasizing the amount, and I wondered if he were expecting me to pay for it simply because the idea had been mine. Finally he dropped the subject when it became obvious he was beating a dead horse.

When I ran into Jerry in the House Rotunda the Monday following his trip he was in a rush, but he stopped to say: "Listen, thanks for getting me to that meeting Saturday."

"Was it important?"

"It was important," he said, "in more ways than one." He laughed. "This town is full of hungry people, isn't it?"

I said: "You're just finding that out?"

He laughed and hurried off.

Perhaps it was Ford's lingering naïveté that got him into a few scrapes as time went on. On the other hand, maybe it was his growing lust for power and money, once he started getting some of both. One scrape involved Earl "Red" Blaik, who had been one of Ford's football coaches in college. Blaik later went into public relations and then became a Washington lobbyist for

Avco, a division of Philco. One day when Blaik was visiting the hotel suite of Fred Black, a lobbyist for North American Aviation, he had a phone conversation with Ford. As it turned out, the FBI had a tap on the phone. The monitored conversation showed that Blaik had enlisted Ford's help in preventing an investigation of an Avco defense contract. After this became public, Blaik became persona non grata around Ford's office. The matter was quickly hushed up, now that Ford had risen to a level in the Establishment where he could have such things done.

Another scrape involved the Old Kent Bank and Trust Company of Grand Rapids, the largest bank in Ford's district and one of the most powerful in the state. The bank's president, Richard M. Gillett, had been a close friend of Ford's for fifteen years, as well as a lifelong Republican. Over the years, Gillett had raised funds for Ford, made personal contributions to his campaign. On January 22, 1968, Ford was named a director of the bank. To qualify, Ford had to buy a hundred shares of the bank's stock, then worth $33 per share. Ford told me that Gillett advanced him a cash loan to buy the stock. For attending four board meetings a year, Ford was to be paid $1,000 annually.

Ford made no effort to make a secret of his directorship. It would have been difficult to do so in any case, and besides, his membership on the board was too much to the bank's advantage to hide Ford in a closet. But when public objections to Ford's connection with the bank began to be voiced, Ford couldn't understand it. He told the reporters: "I don't see any ethical problems whatsoever. I do the director's job. I can be in Grand Rapids for the meetings and in my judgment it is a mutually beneficial association that will contribute to my knowledge." And Gillett said: "More members of Congress ought to be doing things like this. There should be better cooperation between us and Congress and there is no better way for a Congressman to learn about our economic and social problems." That was all well and good, but it disregarded the fact that the Old Kent Bank was affected by all federal banking laws and obviously had an interest in any new bank legislation. It certainly did no harm to have a friend like the Minority Leader at court. With assets of more than $500 million, the bank quite naturally would have an interest in any new bank legislation. Moreover, the bank did a tremendous amount of business with federal projects in the Grand Rapids area, and other banks in the vicinity could rightly claim that, with the Minority Leader on its board, Old Kent had an advantage over them in getting more business. The bank was already one of the largest developers in the federal urban renewal program for downtown Grand Rapids. Members of its board included an architect as well as other businessmen who had government contracts. Perhaps it would have been a good idea for Jerry Ford to learn more about banking, but it would have been wiser of him to take a correspondence course than to jeopardize his career by openly taking a soft job with the very vested interests whose policies and practices often came before him for judgment and determination in his capacity as a member of Congress.

The public criticism grew. On Tuesday, November 19, 1968, I saw Ford in Washington, and we talked about the Old Kent. Ford said that he regretted taking the directorship. He still felt he had done nothing wrong, but he admitted that the circumstances could be used against him in the hands of the wrong person. So he said he would be resigning from the bank soon. He added, however, that he was keeping the bank stock he had bought. Actually, then, all Ford was losing was his $1,000-a-year fee and his key to the executives' john. There was no way to tell what the bank was losing, if anything.

I had known Jerry Ford about a year or so when one day he said to me: "Bob, I want you to know how much I admire your political acumen and your know-how." I realized that he was telling me that I was lucky I had the sense to give him a check whenever I asked him a favor. Ford was the only politician I met in Washington who, to the best of my knowledge, would not accept a campaign contribution in cash. He always insisted on a check, and he always specified how he wanted to have the check made out. Sometimes it was to an individual Republican who was running for public office somewhere in the country and needed financial help. Sometimes it was to the Kent County Republican Finance Committee. Most of the time it was to the Republican Congressional Boosters Club, a sort of kitty from which party leaders doled out funds to candidates when they needed them in a campaign. Obviously, Republicans in office who brought in the most money would have the least trouble getting it back when they needed it. And when Jerry was running for office himself, he accepted checks made out to the "Ford for Congress Committee."

As time went on, Jerry acquired a taste for money. Where he had been hesitant and shy two years before, he was now arrogant and brusquely sure that money was the name of the game. He often repeated this phrase to me. He was a good example of power corrupting what had been, in my estimation, one of the few honest and sincere men in Washington.

In November 1970, Ford, like all members of the House, ran for re-election. Ford won easily. Unlike most candidates, Ford himself acted as treasurer of his "Ford for Congress Committee." By Michigan law, Ford had a ceiling of $10,500 on his campaign, and he subsequently submitted sworn financial statements in that amount to his state and to the Clerk of the House. In February 1971, the Associated Press disclosed that Ford had failed to report $11,500 that had been given to him in November by "stockbrokers, an oil man, bankers, doctors and a union group." Ford admitted receiving the checks, but said he had endorsed them over to the Republican Congressional Boosters Committee, a fund for candidates who may have had difficulty raising enough campaign money on their own. However, that group, the Republican National Finance Advisory Committee, plus a second group run by the same man in GOP headquarters in Washington, sent various checks totaling $12,233 back to Ford's district to pay off the post-election bills of two citizens' groups—Latvians for Ford and Veterans for Ford—plus a printer and an advertising agency. Ford disclaimed any knowledge of these payments, and added that in his opinion what had occurred was "within the law." In fact as this loopholed law is stated, it was. According to the 1925 Corrupt Practices Act, a candidate is accountable only for the expenditures that he personally knows about but not for any expenditures of independent committees organized in his support. Thus ignorance is a candidate's prime defense.

In many discussions I had with Ford on the subject of campaign contributions, Ford told me that if he were ever faced with the problem of accepting excess campaign contributions, this was the neat—and legal—method of circumventing the problem.

Unlike Speaker McCormack, who was always ready and willing to accept a campaign contribution in cash, Jerry Ford always insisted on checks. I never knew him to accept cash from anybody. And once the money issue was settled, Jerry Ford probably worked harder to carry out his end of the bargain—that is, to pay a favor for value received—than anybody else I knew in Washington.

One client of mine for whom Ford worked hard was Francis Kellogg, president and a major stockholder of the International Mining Company, in New York. Although only in his fifties, Kellogg wanted to retire, but he didn't want just to sit around. He had an income of about $150,000 a year, and retirement would decrease this a bit. But his wife's independent income was even larger—she was a Wanamaker and a Munn—so they had no financial worries. Kellogg loved big-game hunting. Each year he spent several weeks at it in Africa, where he had a 15,000-acre ranch in Kenya, and he had been to Africa so often that he had learned to speak Kiswahili. Thus Kellogg decided in 1968 that it would be fun to become the American ambassador to some African country and spend the rest of his life big-game hunting and chatting with the natives in the lingua franca. He hired me to help him get an appointment.

This was a Presidential election year, with important elections at the state and local levels, too. Francis Kellogg was a Republican. I pointed out to him that (1) there would have to be a Republican administration in Washington for him to have any hopes of an ambassadorial appointment and (2) he should optimistically give his financial support to Republican candidates in New York State so that they would owe him their political support when he needed it. Kellogg contributed about $30,000 to the New York State Republican Campaign Fund, headed by Maurice H. Stans, later Secretary of Commerce.

After the Republican victory in November, I told Kellogg: "Now you are ready for the 'big time.'"

"What do I do?" he asked.

"More of the same," I said. "Only now you give your support to the National Committee."

"But I gave to Stans," he protested.

"That was to the state fund," I pointed out.

"Okay, then. How much?"

"What you gave the state, I'd say."

"My God, another thirty thousand"

"At least."

He frowned. "This is getting expensive. I don't know if I can afford it. It isn't tax deductible, you know."

"I know. It's up to you. But just think of all the fun you'll be having in Africa for the next eight years."

He seemed to be listening to the sound of distant drums. "Don't the regulations limit me to a $3,000 contribution?"

"Yes. Just like before. Three thousand *at a time*. You just write out ten checks for three thousand each and I'll dole them out to Jerry Ford one at a time, as we progress." Now *I* could almost hear the drums.

He said: "All right. Talk to Ford."

I was surprised by Ford's reaction. "No dice, Bob," he said. "An ambassadorship is too important to play games with. Besides, I never heard of this man. Who is he? What's his background? What are his qualifications for Africa?"

I said: "He can speak Kiswahili."

"Big deal."

"He's a crack shot."

"Is he planning on starting a war?"

"He's a good Republican."

"So are a lot of people."

"He contributed $30,000 to the campaign in New York."

"That money went to the state." He thought for a moment, then said: "I really don't have the time to involve myself in this sort of problem, anyway. I'm too busy."

I said: "He's willing to give another thirty thousand to the National Committee."

Without changing his tone or expression, Ford said: "He is? Tell him he can see me whenever he wants. I'll try to help."

"Thanks." I turned and headed for the door. Before I got there, I was hit by that wave of nausea I had often carried out of a Democrat's office. I stopped and looked back at Ford, and I guess my feelings showed. I said: "Jerry, this is a hell of a note."

"Don't let it bother you, Bob," he said. "Money is the name of the game. Without it, you're dead."

Ford was unable to get Kellogg an ambassadorship in Africa or anywhere else, despite Kellogg's gift for languages and his speed at writing checks. But Jerry got him appointed, appropriately enough, to the Finance Committee of the Republican National Committee and did manage to get him back to Africa briefly. Kellogg was on the team that represented the United States at a conference of African nations in Morocco. I don't know whether he got a chance to show off his Kiswahili. But he told me to keep working on the appointment, so I did.

It was during Ford's campaign for re-election that I found out how close he was to Richard Nixon. At the time, I had known Jerry for about five months. On Wednesday, September 21, 1966, I was in his office around ten-thirty in the morning and, in the course of a general conversation, I mentioned to him that Jack Slater, who was the fund-raising head of the Republican Party in the Detroit area, had approached me for contributions from my friends, and I asked: "Jerry, would it be helpful to you if I contributed something?"

"It would be nice of you if you did," he said. "But now that you've mentioned it, I'm having a fund-raising dinner in Grand Rapids on October 25, and it would be more important to me if you contributed to that. How about taking five tickets?"

"How much are they?"

"A hundred apiece."

"Okay."

"Swell."

On Monday, October 17, I delivered my check, made out to the Kent County Republican Committee, for these tickets personally to Jerry. He was delighted. He said: "I hope you'll be there, Bob. I don't want to look at the same old faces."

I assured him I would. I knew that many lobbyists bought tickets to such events because they knew they had to, but most often they gave the tickets to the politician's staff so that they could attend the event in a show of devoted loyalty that wasn't costing them anything. But I already had a lot riding on Jerry Ford, and I was determined to attend the dinner even if I had to walk to Grand Rapids. Actually, I flew to Detroit where a friend of mine met me and drove me to Grand Rapids. With us at the dinner that night at the Grand Rapids armory were Alice Weston, to whom I had originally paid the $1,000 for the introduction to Ford, and her brother, Pete Boter, who had written Ford the letter which had led to the introduction.

There were about 800 people at the banquet, and the star was Richard Nixon. Ever with his eye on the White House, Nixon rarely missed a chance to appear at a Republican event, keeping his name in people's minds and picking up the indebted loyalty of candidates he was helping by his appearance. Nixon didn't have to worry about Ford's loyalty. In the short time I had known him, Ford had assured me many times that he and Nixon were close friends. This was borne out by the speeches. Nixon told the audience that Ford was going to be the next Speaker of the House of Representatives. Ford told the audience that Nixon was going to be the next President of the United States. In the middle of his speech, Ford startled me by turning in my direction and saying: "And I want to thank my good friend Bob Winter-Berger for coming all the way out here from New York for this dinner." There was an uncertain sprinkle of applause. Nobody knew who I was, which, as a lobbyist, was the way I wanted it.

It was after the banquet, while Alice Weston, Pete Boter, and I were chatting with Nixon and Ford, that the lobbyist from General Electric approached and took Ford and then Nixon aside to discuss the future appointment of Thomas O. Paine as director of NASA. This was when I heard Nixon say that any friend of Jerry's was a friend of his and that if he—Nixon—were ever in a position to be helpful he would be.

That evening, as Nixon and Ford returned to our group, Ford was shaking his head and, in effect, said: "That guy. G. E. has made a contribution, of course, but they're contributing to the Democrats, too."

Nixon said: "He's a smart boy. He can't lose. But I don't play it like that. When I'm watching a football game or a baseball game, I get my biggest thrill by betting on one team at a time."

Ford said: "Bob, here, obviously agrees with you. He's only betting on the Republican team."

Nixon seemed pleased. He said: "That's the best way, although it isn't always the most effective way to play the game in Washington. But I'll tell you how I feel about these things. I am a man of strong loyalties, and for better or worse I will always back up to the nth degree those who have helped me financially when I really needed it. Bob, I will never forget you and your efforts on Jerry's behalf."

That was nice to know. It was also good to know the way Nixon operated. Whereas Jerry Ford had arrived in Washington as an unabashed country bumpkin, Richard Nixon had come in like a tiger. His victorious 1950 contest for the Senate seat of Helen Gahagan Douglas is best remembered for its infamy. This campaign, as well as his two earlier successful House contests, was masterminded by Reese Taylor, chairman of the board of the Union Oil Company. Nixon won, and one of his early feats in Congress and later when he was Vice President was to lead the fight which won for Union Oil the offshore oil rights at Santa Barbara. Years later, defects in the company's equipment ruined the beaches at Santa Barbara.

Reese Taylor helped Nixon in many ways. In 1957, while Nixon was Vice President, to cite one instance, the Union Oil Company built a service station on a vacant lot owned by his mother, Mrs. Hannah M. Nixon. According to court records in Los Angeles County, the assessed value of the lot for tax purposes in 1956, before the service station was built, was $13,000. Its estimated market value was $52,000. (Los Angeles property values are assessed at 25 per cent of the estimated market value.) Ten year later, after the service station had been built, the assessed market value of the property had jumped to $40,920, for an estimated market value of $163,680. Reese Taylor and Richard Nixon were always willing to do each other favors.

After Nixon lost the Presidential campaign of 1960 to John F. Kennedy, he returned to California and joined the law firm of Adams, Duque, and Hazeltine. Another partner in the firm was Waller Taylor II, son of Reese Taylor. After Reese Taylor died in 1962, it was Waller Taylor who saw to it that Walter H. Annenberg, the Philadelphia publisher, remained financially loyal to Nixon during the lean years prior to 1968. As a reward for this loyalty, Waller Taylor then saw to it that, after Nixon's inauguration, Annenberg was appointed ambassador to the Court of St. James.

What Nathan Voloshen was to Speaker McCormack, and what Eddie Adams was to President Johnson, Waller Taylor became to President Nixon. There is scarcely an important man in the Nixon Administration that Taylor does not know on a first-name basis. To watch him in action at a political gathering is like watching a neurotic butterfly. A tall, good-looking, aristocratic—but ultra-nervous—man in his middle forties,

Taylor has none of the poise one would expect given his background. His foreground seemed to have consumed him and he appeared to be under constant tension—which he was.

I went to President Nixon's inaugural festivities in Washington with Waller Taylor, his wife, and his aunt, Elizabeth Taylor Dunnington, Reese's sister. We were at the celebration at the Sheraton Park Hotel where we sat with the California delegation. For part of the evening, we were joined by Rose Mary Woods, for seventeen years Nixon's trusted personal secretary, and her FBI escort. I remember being surprised that, even during these gala festivities, Taylor wanted to talk business with Rose Mary. I heard him say that he wanted an appointment with Nixon as soon as possible to discuss the appointment of a client of his to an ambassadorship. Rose Mary told him to call the White House in a few days to line the date up. After Rose Mary left, Taylor apologized to me for discussing business with her, but he said this was something he had to take care of quickly. The client was Vincent de Roulet, son-in-law of millionaires Mr. and Mrs. Charles Shipman Payson. Vincent de Roulet's notable accomplishment in life, besides marrying a millionaire's daughter, was to be elected mayor of the village of North Hills, Long Island, which in reality was the family estate. Waller Taylor told me that evening that Mrs. Payson had been a loyal supporter of Nixon, contributing $250,000 to his campaign. She had also given Taylor $100,000 in cash which, he told me: "I gave to Dick." For her loyal support, Mrs. Payson wanted an ambassadorship for her son-in-law, and Waller Taylor thought this matter was important enough for him to get on it even before Nixon was officially in office.

This reminded me that Francis Kellogg still wanted an ambassadorship, too. Besides the $30.000 he had promised the Republican Party through Jerry Ford, he was ready to go for another $30.000 if only somebody in the State Department would give him an embassy in Africa. Kellogg's boss at International Mining was Lewis B. Harder, chairman of the board. Harder was a personal friend of Spiro T. Agnew and had contributed heavily to the campaign. On April 10, 1969, Harder managed to get an appointment for Kellogg to speak with Spiro Agnew in the Vice-President's office. After hearing Kellogg out, Agnew said, as Kellogg later reported to me: "I'm helpless. You're talking to the wrong man. You must cultivate the President. I am only a puppet on a string around here. I do and I say what I'm told."

Two weeks later, Waller Taylor came to New York, and I met him early on the morning of Wednesday, April 30. I told him about the problems Kellogg was having. Although Kellogg had the support of several Republican Representatives and Senators, Jerry Ford the most important of them, things were not moving as fast as Kellogg wanted, and he was getting nervous and impatient. Taylor was sympathetic. He told me he had been having similar troubles obtaining an appointment for Vincent de Roulet. Taylor conceded that the $30,000 Kellogg had given the New York Republicans, plus the $30,000 he had pledged the National Committee, amounted to an impressive total, but he pointed out that Mrs. Payson had already given almost ten times that to Nixon's support, indicating that Kellogg didn't have all that much to complain about.

I asked Taylor if he would help me calm down Kellogg by telling him the background of the de Roulet case, and he said yes. We walked over to Kellogg's office. Kellogg had heard about Waller Taylor from de Roulèt, and so he was impressed by an unexpected visit from such a notable personage. After listening to Kellogg's tale of woe, Taylor said the only way to get the appointment was to get the ear of President Nixon and his personal aide Peter Flanigan, both of whom Waller said were his close friends. Taylor said that he would be happy to try for Kellogg but that he would need a cash payment of $65,000 to take care of his time and the needs of both Nixon and Flanigan. Kellogg agreed to have the money for Taylor that afternoon, and we arranged a meeting for later in the day in Kellogg's office.

When Waller Taylor arrived at the appointed hour, he was carrying a large attaché case. Kellogg had the money ready, in $100 bills, 10 to the packet, 65 packets, and they were piled into Taylor's attaché case. As Taylor and I were walking up Park Avenue later, he casually swinging the attaché case containing $65,000 in cash, he told me that he would keep $10,000 for himself, give $10,000 to Peter Flanigan, and the remaining $45,000 he would give to President Nixon. Taylor offered me $5,000 of the President's share as a commission. I refused because, as I told him, Kellogg had promised to pay me out of his own pocket. Besides, with the business already beginning to smell, I didn't want to be in the position of taking money from both sides. I never learned whether Nixon and Flanigan got the money.

I hoped that Kellogg would relax now. But summer was coming on and he was growing restless. He wanted to head for his ranch in Kenya, but he wanted to arrive

as the new U. S. Ambassador. A couple of weeks after
the Waller Taylor incident. I went to a cocktail party
and ran into Peter Cusick. Around town, Peter Cusick
was referred to as a "man of mystery." Nobody seemed
to know exactly what his job was, but he frequently
traveled all over the world either with Jacob Javits or
for Javits. Cusick was a tall, handsome man, and he
affected a British accent.

Cusick knew what I was trying to achieve for Francis
Kellogg. Javits had already come out for Kellogg and
had written a few letters supporting him. At the party,
Cusick asked me how I was doing. Without going into
detail about Waller Taylor, I said that things had taken
a turn for the better, and I said that I wished Kellogg
would stop nagging me about his appointment. Cusick
said: "It might be a good idea, Bob, if you got John
Lindsay behind Kellogg. After all, Lindsay is the
Number One Republican in New York City. You ought
to be able to give Washington the impression that all the
leading Republicans in New York are supporting your
man."

This was in May 1969. John Lindsay was running for
re-election as mayor of New York. I realized he needed
campaign funds, especially since his chances for re-election didn't look very good. I asked Peter Cusick: "How
much is this going to cost?"

He said: "I don't know. I'll talk to Dick Aurelio
about it. I'd say twenty thousand."

Richard Aurelio had been a newspaperman who had
gone into public relations and was a masterful campaign
manager. He had run two of Jake Javits's campaigns
with great success and was now running Lindsay's battle for re-election. Aurelio subsequently became deputy

mayor of New York, known as the man closest to John Lindsay. I said to Cusick: "Let me know."

Peter Cusick set up a meeting for me with Dick Aurelio for Friday, May 9, 1969, at 10:15 A.M. at Lindsay's campaign headquarters in the Roosevelt Hotel. Meanwhile, I had sounded out Francis Kellogg. He was not happy about shelling out more money for a job he felt he had already paid for amply, but he knew he could use all the help available, so he authorized me to go ahead with the meeting. It was raining that morning. I met Kellogg in front of his apartment around nine-thirty in the morning and walked down Park Avenue with him to his office at Forty-eighth Street. He still felt unsure about the importance of Lindsay's endorsement.

I left Kellogg at his office and went to the Roosevelt Hotel. Peter Cusick was late; I waited almost an hour for him in the lobby. When he arrived, he blamed the weather and the difficulty of getting cabs for his tardiness, and we went upstairs to Dick Aurelio. There wasn't much to discuss. Aurelio assured me that he could set up a meeting between Francis Kellogg and Mayor John Lindsay, as a result of which Lindsay would publicly endorse Kellogg's appointment as our ambassador to Kenya. The price: a $20,000 campaign contribution. I reported this to Kellogg, and he said he would think it over.

The next time I saw Kellogg, he said: "I have checked this out with a good friend of mine in Washington. He said I should forget it. He said Lindsay doesn't carry that much weight with the Republican Party any more and his endorsement really wouldn't do me any good. Javits feels the same way." By then I was aware of Kellogg's habit of referring to Senator Claiborne Pell as his "good friend" in Washington, so I assumed he had checked with Pell and Pell had checked with Javits. The proposed exchange of favors fell through. Cusick kept checking me on it, the price dropping to $5,000 in a few weeks.

Kellogg was willing to ride along now that Waller Taylor had entered the picture, more confident that things would finally start moving. A prospect he enjoyed was knowing that upon his appointment he would be able to dispose of his large block of International Mining stock which he could not sell at the time because he was still president of the company. But his hopes were premature. Things moved, but very slowly. As weeks passed and little happened, Kellogg's friends began to bombard the White House with letters in his support. On Friday, August 8, when Nixon was on one of his working vacations at San Clemente, California, Kellogg received a telephone call from Presidential aide Herbert W. Kalmbach. But Kalmbach's only message was to assure Kellogg that Nixon had not forgotten about him and ask Kellogg to remain patient. Kellogg's impatience was reflected in a letter he wrote Kalmbach on August 11, in which, among other things, he said:

> I very much appreciated the time and interest you took in calling me last Friday. . . . Many friends have written letters in my behalf to the President, the Secretary, and top officials at State and to the White House staff. You undoubtedly know Waller Taylor, who can give you his opinion as to my ability and personality.
>
> Very truly yours,
> F. L. Kellogg

P.S. Believe me, your assistance is very greatly appreciated. I could come out to California if you thought it propitious.

Two weeks later, some ambassadorial appointments were announced. Vincent de Roulet got Jamaica. Kenya went to Robinson McIlvaine. Kellogg's heart was broken. But he fought on. On November 25, six months after the $65,000 payment, he wrote to Taylor:

Dear Waller:
It's a long time since we touched base—hence this note, together with the latest two letters to Washington which will bring you up-to-date.
Very little progress to report as you can see. I think the only end of road blocks is through a meeting with the President.
Could you possibly consider arranging this in my behalf?

Yours very truly,
Fran

In a nice way, Kellogg was calling Taylor's bluff, but it didn't get him far. It was during this stalling period of over a year that Kellogg was tossed the crumbs consisting of jobs on the Finance Committee and a trip to Morocco. Previously, Kellogg had been secretary of the American Immigration and Citizenship Conference, a position he had obtained through the proddings of its conference directors by Senator Claiborne Pell, his "good friend in Washington." Pell himself had been a director and the conference secretary.

When Kellogg finally got a government job, it was in

this general area. In May 1970, Kellogg had a private meeting with President Nixon. At the end of the year, he was given an appointment as special assistant to the Secretary of State for Refugee and Migration Affairs, and the job carried a special ambassadorial title. He was sworn into office by Secretary of State William P. Rogers in February 1971. Paid off at last, he was happy. I, however, found myself less than happy; he forgot to pay me. For my efforts for him for over a year, I had received from Kellogg only $950.

After Richard Nixon lost his bid for the governorship of California in 1962, he moved to New York and joined a law firm that became known as Nixon, Mudge, Rose, Guthrie, Alexander, and Mitchell. The Nixons were not very social, but soon it became the chic thing to do in New York society to let everybody know when you had been to some social event at which the Nixons were present. The fewer the other people present, the more chic you were. For a while, I heard so much of this Nixon name-dropping that I wondered if the Nixons ever stayed home. On November 16, 1965, I attended a dinner party at which I met Dr. Arnold Hutschnecker, an M.D. who, I already knew, was a psychotherapist specializing in patients who were important industrialists, successful actresses, or rich socialites. Henry Ford and his daughter Charlotte had been Hutschnecker's patients. So had Celeste Holm, Elizabeth Taylor, and Hildegarde. Until that dinner party, however, I had not known that another patient for several years had been Richard Milhous Nixon.

Hutschie—as the doctor preferred being called— had a habit of using his patients as topics for dinner conversations. That night, dropping Nixon's name was perhaps part of the current fad. As I listened to him, I had the uncomfortable feeling that he was behaving unethically, but then I realized that this was probably his way of self promotion, of advertising. Hutschie did not have to advertise for patients; his wealthy clients recommended him to each other. But just as some men use money or power to advertise their manliness to women, Hutschie advertised his manliness by exposing the weaknesses of other men. Hutschie was a small man, slight, ugly, a forceful and overpowering braggart. Half German and half Eurasian, he lent himself to the description "inscrutably arrogant."

That night, Hutschie told us that his greatest difficulty with Nixon as a patient was teaching the man not to try to think on his feet. "Nixon," said Hutschie, "is the sort of man who should rehearse even a casual conversation." Hutschie cited the press conference Nixon held after losing the California gubernatorial campaign. Instead of simply announcing his retirement from politics, Nixon used the occasion to tell members of the news media that they'd had their last chance to take pot shots at him. This was a foolish thing for so prominent a man to say, and it became even more foolish when, shortly afterward, Nixon made a fresh target of himself by acting like a candidate and giving speeches all over the country. In the wake of the ridicule that followed the remark, Nixon sent for Hutschie again.

Hutschie adhered to the Pavlovian precept of conditioned reflex. He also held that the way your mother damaged your psyche by scolding you one day when you were two years old can be overcome psychologically by the way you decide you are going to scold your mother tomorrow. Another Pavlovian precept

Hutschie practiced was that thoughts could be presented in carefully chosen words in a way that could shape the reactions of the listeners to whatever you wanted, regardless of what the facts were. The Russian Communists during the 1920's and the German Nazis during the 1930's applied these principles of human behavior with considerable effect, and Hutschie said he tried to instill them into his patients who were in positions of decision. Evidently, they do not always work. Much later Hutschie told me that, in May 1970, after the violent national reaction to Nixon's announcement of the invasion of Cambodia, Nixon went to his Florida home for the weekend and Hutschie was there making an emergency house call, trying to piece together Nixon's shattered ego.

At the dinner party, Hutschie told us about the unusual relationship between Nixon and Dwight D. Eisenhower. Hutschie said: "Eisenhower took on a father image for Nixon. Eisenhower was always telling Nixon to straighten his tie or pull back his shoulders or speak up or shut up. Nixon resented this whenever Eisenhower was too blatant in front of other people and yet I expect he enjoyed it. Nixon is happiest either when he has no responsibility or when he has it all. When he has no responsibility, he can't be criticized for anything and he can relax and be a little boy. When he has all the responsibility, he feels he has the right to exercise it as he alone sees fit, and he can't bear to be criticized for anything at all. That's when he says or does shortsighted things, and I get a call. I don't know how many times I've told him that a good administrator puts up a calm, controlled, and positive front and lets somebody else in the organization do the dirty work that draws the critics out of the wall."

One of the things about Hutschie that amused me over the years was knowing that he was, politically, a liberal and that most of his patients were arch conservatives. I often wondered what subtle, subconscious influences Hutschie was exerting on these patients as he treated them, but I never saw much evidence of change in the more prominent of them. At one point, Jerry Ford told me that the pressures of being Minority Leader were beginning to make him irritable, nervous, and depressed. I told him about Hutschie and about Nixon, suggesting that he ask Nixon if Hutschie were doing him any good. This was how Ford became a Hutschie patient for at least a year.

I'm sure that nobody at the dinner table that night in 1965 considered for a moment that Richard Nixon would ever again be the Republican candidate for the Presidency. As for myself, I just wondered which woman at the party Hutschie was trying to impress. Then, in 1968, as the Miami convention drew near, Richard Nixon surprised us all with how—with his calm, controlled, and positive front, no matter which view he took on an issue in any part of the country—he had sewed up the convention before it began. I worked for him.

About a week before the November election, I was having dinner with a friend who happened to say: "I talked with Hutschie last night. He told me that Drew Pearson had called him and asked if Dick Nixon is a patient of his."

I braced myself. "What did Hutschie say?"

"He said yes."

"My God!"

I telephoned Hutschie as soon as I could; he confirmed Pearson's inquiry and his answer. Hutschie couldn't understand why I was upset, and he said: "I saw no reason for denying it. Lots of people have doctors." Hutschie was not a psychiatrist, although he was a psychotherapist. The difference can be more a matter of aura than ability, and Hutschie never bothered to correct anybody who inadvertently promoted his professional status.

I called Jerry Ford in Washington, but he was out. Convinced that this was a serious situation, I caught an early shuttle to Washington the next morning. When Jerry saw by my face that I had something important on my mind, he cleared his office. I told him: "Drew Pearson knows that Dick Nixon is one of Hutschie's patients."

He frowned. "How did he find out?"

"I don't know, but I do know that Hutschie himself confirmed it for him."

"Damn. Do you think he'll use it?"

"I doubt that he'd check on it just out of idle curiosity. He's for Humphrey, you know. He's got some dynamite now."

"Do you really think it's that serious?"

"How do you think people will feel when they find out, a few days before the election, that the Republican candidate has his own head shrinker?"

He shrugged. "A lot of people do."

"A Presidential candidate shouldn't. Even though Hutschie is little more than Norman Vincent Peale with a couch, the fact remains that he is a psychotherapist, and that's enough for Pearson to make Nixon look like a raving maniac."

Jerry shook his head. "I don't know what to suggest."

I didn't either. Approaching Pearson directly for a

fair treatment of the story would have been completely unrealistic. Trying to approach him through his Democratic contacts in Congress would have been equally unrealistic. Most of them would have relished the story, knowing the damage it could cause in the last days of a campaign that looked as close as this one. I was acquainted with several editors whose newspapers carried Pearson, but not enough of them to create the desired effect. I realized I would have to move higher. I knew two publishers who owned chains of newspapers in different parts of the country, and I knew they supported Nixon. I telephoned each one and explained what was about to happen. Without making any specific suggestions, I was quite clear about the great harm that would be done to Nixon's image if this information about him became public before the election. Each publisher pointed out that Drew Pearson was too powerful a journalist and too proud a man to let any evidence of efforts to kill one of his columns slip by him without a stormy response. I suggested that the column didn't have to be killed but that, as with most syndicated columns, the publisher had the right to reschedule material unless the author's contract contained specifications to the contrary. I also thought that, if approached with proper obeisance, Pearson himself might even agree to postpone the column on the grounds of fair play. This, in fact, was what happened.

Drew Pearson's column on Nixon and Hutschie appeared—but only after the election. By then, Ford had told me that he had had a telephone conversation with Pearson. It had included an exchange that went something like this:

> PEARSON: "I get the impression that somebody is trying to kill a column I've done on Richard Nixon and his psychiatrist."
>
> FORD: "Is that right?"
>
> PEARSON: "Yes, I was wondering if you knew anything about it?"
>
> FORD: "No, I don't."
>
> PEARSON: "Have you heard anything about the subject?"
>
> FORD: "Just that you might write it."
>
> PEARSON: "Who told you that?"
>
> FORD: "Bob Winter-Berger."
>
> PEARSON: "Who's he?"
>
> FORD: "He does public-relations work in New York. He's helped on the campaign."

I doubt that Drew Pearson made a note to himself to "get" Winter-Berger. Two years later, however, it seemed to me that Jack Anderson, Pearson's former collaborator and then his journalistic heir, went out of his way to include my name in his column whenever he wrote about Nathan Voloshen or Voloshen's deals, practically mentioning me parenthetically. I was told that some Democrats were feeding Anderson information about me, hoping through my association with Jerry Ford that some Republicans would be drawn into the Voloshen scandal.

After Richard Nixon and John Mitchell left their law firm and went into government, the firm changed its name to Mudge, Rose, Guthrie, and Alexander, better known on Wall Street as Mudge Rose and still often referred to as Nixon's firm. An old and respected firm, Mudge Rose has always preferred long-term clients; but when Nixon entered the White House, the firm began to get a lot of one-shot offers, some of them with heavy political overtones. Many of these offers were discreetly detoured to Waller Taylor. Taylor told me once that Nixon had offered him several government posts, but he had declined on the basis that he could not afford to live on a government salary.

Even so, Taylor was rarely far from President Nixon. His frequent visits to the White House made him an intimate member of the White House family. But, like a good political operator, he pointedly avoided publicity about his friendship with Nixon and his role in the White House, never letting himself be photographed in the White House or with Nixon if he could help it. One picture that showed him in the midst of things appeared in *The Los Angeles Times* on Wednesday, August 27, 1969. An accompanying article told about a big party for the members of the summer White House and their wives. The picture caption read: "At Dana Point, warm summer skies brought allure to Western scene for DuBridge-Ward Mexican Fiesta Monday. Guests included (left to right) Mr. Waller Taylor, Mr. and Mrs. James P. Kennedy, Dr. Arthur F. Burns, who was counselor to President Nixon, and Mrs. Waller Taylor." Dr. Burns was quoted as saying: "This is the heaviest gathering I have seen outside the White House." That's why Taylor was there.

Taylor was the lawyer's lawyer for lobbying in Washington at the White House level. Taylor had an almost unblemished record for delivering. His unofficial connection with Mudge Rose was one of his aces in the hole. He got the one-shot political referrals that the firm didn't want.

One of the incidents that raised questions of propriety involving Mudge Rose pertained to the El Paso Natural Gas Company. Between 1961 and 1967, the company paid Mudge Rose over $700.000 for representation in an antitrust case. Two months after Nixon and Mitchell took office, the Justice Department dropped the action. Another incident dealt with the Penn Central Railroad. In 1970, while the railroad was in bankruptcy proceedings, the Nixon Administration offered a $200-million loan guarantee. The offer was withdrawn when Representative Wright Patman of Texas disclosed on the floor of the House that the railroad was being represented by Mudge Rose and that Nixon had been a director of Investors Diversified Services, a major Penn Central stockholder. Also, it seemed more than coincidental that Nebraska, New Jersey, Kentucky, and West Virginia, all having Republican governors, should promptly turn over their tax-free bond business to Mudge Rose, giving the firm fees of over $1 million a year. In January 1971, Mudge Rose appeared before the Justice Department on the matter of the merger of Warner-Lambert Pharmaceutical Company and Parke Davis. Mitchell disqualified himself, but Deputy Attorney General Richard Kleindienst let the merger go through. A key figure in the deal was the little known Elmer Bobst, former chairman of Warner-Lambert, and a close friend of Nixon's since the Eisenhower Administration. A self-educated man, Bobst's success in pharmaceuticals earned him the title of "the Vitamin King." In August 1971, Arizona Democrat Morris K. Udall, chairman of the House Postal

Service Subcommittee, asked Postmaster Winton M. Blount to postpone a $250-million bond issue, scheduled for October, until he could finish an investigation. Udall had found out that the legal advisers to the five underwriters were Mudge Rose and that a White House aide, Peter Flanigan, once worked for one of the underwriters, Dillon, Read & Co., and Udall wanted to determine whether this was all coincidence.

For all the aura of middle-class holier-than-thou-ism that surrounds the Nixon Administration, its members seem to have lost precious little time adapting to the wheeler-dealer tactics of everyday Washington. For me, who had crossed the aisle, as it were, in the hopes of finding a somewhat less polluted political air on the Republican side, the experience was especially revealing— and discouraging. The only real difference I could detect between the Nixon Republicans and the Democrats was that the Republicans affected an air of morality, which I strongly suspected rested on a firm basis of bigotry.

Once while I was attending a large social event in Washington where the guests were supposed to be close to the hierarchy of the Nixon Administration, my date surveyed the crowd and remarked: "Looks like all the bigots in town are here."

Yes indeed: a nice bunch of people.

My host said: "Bob, I want you to meet Perle Mesta."
So I was introduced to Perle Mesta for the umpteenth
time, evidently never yet having made much impression
on her. But in her later years, very little got through to
Perle, so I didn't mind. Besides, this was a Washington
party, so by definition the only people who mattered
were people you were working on.

Like New York, where a party or dinner often mixes
business with pleasure, a Washington party is an inte-
gral part of the business of politics, the business of making important connections. Since the days of Dolly Madison, Washington parties have been business expenses
for the people who give them, and they have been worth
the price. Perle Mesta once said: "I like to have guests
who are in the thick of things so that my parties can be
a place where differences can be settled or important
matters worked out." If those differences and policies
pertained to any company Mrs. Mesta held stock in, the
party was a success. That is the point of it all.

Some Washington parties have a social aura about
them, depending on who gives them and who is there,

but most parties are virtually open-house affairs, with the hosts not knowing most of the guests who are there. Soon after I started lobbying in Washington, I began to receive invitations from people I didn't actually know but whose names were politically or socially prominent in the city, and I wondered why they were inviting me. Then I learned that my name had somehow been added to the "approved" guest lists swapped by hostesses. As another bachelor in town, I had been invited to help fill the need for an extra man. I was a convenient suit, and although I tried to keep out of the Washington limelight I was known to have important connections.

I went to a few of these parties because I wanted to see the inside of some of the Washington mansions I had heard so much about. Almost invariably during the evening some man would turn to me and say: "Good to see you again, Ed." The name varied.

I'd say: "I'm Bob."

"Of course. Bob Twillingham, isn't it?"

"Bob Winter-Berger."

"Of course. I'm sorry. Well, Bob, how's the lumber business these days?"

"I'm in public relations."

"Oh, really? That must be interesting."

The party-going aspect of it certainly wasn't, but such a typical exchange clearly demonstrates "a gathering of friends" according to Washington party standards. You don't even need an invitation to attend many Washington parties. You just have to know about them. No Washington hostess would allow a servant or a security guard in black tie to ask you who you were. You might turn out to be a new undersecretary of some department and she wouldn't want to risk insulting you. Most of the bigger parties, those with 300 or 400 guests, are given to impress somebody, and Washingtonians are easily impressed. Most members of the Congress, for example, come from middle-class backgrounds in smaller communities across the country. They are dazzled by money. They are dazzled by big names. Being courted by any of Washington's famous hostesses is a heady experience for them. When the hostess calls them from time to time and tries to influence their vote on a certain matter or asks them to hurry certain documentation through a government agency, they go along with her because she is a friend and they have no idea that they are being used—or they don't care if they are.

Washington hostesses have their own brand of lobbying down to a science. First, there is the big party to impress the guest of honor, be he a member of the Congress or the cabinet, a department head or a visiting dignitary. If the dignitary is important enough, he is used as bait to impress the locals who will be riper for lobbying later on because they themselves feel they had to be important in order to be invited. Continuing, the hostess presses her prey by inviting him to smaller and smaller gatherings, until she is down to a dinner for twelve or less and her victim feels he has finally made the "in" crowd. After that, he is a pushover.

Washington had its great hostesses in the 1920's and 1930's in women like Mrs. John Henderson, Evelyn Walsh McLean, and Eleanor "Cissy" Patterson, who never mixed business with pleasure. But the one hostess who capped them all was Pearl Reid Skirvin Mesta, a woman who never gave a party without a purpose, and she was well rewarded. Born in Sturgis, Michigan, in 1892, Pearl was the eldest daughter of William Balser Skirvin, an oil millionaire and real estate promoter in

Texas and Oklahoma. He finally settled in Oklahoma City and built Oklahoma's largest hotel, the Skirvin. Pearl married George Mesta, a considerably older man who started out making machine tools in Pittsburgh and then went into the business of making huge machines to roll out sheets of steel, great turbines for dams and electric plants, and propeller shafts for the largest ships. When the Mestas settled in Washington in 1917, they were millionaires in their own right, many times over. Money was never a problem for Pearl at any time in her life.

In Washington, a good hostess must have money, time, drive, and purpose, and Perle—as she later spelled her name—had all four in abundance. The Mestas moved to Washington because World War I had made the U. S. government Mesta's major customer. They settled at the old Washington Hotel, and Perle began to throw the parties which brought in the government people who had roles in awarding contracts. Not only did Perle entertain with benefits for her husband's company in mind; she herself was also a partner in many of her father's oil deals. The Homestead Act had allowed pioneers to acquire land on the Western plains by settling on it and paying a small fee for five years, but the government retained the right to the gas and oil in the ground. To get those rights, promoters first had to obtain approval from the Department of the Interior before making a deal with the farmer. Most of the farmers were poor and were willing to cooperate for several thousand dollars. It would be impossible to estimate how much more than that the promoters spent around the Department of the Interior to get the action going. Living in Washington, Perle was in a good spot to make connections for her father. After her husband's death in

1925, she became the major stockholder in his company and continued to be its Washington contact for government contracts.

A lifelong Republican, Perle Mesta backed Democrat Robert S. Kerr when he made his successful bid for the Oklahoma governorship in 1942. Kerr had been president of the Midcontinent Oil and Gas Association for many years. Perle backed Kerr again when he ran successfully for the U.S. Senate six years later. In Washington, the two of them became partners in numerous oil transactions and other business deals, both of them making millions. For a Republican, Perle did very well with the Democrats. In 1944, she stumped for Harry Truman's Vice Presidential candidacy at the Democratic convention, securing his friendship from then on. Because Bess Truman disliked parties, Perle was Truman's unofficial hostess. In 1947, she served as national cochairman of the February 19 Jackson-Jefferson Anniversary dinner. Not only did she herself contribute heavily to Truman's 1948 campaign, but she was also the source of so many other big donations that *Time* magazine described her as "a money raiser extraordinary." In a position to do favors for people all over Washington, she had no trouble raising funds when vested interests were at stake.

During and before the Truman Administration, Perle became good friends with Sam Rayburn, John McCormack, and Lyndon Johnson, and part of her reward was to be named minister to Luxembourg in 1949, after Denmark—rather embarrassingly—turned her down. The appointment was a farce and everybody knew it. Out of it, Irving Berlin wrote his hilarious *Call Me Madam,* a satire which Perle mistook for a salute. Ethel Merman's raucous portrayal of Perle as the pratfalling ambassador lacked only one Mesta trait: Perle's arrogant, two-fisted assault on anybody in her way.

Perle's star began to wane during the Eisenhower years, probably because Republicans would not forget her Democratic ties. In 1960, she returned to the fold by supporting Nixon, which turned out to be another mistake. But more than party loyalty was involved. Perle Mesta disliked the Kennedys. She often denigrated John Kennedy by telling the story of how, in April 1949, when he was a Congressman, he had arrived at one of her formal dinners in a tuxedo and brown loafers. The truth was that she was aware of the political feud between the Kennedys and Speaker McCormack, her close friend, and she took McCormack's side. In 1968, she backed Nixon again. I saw her at the Inaugural Ball at the Sheraton Park Hotel, looking slightly gaga in a large blond wig. Hopeful of returning to her throne as Washington's Number One hostess, she had gone on a diet and trimmed down from a size 16 to a 10. It didn't help. Her age was beginning to show. There had always been something misty about her, but now it appeared as if she weren't quite sure where she was.

On Easter, 1970, Perle Mesta appeared at the Metropolitan Club in New York. At one time, her presence would have attracted everybody in the New York Social Register. On this occasion, her escorts were some rather obvious effete snobs. Also in 1970, Perle threw one of her fabled parties for 300 people at Washington's Sheraton Carlton Hotel. Her guests included three Nixon cabinet members and the President's social secretary Lucy Winchester. The guest of honor was Ethel Merman, and everybody at the party would have paid to see her.

Without a doubt it was Perle Mesta who laid the ground rules that turned Washington parties into a battlefield for wheeler-dealing. Other women have learned well from her. I believe that Perle was not so much replaced by the other women as by the fact of her advancing age. Eras fade, and although Perle Mesta could still draw a crowd as long as she was willing to pay for it, the fist that once held Washington's politico-society in its grip was now lucky to be able to wave across the room.

One of Perle Mesta's competitors during her heyday was Mrs. Morris Cafritz, widow of a millionaire builder in Washington. The two of them constantly battled to get big names at their parties, Perle holding sway for years. When Perle left Washington for Luxembourg, Gwen Cafritz came into her own. By the time Perle Mesta returned in 1953, Gwen Cafritz was solidly entrenched, and it was she who was the "in" hostess during the Eisenhower Administration.

Gwendolyn Cafritz came from Hungary via Brooklyn, where she married Morris Cafritz. Shortly after their marriage they moved to Washington, where Cafritz became the city's bowling king before going into building in a big way. When he died in 1964, he left a $24 million fortune. As a builder and financier, he put together a company which is still the largest builder in the Washington area. Cafritz owned several office buildings, hotels, and apartment houses in Washington. He built, among others, the Westchester Apartments, the Universal Building, and the Washington Hilton Hotel. Some of his buildings were leased in whole or in part to various departments and agencies of government, to such an extent that they often cost him very little to build, because of the amortization of the government leases. For example, NASA had about ten floors in one of the Cafritz buildings in downtown Washington.

Gwen Cafritz's parties paid off because her guests knew the government's building plans and enjoyed passing this information on to her. Knowing beforehand what the specifications would be gave Morris Cafritz and his three sons a head start in preparing their bids. Personally knowing the men who would make the decision on bids didn't hurt, either. As the three sons married, their wives adopted Gwen's party-giving technique for getting on the inside track, which was doubtless why the company continued to grow.

Gwen Cafritz was less dedicated to her party-lobbying than Perle Mesta was. Perle once said: "I never give a party without a purpose." One purpose for which she rarely gave a party was for the benefit of any philanthropy except her own. The Cafritz family—Morris's brother Edward was a renowned and respected doctor —supported many philanthropies, and it was possible to go to a party at the Cafritz home where the main topic of conversation wasn't politics but a charity. Also, Washington was home for the Cafritzes. For Perle, who always lived in hotel apartments or occasionally a rented house, it was a base of operations.

Less well-known and ostentatious was Patricia Firestone Chatham. She was the widow of Representative Richard Thurmond Chatham, Democrat of North Carolina, who, at the time of his death in 1957, had been chairman of the board and president of Chatham Mills. The Chathams lived in one of Washington's most magnificent residences and landmarks. Called Prospect House, it was located, appropriately enough, on Prospect Street in Georgetown, and the Chathams had bought it in 1951 from the widow of one-time Secretary

of the Navy James Forrestal for well over $200,000.
While the Trumans were living at Blair House during
the repairs on the White House, Prospect House had
been the nation's guest house. The Shah of Iran and
other notables had stayed there. In 1967, Pat Chatham
put the house, guest house, and property up for sale at a
price of $2 million. If she had sold it, she wouldn't have
had to worry about a place to live. She also had a 10-
acre Maryland home and a 500-acre Christmas tree
farm in North Carolina.

I met Mrs. Chatham the evening before Nixon's inauguration in 1969. I was with the Waller Taylors and
others and we stopped off at Prospect House on our
way to a party by the California delegation at the Army
Club, the "in" event of the evening, Nixon being a Cali-
fornian. Pat Chatham was having a party in honor of
her husband's cousin and his wife. Everybody was
there, even the President's brother. I was impressed by
Mrs. Chatham's simplicity on such a gala night. Perle
Mesta and Gwen Cafritz would have been done up to
the teeth, but here the hostess was wearing a short,
plain black dress, with no jewels. With her on the receiving line were her younger son Walter, and the guests
of honor. I took Mrs. Chatham for a wealthy widow
who occupied her time with her children, gardening,
and charities.

Late in November 1969, I received a call from Mrs.
Pierre Gabard, whose husband had been the French
consul in Philadelphia. Barbara Gabard and Pat Chatham were close friends. Barbara Gabard said she wanted
to talk to me about something, and so we made a date
for lunch at her Park Avenue apartment for December
4, a Thursday. That day Mrs. Gabard told me that Patricia Chatham had been a lobbyist for the tobacco in-

dustry for several years. In 1964, the Surgeon General's office had issued a lengthy report definitely linking smoking to cancer and other diseases, and action had begun to put a health warning on cigarette packs and to eliminate smoking commercials from radio and television. The tobacco people had hired Patricia Chatham to prevent that, and for five years she did. Through her parties and follow-up contacts, she had been able to persuade her Congressional connections to block efforts by private and public health organizations to push through the warnings. By 1969, the public pressure had built to the point where the tobacco industry lost the fight. Patricia Chatham lost her client.

At lunch that Thursday, Mrs. Gabard told me that Patricia Chatham wanted to go into partnership with me as lobbyist. I was supposed to track down the clients; Patricia would do the actual lobbying with Congressmen and government officials through the network of her social contacts in Washington. For her part in bringing about this alliance, Mrs. Gabard wanted Patricia and me to pay her $25,000 a year. Mrs. Gabard was so direct, specific, and unabashed during this discussion that she sounded as if she were peddling concubines. I expressed surprise at Patricia Chatham's sideline; I had thought she was already wealthy. Mrs. Gabard explained that Patricia practiced her avocation for operating funds for Prospect House. By this time, my own career as a lobbyist was practically over, and I had no desire to go back into it, even behind such a respectable front as the mistress of Prospect House. I turned the offer down.

Another hostess who entertains lavishly, but controversially, is Gabrielle Lagerwall. She shuttles back and forth from New York (where she lives) to Washington. *The New York Daily News* has referred to her as "The

Jet Set's Most Controversial Woman." An electrifying person, she is a modern-day Jennie Churchill. One of the world's last great professional beauties, her admirers are legion—mainly, fabulously rich, internationally prominent industrialists and politicians. In the early fall of 1963, she hired me as a public-relations consultant to help her expand her personal social network, and to try to create an image of her as a respectable matron. It was not an easy assignment.

She was supposed to be Mrs. Adahan Lagerwall; in reality, there was no Adahan. I invented the name, to provide her with a respectable escort to the opening of the 1963 season of the Metropolitan Opera. Suzy, who then wrote for New York's now defunct *Daily Mirror,* noted in her gossip column: "Yes, Virginia, there is a Mr. Lagerwall." Adahan Lagerwall was in reality William Klopman, the textile tycoon, who was Gabrielle's most ardent and generous suitor. Since he was in the middle of a divorce at the time, we had to disguise him. A cosmetician darkened his sandy hair and gave him a mustache for the occasion. According to what I carefully planted in the society columns, Adahan was supposed to be a Dutch multimillionaire who had made a fortune in rubber in Java, lost it during World War II, but found another fortune in oil later in the same part of the world. Gabrielle had got to know him, my story went, because of her own Dutch family holdings in Java. Adahan, much older than his wife, was supposed to be a recluse who preferred to spend most of his time alone in his Swiss palace, while his lovely wife traipsed around the world. Actually, the real Mr. Lagerwall in Gabrielle's life was a G.I. whom Gabrielle had married in Europe after the war in order to get to America. Once here, she had promptly dumped him.

The New York Daily News reported that Gabrielle had helped set the traps that had resulted in the divorce of William Klopman, Sr., her swain, and also that of his son Robert, a Yale zoology instructor. In both cases, the trap was allegedly the same man: one Fernando Gallo, the U.N. correspondent for a South American newspaper. Within the space of one year, Gallo had apparently managed to entice the wives of both Klopmans to his suite in the Hotel Alrae and persuaded them to undress. Then, in classical fashion, he had excused himself to shave, and during his well-timed absence photographers had entered the room and photographed the naked women. Both Klopmans had used the pictures as evidence of adultery in getting divorces. Gallo was supposed to be one of Gabrielle's close friends, but she said she could only recall meeting him once, when he accompanied a friend of hers to a party she gave.

In order to live in the manner to which she had accustomed herself, Gabrielle had to continue to meet men who could afford her expensive tastes. She managed this well enough on her own. When I first met her, she had a huge cooperative apartment in New York's exclusive Hotel Pierre, a mansion on Long Island, designed and built for her by world famous architect Edward Durrell Stone, and owned well over $2,000,000 in diamonds. But she had one major failing: she had a raging passion to socialize in the circles of her courtiers, and quite understandably, she ran into a bit of trouble. The problem was that too many other women, among New York's Four Hundred, had achieved social status in the same way Gabrielle was trying to: thus they recognized her on sight—and they loathed her. In the early days, she could hardly get an invitation to a wake.

Gabrielle's main problem was her beauty. When she

entered a room, her poise, her alabaster skin, her crown of braided auburn hair, her expensive gown, and her sparkling array of jewelry brought the place to life. Every other woman there suddenly turned drab. Gabrielle had style. She was dazzling—a throwback to "La Belle Epoque," when the only interesting women in Paris and New York were those cultivated by interesting men. Whenever Gabrielle entered a room, there were almost inevitably a few men present who had contributed to her wardrobe or her jewelry collection. Their wives suspected it, and they hated Gabrielle—if only because the dress or the diamonds looked better on Gabrielle than they would have on them.

Gabrielle was expensive, but she was also expansive —outgoing, generous, regal; she entertained lavishly, a grande dame in every sense of the term. Most women didn't like that, so most women didn't like Gabrielle. What worried these women more than losing a man to Gabrielle was losing the man's money. With a wealthy husband supposedly tucked away somewhere in the Swiss Alps, Gabrielle obviously had no need to shop for a new one.

In New York, however, there were a number of social events each year which, because of their nature, were open house. Be it a fund-raising for an animal shelter or an art museum; an opening night at the Metropolitan or the Horse Show; a benefit for the Apaches or for Albert Schweitzer's hospital; if you could afford the traffic and you dressed right, you could get in. Gabrielle always subscribed very generously to these affairs—entertaining between ten and sixteen at dinner at $100.00 a head. Since most of the men she knew were married, they could not very well escort her, and on these outings that task often befell me. I looked on these occasions as a pleasurable and unexpected fringe benefit. Time and again, after these glittering events, the next day's papers would show Gabrielle smiling and seemingly chatting with Blue Bloods—whose blood boiled when they saw their names publicly linked with hers. Her technique was to manage, with remarkable finesse, to place herself with someone famous—a diplomat, ambassador, an industrialist, or a plain old millionaire—just as the photographer began to click away. But the fact was, in spite of any disclaimers on the part of the diplomats or millionaires, Gabrielle often knew them very well indeed.

Although she continued to fascinate me, the time came when, because of the pressures of other work, I realized that I would have to give her up. She is nonetheless still flourishing, more successfully and beautifully than ever. Unlike other hostesses who entertain in Washington with government contracts in mind, Gabrielle entertains with government *and* industrial contacts in mind. In both cases, the end product is the same: money.

The "in" hostess during the Johnson years was Barbara Howar, who was the wife of Edmond Howar, a multimillionaire Washington contractor. They were divorced in 1967. She was born and raised in Raleigh, North Carolina, and met Howar at a cocktail party in Washington while she was working as a secretary. Even after becoming the wife of a rich man and entering Washington society, she continued to work. "Not to work," she once said, "is unchic." Although she worked mostly in fashion, she also had a TV interview show on Metromedia's Washington station WTTG, interviewing everyone from Supreme Court justices to theatrical personalities. The show put her in the unique position of promoting, by television exposure, authors, politicians, and others who, as a result of their appearances, felt beholden to her. She later teamed up with Joyce Susskind on a television discussion program that was universally panned as boring.

This was unlike Barbara Howar. The woman had tremendous energy, great push, unlimited audacity. She could be utterly irritating, but she was never a bore. In March 1970, Barbara Howar led the Women's Liberation siege on the *Ladies' Home Journal* in New York, making her way into the office of editor John Mack Carter and telling him what was wrong with his magazine. This was more like her.

Barbara's parties—she preferred to call them gatherings—were off-beat and kooky. In 1966, as E. William Henry was resigning as chairman of the Federal Communications Commission, Barbara gave a Batman party for him at a Georgetown "girlie" bar called Tomfoolery. Guests were asked to come in appropriate costumes. Her social set at the time was the beautiful people left over from the Kennedy crowd and the younger Johnson group, and there was a lot of tomfoolery. Barbara was a beautiful person herself, and sexy. Jerry Ford once said to me: "Barbara Howar has got a tongue that must have gone to college." Others thought differently about Barbara's tongue. She could also be sarcastic, snide, vicious, with a few well chosen words.

Barbara Howar got to know the Johnsons in 1964 when she became one of the Ladies for Lyndon at the Democratic Convention at Atlantic City. On the campaign train, she pinch-hit for Ladybird's hairdresser;

and with her drive and wit and flair for clothes she captivated the Johnson girls. She was always close by with helpful hints. She helped with Lucy's wedding. With a White House passkey at the family level, Barbara was extremely popular and powerful during her "reign." Because of her Democratic affiliations, the Nixon Administration edged her toward the sidelines, though not completely. She was frequently dated by Henry A. Kissinger, Nixon's Assistant for National Security Affairs, one of the three or four most influential men in Washington and one of the most sought after bachelors for parties.

Kissinger often went to parties at the apartment of Anna Chan Chennault, the Peking-born widow of General Claire Lee Chennault, the Leader of the Flying Tigers during World War II, and he learned not to take Barbara Howar there. The two women loathed each other, perhaps because they knew they were sisters at heart. Anna Chennault became part of the Washington scene in 1959, about a year after her husband died. She bought into his company—the Flying Tigers, an air cargo line—and became a working vice president. She was also purportedly a registered agent of the governments of Formosa and South Vietnam. A Republican, she was in social limbo from 1960 to 1968, although she was fairly active as a lobbyist. It was during this period that she developed her close friendship with Tom Corcoran, a New Deal Democrat who had spent a lifetime in Washington as one of the capital's most powerful lobbyists.

After spending an eight-hour day at her office, Mrs. Chennault entertained evenings at her luxury duplex apartment in the swanky Watergate Towers. She too never gave a party without a purpose. Anna secured her role in Republican circles by raising over a quarter of a million dollars for the Nixon campaign in 1968. Not long after the Republicans took over, the Flying Tiger Line was awarded a lucrative trans-Pacific cargo route and airmail contracts. This perhaps was just coincidental, although such things rarely are in Washington.

Widely known around Washington as a Vietnam hawk, Anna Chennault was close friends with both President Thieu and Vice President Ky, though the two men themselves were hardly friends. In the early fall of 1968, she tried to sabotage the Paris peace talks by persuading General Ky to change his mind about going to Paris. On learning this, President Johnson blew his stack, and therafter he referred to Mrs. Chennault as the "Dragon Lady." She was the Dragon Lady, in a way. Small, around five feet tall, she wore an air of intrigue as though it were an Oriental perfume. Slippery and mercurial, she was also fierce and forceful. When ever I was near her, I kept expecting Sidney Greenstreet to show up and slip her the combination of the Fort Knox vault.

One night at a party at Patricia Chatham's, I happened to approach Anna Chennault while she was talking to Waller Taylor, and I heard her say: "Everybody knows why we're in South Vietnam and that we have to stay there."

I couldn't let that pass, so I said: "I don't know why we're in South Vietnam. Why are we?"

She shot a snarl at me and said: "You are stupid!" I started to retort, but thought better of it.

Mrs. Chennault doted on publicity. She invited members of the society press to her parties and she freely passed out copies of her guest list to the press in advance. Among her close friends and frequent guests were J. Edgar Hoover, Attorney General John Mitchell, Senator Russell Long, Henry Kissinger, Senator Barry Goldwater, C. I. A. Director Richard Helms, the Chinese and South Vietnamese ambassadors, plus many more of this ilk. Jerry Ford once said to me: "At Mrs. Chennault's, you see all the most important people in Washington, even some prominent Democrats. She really is important, Bob."

Mrs. Chennault's detractors said she mainly ran a salon for Vietnam hawks, of whom there were plenty in the Nixon Administration as well as in the Pentagon. The detractors also said that if the Vietnam war ended tomorrow, Mrs. Chennault's power and popularity would diminish the day after. But some of these detractors were competing hostess-lobbyists who were invited to the White House as often as Mrs. Chennault was, so perhaps the denigration was more hope than fact.

A hostess-lobbyist who would never have to worry about her future was Louise Gore, who was to the manner born. She was the daughter of H. Grady Gore, who headed a real estate investment business that owned apartment buildings, hotels, and restaurants. All four of the Gore children were associated with the multimillion-dollar family company. The family was active in politics. The one-time Democratic Senator Albert Gore of Tennessee was a second cousin. Louise was a hardcore Republican.

A completely political animal, Louise had been on the staff of the Thomas E. Dewey national campaign headquarters in New York in 1944. She was the head of the Dewey Button Girls in 1948. From 1954 to 1959, she traveled more than 300,000 miles organizing women's clubs for the Republicans. In 1962, she was elected to the Maryland State Assembly; in 1966, she be-

came the first woman to be elected to the Maryland
State Senate. In 1967, she introduced her old friend
Spiro T. Agnew to Richard Nixon at a meeting in New
York. Agnew had already come out for Nelson Rockefeller for President, so there must have been more than
a few anxious moments as the meeting began. But
Louise Gore knew both men well, as men and as politicians, and apparently her matchmaking worked. Politically, Louise was known as an extreme reactionary.
Some of her friends said that she stood just to the right
of Attila the Hun. Oddly enough, she was close to John
and Bobby Kennedy, the three of them all loving a good
political battle.

Louise Gore was a member of the Maryland delegation to the 1968 Republican National Convention in
Miami. She was chairman of the Nixon-Agnew campaign in Maryland and chairman of the women's division of the United Citizens for Nixon-Agnew. She was
also chairman of Agnew's Vice Presidential reception at
the inauguration. Louise liked to identify herself as "the
sensible advocate for Women's Liberation." She worked
as vice chairman and legislative chairman of the National Women's Party to get the equal rights for women
amendment passed by Congress. She urged President
Nixon to appoint women to key posts in government,
advising him to seek out women who were already active and outstanding in their fields—judges, doctors,
lawyers. Nixon followed through by appointing her the
ambassador to UNESCO.

Louise had tried to help Francis Kellogg get his own
appointment to an ambassadorship, entertaining for him
in Washington in 1969 and later. He finally became, as
we have seen, special assistant to the Secretary of State
for Refugee and Migration Affairs. After she became an

ambassador, Louise complained to Kellogg that she was not being allowed to give her own speeches, that the State Department people were always peering over her shoulder. She didn't like that a bit and she told the President so. She said that if she were going to stay on in her post she intended to speak her own mind.

Such a formidable woman could move mountains in Washington. The only entertaining that Louise did that was not political was the poker games she enjoyed with a few close friends and occasional fetes for charity. Everything else was business. She had her axes to grind, usually of a political nature, and she knew how to bring the right people together to get things done. By birth, by experience, and by heavy contributions to campaigns, she had come to know all the right people, and she was amazingly effective. Besides her political interests, she was part owner of the Jockey Club Restaurant with her brother James and her sister Mary Dean, the widow of Gordon Dean, who had been chairman of the Atomic Energy Commission. The restaurant, for a while the "in" place to dine, was in the Fairfax Hotel, owned by the Gores. Louise entertained at the hotel, at her house in Annapolis, and she held her charity benefits at the family estate—Marwood—near Potomac, Maryland. She also had an apartment in New York. A restless schemer and plotter, she nevertheless had her good side. One day, for example, while touring a mental hospital, she observed that the windows were, for the protection of the inmates, placed so high on the walls that little light came in and nobody could see out. Louise had renovations made which corrected these faults but still provided protection, and she did so at her own expense.

There is, for that matter, a good side to some Washington parties, depending on who is giving them. This category is not overcrowded, however. The Paul Mellons would head the list. Whether they were giving a small dinner party at home or a big party that required the main hall of the Mellon Museum to hold it, their guests never felt like part of the furniture or parts of a plot. On the list, as well, would be Kentucky Republican Senator John Sherman Cooper and his wife Lorraine. Mrs. David E. K. Bruce. Kay Graham, publisher of *Newsweek* and *The Washington Post,* a no-nonsense woman whose low-key, relaxed gatherings were attended by people she considered interesting, not influential.

With few exceptions, I never went to a Washington party without the feeling that I was working overtime. When I first started lobbying in Washington, I went to some parties because I was curious, but most of the time I went because I felt obligated. After I worked my way down the receiving line and said hello to personal secretaries who were making mental notes on who showed up, I'd look for a side door and head back to New York. But after my name got into the papers and I became "bad news" to a lot of people, the invitations stopped. It was a relief.

When Abraham Lincoln defined the Union as a government of, by, and for the people, he omitted one word: rich. Lobbying and public relations have taken me into the homes of some of the richest people in this country. No matter where I found them—New York, Newport, the Hamptons, Washington, Miami, and Lexington, Kentucky—I found them to be deadbeats, hypocrites, bigots, and so condescending to anyone they consider beneath their class that when they shake your hand you are supposed to feel that you have just received a papal blessing. And yet these are the same people who, because of their money, wield vast influence, controlling a terrifying majority of the country's politicians at all levels. Many members of Congress are in Washington today because some multimillionaire once recognized them as ready and willing tools eager to rise above their middle-class backgrounds. The gratitude these politicians express when they're allowed to socialize with the rich verges on adulation. I once arranged for Jerry Ford and his wife to spend the Kentucky Derby weekend at the home of a Lexington multimillionaire, and Ford came back absolutely starry-eyed. For days, all he could talk about was what kind of thank-you gift to send.

Most members of Congress come from middle-class backgrounds, and generally they have little exposure to real wealth until they become politically promising. If they don't already know it, they soon learn that money —which happens to be the social denominator in this country—buys power. It is this simple equation that explains why many of our politicians are so easily corruptible. I know this because I have had my share of experiences with the corrupt rich.

In February 1964, for example, I met one Dwight Deere Carter, an heir to the John Deere tractor millions. He had been named after his maternal grandfather, Dwight Deere Wiman, who had been a famous Broadway producer. The boy's mother was Trink Wiman, and she had married William Carter. The marriage had ended in divorce. Trink Carter had then married William Wakeman, and at the time I met their son, they were living in Palm Beach. With parental consent, young Dwight had joined the U.S. Marine Corps at the age of seventeen, an impulsive act he had promptly regretted. Over the next three years, he had gone AWOL a number of times and had often been in trouble with his superiors. In December 1963, he had been in a car accident and suffered a serious leg injury. He was convinced that the Navy doctors at Camp LeJeune, North Carolina, where he was stationed, were not giving him proper treatment. With about two years of his enlistment still facing him, with extra time for his AWOL periods, Dwight wanted desperately to get out of the Marines.

I met Dwight through mutual friends. They asked if I could do anything to help get Dwight out of the Marines. I realized that I was too new at lobbying to accomplish anything at that level by myself, but I offered to talk to Nathan Voloshen. Voloshen's eyes lit up as I gave him the background. He knew that Dwight's family was still in the tractor business and that an uncle, William F. Hewitt, then president of John Deere, was heading a fund-raising committee of industrialists for Johnson's Presidential campaign that year. Voloshen was confident he could help Dwight, but he said that it would cost "at least $5,000 plus."

Since Dwight was still a minor, I felt that a final decision on something like this would have to be made by some older member of the family. Before I called Trink Wakeman in Palm Beach, I phoned her mother, Mrs. Mimi Wiman, at her Park Avenue apartment. Mrs. Wiman met with me and said that although she was sympathetic, she felt this was her daughter's problem, not hers. I contacted Dwight's father. Carter said that, in the first place, he no longer had any money, and, in the second, he felt Dwight should stay in the Marines— perhaps they would shape him up. I called Trink. To my surprise, she was willing to go along if Voloshen could get Dwight a medical discharge on psychiatric grounds.

There must be some truth to the adage that it takes one to know one because, when I told Voloshen about Trink's questionable plan, he would have no part of it at all. He had a plan of his own. He wanted Dwight to sign three $10,000 promissory notes, payable to me and dated after his twenty-first birthday. Whether Dwight would be out of the Marines within the five months that remained until his birthday was not as important to Voloshen as that piece of paper that was supposed to be tantamount to legal tender. Dwight signed.

Voloshen went to work, which meant that he put House Speaker McCormack's office to work. I had lunch one day with Voloshen and Martin Sweig at the Speaker's table in the House dining room when Voloshen discussed the Carter case with Sweig. Sweig offered to turn loose the powers of the Speaker's office for $2,500. Voloshen said he would pay. I never found out if the payment was actually made, but Voloshen insisted several times that he had paid Sweig out of his own pocket. McCormack's office certainly became active, with letters and telephone calls to Camp LeJeune and Marine headquarters in Washington. A memo to the commandant of the U. S. Marine Corps in Washington, from W. J. Van Ryzin, commanding general of the Second Marine Division, Dwight's outfit, noted, on April 18, 1964: "As a matter of additional interest, it is understood locally that the office of the Speaker of the House of Representatives has more than once contacted Headquarters, Marine Corps, on Carter's case." This was an understatement. Dwight Carter and Speaker McCormack had in fact met during this period. They were both Catholics, and this seemed to be the bond between them. Carter wrote McCormack several personal letters and McCormack seemed pleased when he mentioned them to me. They got me into the act myself. Usually once or twice a week I went to North Carolina to let Dwight know how things were going and to sound things out locally. I was their errand boy, delivering written and verbal messages to officers of the corps from the Speaker. The main resistance to Carter's release seemed to come from a Captain Norris, who was head of the naval hospital at Camp LeJeune, and his main concern seemed to be the treatment of Dwight's injured leg. I told Dwight these trips were costly; he offered to cover the expenses after he was twenty-one and came into some money. The funds for the trips had been advanced by Ancky Revson Johnson, a friend of Carter's mother, whom I wanted to reimburse. Ancky had given me the money, feeling it was particularly heartless of Trink to turn her back on her son at a time when he most needed her.

From various things Nathan Voloshen said, I gathered that his energies on Carter's behalf were aimed at much more than $10,000. Carter's relatives were still running the huge John Deere Company, and Voloshen had his eye on the company as a future client. But despite all the pressures emanating from McCormack's office, the Marine Corps still refused to budge. Then I remembered that I knew Evelyn Larson, one of the few women to become a commodore in the U.S. Coast Guard. She was no longer in the service, but I knew that having attained that level in the military hierarchy she would be well connected. I also knew that the military would be more likely to do for one of their own what they would not do for an outsider like the Speaker of the House of Representatives of the United States. I went to her. Out of this, Dwight Carter was permitted to go to New York to be examined by Dr. Milton Wilson, the noted orthopedic surgeon, who independently determined on May 13 that Carter was not fit for active duty in the service and probably would not be for an indefinite period. On May 28, 1964, Carter was discharged with a general discharge under honorable conditions because of physical disabilities.

A couple of days later, Nathan Voloshen called me, very excited. "Have you heard the good news?" he said. "Carter is out."

"I know," I said. "I was with him last night at El Morocco."

"Did he say anything about the money?"

We had squared on the travel expenses. "No. I'll put through the promissory note in July."

"Don't forget it."

I put through the note. It bounced. Voloshen was furious. For over a year, he hounded me to get the money out of Carter—on the telephone, in letters which I still have, whenever I ran into him around New York or Washington. As angry as he was about not getting the Carter money, Voloshen said he was even more upset over having given Martin Sweig the $2,500, and he brought up Sweig as often as he brought up Carter. I talked to Carter about it, but he felt Voloshen really hadn't done anything for him. Carter said he was willing to give Voloshen two or three thousand dollars, but no more. Voloshen wouldn't settle. In 1965, in an effort to bring the problem to an end, I wrote to Trink Wakeman at Palm Beach and gave her the full story. In reply, her lawyer said that if I persisted in trying to collect the note she would notify the authorities that what I had done had been accomplished with the aid of political influence. I dropped it. I'd also, by this time, had my fill of Nathan Voloshen and his hysterics, and so for the better part of a year I avoided him, rarely setting foot in his New York office, until in May 1967, Wels began pleading with me to bring Voloshen and Eddie Gilbert together.

Thus I began to learn graphically how painful it is for a very rich person to part with a buck, regardless of how desperate the situation may be. In 1967, Mimi Strong and Gus Ober, then still working for Mimi, told me that one of their clients was thinking of going into politics in Kentucky and was looking for a public-relations man to handle the press during his campaign. He was David Morton Trapp, a handsome, witty, and intelligent man, who had made a fortune in real estate development in the Lexington area. Then in his forties, he had an income of around $80,000 a year whether he worked or not, and he never had to work hard. His decision to go into politics was more than a whim; he felt he could be of service. A Democrat more by habit than conviction, he did not want to enter Kentucky politics via the state's Democratic machine.

When I met him, Trapp had already entered the primary for the Democratic nomination for governor of Kentucky, running as an independent without the official party backing. He had called in an expensive political consultant from California, but nothing right seemed to be happening. During our first conversation, Trapp said: "I want to be in politics, but not if I have to mortgage my income and my ideals. There must be an honest way to do this."

I said: "Mr. Trapp, I was beginning to think I'd never hear a politician talk like that. I'll work with you and I don't want any fee for it."

He said: "I never thought I'd hear a public-relations man talk like that."

Before I went to Kentucky for the first time, Mimi Strong told me that David Trapp's wife was one of the most beautiful women she had ever seen. She had been Juliet Combs. Her father, Leslie Combs, is the millionaire owner of Spendthrift Farm, the country's leading breeder of thoroughbreds, and the innovator of big-time syndication of thoroughbred winners. My visit had been timed to coincide with the Kentucky Derby. David Trapp picked me up at my Lexington hotel and took me to a typical pre-Derby cocktail party. There must have been 500 people there. Glancing at the door at one point, I saw an extraordinarily beautiful woman come in. I asked David: "Isn't that your wife?"

He looked. "Yes. How did you know?"

"Because she's the only really beautiful woman here today."

With the exception of the Trapps, Frank McMahon (probably the richest Canadian alive), and the newspaper publisher Jack Knight, virtually everybody I met in the Kentucky horsey set was both a bore and a bigot. Knight, I found, was an intelligent and sensible man who went to Kentucky to buy and sell horses, and although he mingled with the so-called "beautiful people," he did not share their views. But the rest of this financially and politically powerful group seemed to contain no equalitarians. These people had homes all over the world and, according to the season and the track, would virtually move, as a group, from one state to another or one country to another, associating only with their own kind.

Among the horsey set were Cornelius Vanderbilt Whitney, John Hay Whitney, his sister Mrs. Charles Shipman Payson (owner of the New York Mets), Mr. and Mrs. Theodore Gary, Burnett Robinson (whose hobby was marrying rich women), Barbara and George Headley, Philip B. Hofmann (chairman of the board of Johnson & Johnson); John Hanes (ex-Under-Secretary of the Treasury), John Olin, and many more. Around Lexington, the crowd gathered at the Idle Hour Country Club and the Hunt Club. I have never known an acknowledged Jew, Negro, or Catholic to get into this club—or any other of this crowd's water places, such as

Miami's Indian Creek Island—unless he happened to get in through the back door—that is, unless he worked there. The patrons were strictly white Protestants.

In June of 1967, when I had just returned from a campaign swing with David Trapp through western Kentucky, he took me to a private party at the Idle Hour Club. I already disliked the crowd. Their attitude on the surface was one of fixed benevolence to all. They bestowed their glazed smiles and tepid conversation on each other meaninglessly, dutifully kissing cheeks or patting backs no matter how many times a day they ran into each other at the races or the auctions or the parties. The men invariably greeted each other with the pat and: "Hello, buddy boy." It was all so phony. They were influential people, they knew it, and they made a point of trying to get by on influence. Even David Trapp, who was the only person in that Kentucky set that I really admired, annoyed me when he said several times: "I can do a lot for you, Bob. I know a lot of important people. They need a public-relations man for the social affairs they throw. They need to know somebody like you in Washington. I can do a lot for you."

At the party that night, one of the waiters—all of whom, of course, were black—drew me aside to discuss David's candidacy. Pointing to the crowd, he said: "These people don't give a damn about me. They don't realize times have changed. When I go to the polls to vote I want to know what a man's going to do for me. I want to know what Mr. David is going to do for me."

Before I had a chance to answer him, Burnett Robinson, who was standing with David, motioned to this waiter and yelled: "Hey, nigger, come over quick and give me another drink." The waiter looked at me, hurt and embarrassed, and he hurried to Robinson. His question, I'm afraid, had been answered.

That same evening, I happened to be standing several feet away from Mary Lou Whitney, Cornelius Vanderbilt Whitney's wife. She seemed to be perturbed and upset. I saw her beckon to Mimi Strong, who went over to her, and although she thought I was out of earshot, I heard her say: "Mimi, is Bob Winter-Berger Jewish?" Mimi nervously and quickly assured her that I wasn't. Suddenly I understood how that waiter felt. I thought of what the first great black, vaudevillian star, Bert Williams, had said, when asked if it was difficult being black. "No," he said, "it's no disgrace to be black, but it *is* very inconvenient!" How applicable I thought his comment was, as I paraphrased his quote in my mind, substituting the word Jew for black. No one, I thought, was ever given a medal for being a Jew.

What struck me as most ironic, however, was that this same Cornelius Vanderbilt Whitney had been the confidant of several Presidents, and that he, like all these other wealth-ridden people, was in a sense running the country. He was typical of those who were doing the least for it but getting the most out of it.

For example, all of them, or virtually all of them, were involved in the business of breeding and racing horses. Officially, it was a business, but it was also a legal tax dodge. All the breeders had to do to prove they were in business was to win a race once in a while. One way of accomplishing this was to send their horses to new tracks where they faced inferior competition and could set track records while earning some money. The breeders also sold horses to each other at puffed-up prices, exchanging credit and debit slips instead of cash.

This way, they satisfied the tax laws which required them to show that they were actually doing business and turning a profit within a period of five years. Otherwise, it was a losing proposition because of the great expenses of property, maintenance, staff, travel, and anything else clever accountants could think up. Regardless of how much a breeder earned from his other business interests, he could start his annual income tax report by writing off the breeding as a loss and thereby save huge taxes. In most cases, the only breeding that is done is in the in-breeding of the bigoted crowd.

In January 1968, Haden Kirkpatrick, publisher of racing's bible, *The Thoroughbred Record,* and his wife gave a small dinner party at the Pavillon Restaurant in New York. During dinner, we all started discussing the state of national and international affairs. Haden turned to me and said: "The trouble is and always has been Franklin Delano Roosevelt. He got us in the Second World War on the wrong side." I was speechless.

Several days later, back in Washington, I recounted this story to Mildred Leonard, for many years Jerry Ford's private secretary. Before I could add my personal reaction to Haden's remark, Mildred looked up at me and said: "You know, he's right, Mr. Winter-Berger." I was even more amazed, hearing this in the Capitol of the United States from the secretary of the House Minority Leader.

Haden Kirkpatrick always reminded me of what is said about most rich, well-born, old-line Southerners. They are raised to hate the blacks, to hate the Jews, to hate the Catholics, and always to be hospitable and courteous. One night some of the Kentuckians, including Haden, were in New York and I joined them for a night on the town. We all decided to go to Raffles. As we were about to descend the staircase to the private club, up came some black men who, judging from their dress, were presumably representatives of an African embassy to the United Nations. Haden stopped and said: "I refuse to go anywhere where they serve niggers."

That was not an isolated experience. In 1969, on the weekend after the Annual Flamingo Ball, Mrs. Theodore (Pat) Gary invited me to a party for the racing crowd at the Indian Creek Club on Indian Creek Island, a restricted island development just off Miami Beach. True to form, the late Harry Guggenheim, who certainly qualified as a wealthy breeder, was not invited because he was Jewish. Marilyn Breer, one of the crowd, told me Guggenheim's daughter was invited because she had intermarried and no longer had a Jewish name. I knew Marilyn about as well as I knew the rest of this group, which was casually, and so I was surprised when she called me in New York a few weeks later. She had a problem.

Marilyn Breer lived in a palatial mansion in Grosse Pointe, Michigan. She traveled a great deal and dressed in the best of taste and the highest style. Born Marilyn Wall, she was the daughter of the founder of the Wall-Colmonoy Corporation, alloy manufacturers who supplied parts to Detroit's auto industry. She had married —and divorced—William Breer, the son of Carl Breer, one of the founders of the Chrysler Corporation. For years after her divorce, Marilyn had been the girlfriend of an investment banker with government connections who provided her with all the plush niceties of life despite her own income of about $50,000 a year. The problem Marilyn had could have been resolved by him, but she chose to bring it to me.

Marilyn's twin sons, Albert and Carl, were at that time—in 1968—twenty years old, and they were in danger of being drafted because poor grades were threatening their scholastic deferments. Actually, Carl was still in high school in Connecticut and Albert hadn't passed a course since entering Lansing Community College two years before. Their energies, it seemed, were directed toward cars and girls rather than academics. Marilyn wanted them to keep their deferments, and she asked if I could do anything about it. I said I would look into it. She asked what my efforts would cost. I estimated expenses at around $400 and I set the fee at $2,500. She agreed to both.

I took the problem to Jerry Ford, and he suggested that I approach the assignment at the state level. I got in touch with Jack Slater, head of the Michigan Republican State Finance Committee. Slater felt that something could be done, provided that Marilyn made a contribution to the committee of anywhere from $1,000 to $2,500. Marilyn also agreed to this.

While these developments were taking place, I got a call one night from David Trapp. David's attempt to win the Democratic gubernatorial primary in Kentucky had failed, but he and I nonetheless continued to be friends. I told David about my efforts for Marilyn Breer, and he said: "I appreciate what you've done for me, but I hope you're not doing this free for Marilyn." I told him I wasn't and outlined the agreement. He said: "If I were you, I'd make her pay in advance."

"All right," I said. "I'll ask her for the expense money. But I can't ask her for the fee until I've done the job."

"That's up to you," he said. "Don't say I didn't warn you."

I should have known better. I had associated with the rich enough to know that most of them are traditionally deadbeats. Because of their names, they can easily get credit, but they are slow to pay up when bills become due. The middle class and the poor have to pay in advance, but being rich seems to carry the privilege of living off other people's patience. Time and again I have been stuck with the check or an unpaid bill with someone whose income was a generous multiple of mine. Even so, I decided to risk it again.

After three or four telephone calls Marilyn sent me the $400. On April 25, Jack Slater introduced me to Charles M. Smillie, a member of a local Detroit draft board. Smillie agreed to review the boys' files, but he soon washed his hands of the case. The school records of both Breer boys were so bad that Smillie refused to do anything for them. Over lunch, Jack Slater then approached a Colonel Holmes, head of the Detroit draft board, who recommended Slater to Alfred May, a prominent Republican attorney who was, among other things, a counsel to the Ford Motor Company. May thought that he might help. Knowing that the Detroit draft board would be none too favorably disposed toward the boys, he had both appeals transferred to the Lansing draft board on the premise that Albert was attending college there. His tactics worked, because both boys kept their deferments. Marilyn subsequently retained May to represent her in her long-running and bitter estate battle with her sister.

On May 22, 1969, I received from Marilyn the following letter:

Dear Bob,
    Just a brief note to thank you for your assis-

tance regarding my twin sons. The attorney Mr.
May has been successful in his efforts to obtain a
re-classification for them on a College deferment
basis.

Your friend's choice of Mr. May shall also
prove to be of value to me in the Estate matter,
at least it looks very good at this juncture.

Thank you again Bob for aiding me in this
most important matter. I need not tell you that
the twins are also very grateful to you.

Sincerely,
Marilyn Fraser Wall

I inspected the envelope several times but did not
find the $2,500 check. I wrote her, thanking her for her
note and reminding her about the fee for myself and the
contribution to Slater. No answer. I wrote her again and
again. I thought of suing her, but a friend reminded me
of how Trink Wakeman had reacted when I tried to get
her to fulfill Dwight Carter's agreement, and he suggested: "Why don't you forget it Bob? Why don't you forget that whole pack of hypocrites?"

I decided to heed his advice and I did. But I did not
have to leave New York to watch the rich at their shenanigans. I had known the Skouras brothers for years
and was often a guest in their homes. Like so many rich
people engaged in a variety of business, the Skourases
made campaign contributions to both political parties,
so that whoever won would owe them favors. Howard
Hughes does it. H. L. Hunt does it. The American
Medical Association does it. And so did the Skouras
brothers. It is a kind of insurance. A big operator may
have to deal with one party at the national level, another at the state, and a bi-partisan group at the local level.

So the big operator donates to the campaign of everybody he may come in contact with in any area of government. The recipients know this, and it doesn't bother them. After all, the money is all that really matters. And the candidate who wins knows he can depend on more of it from the same two-faced sources. To be sure, there is nothing illegal about accepting it. This game is one of insurance for a businessman, the playing-it-safe for future favors, no matter who wins. Like the others, the Skourases always played it safe. In 1968, however, I learned that this time the Skourases were supposedly going to give the majority of their support to the Republicans because Spiro T. Agnew, also of Greek origin, was a close friend.

Among the business interests of the Skouras brothers was a shipping company, the Prudential Line, with offices at 1 Whitehall Street, Manhattan. The Skourases got into shipping almost by accident. Back in the 1950's, their friend and fellow Greek immigrant Stephen D. Stephanidis, who founded Prudential, encountered financial difficulties, and the Skourases helped him out by investing in the company. By the time Stephanidis died in 1960, other investors had sold out and the Skourases found themselves the sole owners. The line had two oil tankers out on charter and eventually acquired five freighters which plied the lucrative cargo routes to the Mediterranean. Sailing under the American flag, the Skourases had to pay higher taxes and higher wages than did shippers under foreign flags, but this was the only way they could get government subsidies to build new ships and government contracts to haul government cargo. Both the subsidies and the cargo contracts were acquired through Washington friendships which the Skourases had made by heavy campaign contributions to both major parties over the years. Spyros's son, Spyros, Jr., ran the shipping company, under his father's watchful eye.

It was a family company, with the two brothers and their children on the board, and no written partnership agreements. After George Skouras's death, Spyros began almost immediately to try to oust George's two daughters, Thana and Odyssia, from the board. In time, the two daughters went to court; the case is still pending.

In 1966, Spyros Skouras became a client of Louis Nizer, the famous lawyer-writer, and Nizer was associated with someone equally famous, at least in Washington circles: Arthur Krim, who was very close to Lyndon Johnson and also head of the President's Club, comprised of outstanding campaign contributors. It was generally acknowledged that President Johnson rarely did anything without consulting Krim. In April 1968, the Department of Commerce announced that the government was going to subsidize the building of eleven new ships. Five of them would be Prudential Line vessels. Outside of war time, nothing like it had ever happened to a shipping company before. And something else happened that was even more amazing. Spyros P. Skouras, who had spent all his life making movies, was elected vice president of the Committee of American Steamship Lines, a powerful Washington lobbying group. The president was William T. Moore, head of Moore-McCormack Lines, who had a lifetime of shipping behind him.

In March 1968, Lyndon Johnson stunned the country by announcing that he would not seek renomination by his party and would not accept it under any circumstances. This cleared Hubert Humphrey's path for the

job he had always wanted so badly. But Humphrey
waited a month before declaring his own candidacy. He
knew he had his problems. In the public's mind,
Humphrey was associated with the Johnson policies,
and the public's opposition had driven Johnson to premature retirement. As Vice President, then, Humphrey
was not a free man when it came to criticizing his boss.
But Humphrey had another, equally serious problem:
he had no money. A political campaign at any level
costs money, and the higher the office the more it costs.
It was generally conceded by Washington insiders that
Humphrey would not risk his image in primaries against
the popular Eugene McCarthy and Robert F. Kennedy,
which would spare him that expense; but still he had to
conduct a campaign of some kind, and it would cost
plenty. To find out what kind of backing he could expect from party regulars, Humphrey began making
quick trips all over the country, addressing any audience he could attract and attending small gatherings
where the guests were expected to write checks or at
least make a pledge.

One such gathering was scheduled to be held in New
York on May 23. I heard about it from Nathan Voloshen. Humphrey was to make a speech that night, opening his campaign headquarters at the Biltmore, and this
gathering was to take place before it. The organizer was
the late Edwin L. Weisl, a partner in the law firm of
Simpson, Thatcher, and Bartlett, and a leader of the
New York regulars. Weisl, who was the Democratic
National Committeeman for New York State, had taken
over the Cottage Room in the Hampshire House, on
Central Park South, and had invited about sixty people
for cocktails. In politics, it is rarely enough just to make
a campaign contribution: it is better to make it in per-

son so you can show that your heart is really in it. Voloshen, who preferred regulars to reformers, was convinced that Humphrey would get the nomination at the Chicago convention, and he said it would be a smart move on my part to attend the party. He was going, of course, and I went with him. On the way, he told me that Spyros Skouras would also be there. Knowing how Skouras felt about Spiro Agnew, I was surprised at this.

We arrived early. Skouras was indeed there. Eddie Adams had him in tow. Also present was Richard Wels, the attorney on the Eddie Gilbert case. We sat around chatting and having a drink. Wels wandered off to talk to Meyer Davis, the orchestra leader, who had come in.

Then Adams, who had maneuvered Skouras behind a trellis-screen, said: "Mr. Skouras, when Mr. Humphrey comes in, how much are you thinking of giving him?"

"I don't know," Skouras said. "What should I give?" Adams threw it back. "How much do *you* think?" Skouras said: "I've got $10,000 with me."

"That's good," said Adams. "Check or cash?"

"Cash."

"Good. I prefer it that way."

The room started filling up. Soon Hubert Humphrey came in, accompanied by his executive assistant, William Connell. As they moved around the room, the assistant made the introductions. When they got to Adams, Eddie cut off the introduction with an impatient: "We've met, we've met."

"Of course," Humphrey said. "Hello, Eddie. How've you been?" They shook hands and moved on to Skouras for the introduction and a few words.

Before Connell could move on, Adams took him by

the arm and said: "Mr. Skouras has something for you." I saw Skouras hand Connell an envelope which Connell put into a jacket pocket, nodding his thanks. Then Adams said: "Mr. Skouras occasionally has some problems in Washington."

"Yes, of course," Connell said. "We'll get together." He then looked at Skouras. "Call me anytime."

"I will," Skouras answered.

Connell moved on.

I remembered the government award of the subsidy of five boats which was awarded to Prudential only a month before, and I wondered if this was a campaign contribution for favors done, or favors yet to come.

Hubert Humphrey remained in the room another fifteen minutes, chatting amiably and ebulliently with the guests who made their way to him. Then he thanked us all for our presence and our support, and he left. After that, pledges were solicited and speeches were made.

Humphrey had been in New York two days, opening campaign headquarters, speaking at rallies, attending banquets, and his movements were thoroughly covered by the press. Oddly enough, there wasn't a word in the news media about the cocktail party. Although I subsequently received a thank-you note from Weisl, the gathering itself seemed to be an off-the-record event for persons concerned with vested interests.

On February 2, 1969, *Time* magazine broke the news that Spyros Skouras was going to buy the 24-ship Grace Line from W. R. Grace & Co. The purchase was to cost $44.5 million, and two New York banks, Marine Midland and Chase Manhattan, were backing the deal. Still pending was the approval of the Maritime Administration, which was part of the Department of Commerce. This sort of multimillion-dollar business transaction does not happen overnight. It takes months of negotiations, with every possible obstacle scrutinized long before hand; and if any government regulations are involved, the people who must make the decisions are sounded out well in advance, to eliminate any last-minute surprises. Even the outcome of a Presidential election cannot make any real difference. The network of the Establishment is too well intertwined for the outcome of any election to make much difference to anyone except the party workers whose patronage jobs may be in jeopardy. There is more political power on Wall Street than on Pennsylvania Avenue. There is more political power in Detroit or Chicago, in Pittsburgh or Dallas, than on Capitol Hill. There is more political power in the blue-grass fields of Kentucky than in the marble halls of Congress. Government is in effect a closed shop, and you've got to pay to get in. In this case, Hubert lost, but Spiro won, and Spyros got his boats.

Shortly after leaving office, President Eisenhower made a secret speech, on October 3, 1961, to the faculty and students at the Naval War College. His remarks were not made public for almost ten years. Regarding the military-industrial complex, against which he had already warned the country, Eisenhower said:

> If we are going to solve this particular problem, we have got to recognize that the nation's resources are not unlimited. The Congressman who sees a new defense establishment in his district; the company in Los Angeles, Denver, or Baltimore that wants an order for more airplanes; the services which want them; the armies of scientists who want so terribly to test out their newest views—put all of these together and you have a lobby.

You also have pay-offs, kickbacks, bribes, blackmail, and double-dealing. The heart of the problem is the professional politician's seemingly insatiable need for campaign funds. A study by the Citizens' Research Foundation of Princeton, New Jersey, made public in June 1971, revealed that the cost of the 1968 political campaigns was a record $300 million, 50 percent higher than the cost of the 1964 campaign.

As staggering as the Princeton foundation's figures may seem, I have reason to believe that the total given fell far short of the real mark. Just taking a few examples of which I have personal knowledge or documentary proof gives some idea of the size of that "dollar gap." For instance, the foundation listed Vincent de Roulet, the son-in-law of Mr. and Mrs. Charles S. Payson, whom Richard Nixon appointed U.S. Ambassador to Jamaica, as contributing $44,500 to the Republican campaign. The foundation listed the Paysons' contribution to the same campaign at $28,000. Waller Taylor, who ought to know, told me that Mrs. Payson had contributed at least $250,000 to get de Roulet his ambassadorial appointment. This works out to $177,500 more than the foundation attributed to de Roulet and the Paysons combined—which is quite a gap.

Or take Francis L. Kellogg, whom the foundation listed as a $25,000 contributor to the Republicans. Kellogg, as we have seen, was a client of mine, and I followed his various, dogged effort over the years to obtain an ambassador's post somewhere—anywhere!—in Africa, an effort which cost him $125,000. In this case, the foundation's figure was only $100,000 shy of the mark. If these two prime examples are at all typical, then the foundation's $300 million figure may only represent the visible portion of the iceberg.

The foundation stated correctly that the Democrats had trouble getting donations in 1968 and had to resort to borrowing. Two of the most generous lenders were identified as John Factor, the California realtor better known in the underworld as Jake the Barber, and Lou Wasserman, head of MCA, Inc., each of whom put up $240,000. Nineteen others were listed as having "loaned" $100,000, among them Edwin L. Weisl, New York attorney and former Democratic National Committeeman for New York, who also was the host at the fund-raising cocktail party for Humphrey at the Hampshire House previously described. As the foundation pointed out, these loans are seldom repaid when the ticket loses, or at best are repaid a few cents on the dollar. But reports of this kind, too, can be deceptive. For example, Maurice H. Stans, Nixon's Secretary of Commerce, reported that he had contributed only $4,500 to the GOP in 1968. Actually, as chairman of the New York State Republican Finance Committee that year, he helped raise millions for the party, and the sources and amounts of all the donations will doubtless never be known.

One area of great expense in any election is the primary. The higher up the political ladder the contest is, the more the primary will cost. Unless a candidate has the backing of his party, he has to look elsewhere for financial support. If he has to look beyond the circle of his relatives and friends, he exposes himself to the support of strangers whose big donations will put him into political debt to them if he is elected. A lot of good men, like David Trapp of Kentucky, have dropped out of politics at the primary level either for the lack of funds or for their refusal to sell out to the local machine. More recently, Fred Harris, who should have had a fair opportunity to try for the Presidential nomination, had to throw in the towel, because of his failure to raise enough money to carry on.

The vast and often unrecorded millions spent on every election campaign would soon deplete Fort Knox itself. Because of countless loopholes in existing campaign laws, however, most candidates can, by hook or crook, raise money. But the sums required spawn all kinds of abuses, such as the following:

1. Many contributions are made by corporations— illegally. An officer of a company can personally contribute a flat sum to a candidate, but then his corporation can provide printing services, personnel, and automobiles. All these expenditures are then illegally deducted and charged off as business expenses by the corporation. Illegal as it may be, it is done all the time.

2. Many contributions are made in cash. Illegal, yes, but done all the time.

3. Dummy committees are formed and, in most states, are not required to account for funds received or spent, so there is no way to trace the money to its source. Not right, but done all the time.

4. Contributions are disguised as loans that are never repaid, or are repaid only in part. Illegal, yes, but done all the time.

The big donors who hide behind these subterfuges are essential to the success of the modern multimillion-dollar Presidential campaigns. A candidate has to have the money to pay salaries, travel expenses, advertising, and stadium rentals before he can get his campaign moving. Small donations really don't help much. Fund-raising dinners pay off only when the candidate can attract a big enough crowd willing to pay enough per ticket to cover the high overhead of such events and still leave a hefty addition to the campaign fund. The candidate for the Congress or the White House soon finds himself beholden to a handful of extremely wealthy people who can produce the cash from their labyrinth of private interests—which is why they have such power over the candidate when he wins.

Marvin D. Rosenberg, a well-known Democratic fund raiser in the 1960 and 1968 campaigns, said: "That's the way American politics is paid for, for better or worse." It can only be for worse, and the situation will deteriorate even further unless the system is changed.

Big spending does not always guarantee victory, of course. In 1970, Howard Metzenbaum in Ohio and Richard Ottinger in New York both won the Democratic primaries for the Senate essentially on big TV spending. During the campaign itself, Metzenbaum and Ottinger continued their big spending. Both lost the election, however, and the fact that they had gone overboard on their spending was cited by some pundits as perhaps the reason the voters had reacted against them. Later, in November 1971, the voters of New York State reacted in a similar way to the Bond Issue (a vain effort to keep New York City's 30¢ transit fare) at the polls, despite a prestigious TV campaign in support of the bill and despite the unholy alliance of Nelson Rockefeller and John Lindsay in its support. The voters, in these obvious examples of monetary superiority, seemed to resent the pressure and voted their preference.

Money wouldn't be such a problem in politics if there were national laws that put a ceiling on the amount that could be spent for a particular office. The May 17, 1971 issue of *Time* magazine suggested that a floor be set for each particular campaign and that public funds be provided to qualified candidates. But *Time* also suggested that candidates be allowed to accept any additional campaign contributions they could get. Though this would be helpful to some extent to the newcomer with few connections, it would still give the advantage to the machine-backed incumbent, or a rival who had the support of vested interests. As things are, no candidate could run for Congress on the small donations he receives from the average voter. A big campaign requires big money, which comes from only a few sources—and always with strings attached. If there is to be fairness and honesty in a political campaign, then all candidates must have equal time, equal space, and equal opportunity.

Every candidate who manages to get his name on the ballot has a right to a reasonable exposure of his person and his ideas. To preclude dishonesty, each candidate should be provided with an amount based on the vote cast in the previous election for the office he seeks. Thus, through television and other means, he would have an equal opportunity to apprise the electorate of his plans, his program, and his personality. The money would be appropriated by Congress.

No changes in legislation pertaining to campaign costs would be valid without appropriate and stringent controls of primary spending and fund raising. If we cannot have all campaigns underwritten by public funds, then we must have full disclosure of private resources. As fate would have it, the legislation we need must be written by legislators who don't want it. Being in office is half the victory in a campaign; thus incumbents are reluctant to write laws that might give challengers an even break. Too often, newcomers to the Congress are too eager to join the club, too ready to drop the ideals which turned them to politics in order to gain favor with senior members who pull the strings and make committee appointments. There have been some exceptions to this rule recently in

such outspoken, apparently sincere, and courageous
public servants as Congresswoman Shirley Chisholm,
Congresswoman Bella Abzug, Congressman Edward
Koch, Congressman Paul N. McCloskey, Senator Mark
Hatfield, Senator Edward Kennedy, former U.S. Attorney General Ramsey Clark, former Congressman Al-
lard Lowenstein, and former U.S. New York Attorney
Robert Morgenthau, among others, or such oldtimers as
former Supreme Court Justice Arthur Goldberg, Senator Mike Mansfield, and Senator J. W. Fullbright.

People like these can lead the crusade to change the
laws that regulate our elections, so that our politicians
do not have to prostitute themselves to the rich and the
powerful—and to lobbyists—in order to get the money
to stay in office. It was long known on Capitol Hill that
Nathan Voloshen was a nonregistered lobbyist, an
influence peddler, and a fixer. And, in fact, a lot of people did not want to be seen with him. But, for years, nobody wanted to take any action against him. Nobody
wanted to rock the boat. It finally took someone with
the guts of a Robert Morgenthau to start the action. But
the job remains unfinished. When you want to get rid of
the rats in your house, you don't just set traps and fumi-
gate, you plug up the holes they use to enter.

In his State of the Union address to the Ninety-second Congress on January 22, 1971, President Nixon
tried to convince the members to support his various
programs by throwing a challenge at them. He said:

What this Congress can be remembered for is
opening the way to a new American Revolution
—a peaceful revolution in which power was
turned back to the people—in which government at all levels was refreshed and renewed,

and made truly responsive. This can be a revolution as profound, as far-reaching, as exciting as
that first revolution almost 200 years ago—and
it can mean that just five years from now
America will enter its third century as a young
nation new in spirit, with all the vigor and fresh-
ness with which it began its first century.

For me, the irony was in knowing that if there was
one man in the country who was fully aware that this
"challenge" was an infantile daydream, that man had to
be Richard M. Nixon. Nixon had been in politics for
most of his adult life. He knew all the ins and the outs
of it. He knew its rottenness. And he could not have
been unaware that, among the members of the Congress
seated in front of him that night, there were several who
should have been behind bars. Nixon himself has never
had the reputation of being the boy scout of Washington politics. Fourteen of the persons he named ambassadors were listed by the Citizens' Research Foundation
as among the heaviest contributors to his campaign—
that is, they were pure political appointees. And if
Nixon had no idea that Waller Taylor was running
around the country, both before and after the election,
picking up contributions, then maybe Nixon needed another long session with Hutschie.

In any case, the President stood there and told the
members of Congress that he expected them, perhaps
by some miraculous baptism, to abandon their old ways
of pay-offs, double-dealing, kickbacks, favoritism, and
vested interests, and come out of it all looking like an
interfaith College of Cardinals. Immediately after the
speech, radio and television news commentators generally agreed that Nixon's "driving dream" was impossi-

ble, and that Nixon had merely been laying the ground-
work for his re-election. If the country was still a mess
late in 1972, Nixon would at least have a potential
scapegoat: the Congress.

As I watched Nixon's speech on television that night,
I recognized in his audience a number of Senators and
Congressmen with whom I had worked during my five
years in Washington as a lobbyist, and I found myself
wondering whether there were any truly free men in the
room. It costs money to run for public office—the higher the office, the higher the cost. And it costs money to
remain in public office. Unless an elected official is in-
dependently wealthy—and few of them are—he is
bound to incur a variety of indebtedness the longer he
stays in office, in terms of money, favors, and support,
and his best means of liquidating these debts is to use
his office—that is, his influence—to pay them off. Besides the money needed to pay off his own debts, the
Congressman is expected to raise money for the national committee of his political party. He does this in the
same way: by using his influence. Every member of the
Congress is appointed to several committees which supervise the operations of federal agencies, federal programs, and federal policies. The more important the
man—sometimes in seniority, sometimes in connections, sometimes in experience—the more important his
appointments and the greater his influence. Similarly, as
the man's influence increases, so does that of his staff
members who can speak and act in his name. And yet
every time a member of Congress pays a debt he creates
a new one, sinking deeper and deeper into the bottom-
less pit of political vulnerability.

A man needs connections in Washington to get certain things done, not done, or undone. All that has been

said about Washington bureaucratic red tape is true, and the important man and his vested-interest group will not waste time with it. They know that the members of Congress, usually through committees, control the budgets for all federal departments and agencies. They also know that one telephone call by the member of Congress, particularly if he is on the right committee, gets things done—or undone—a lot faster in the federal departments and agencies than going through the endless governmental red tape, the way ordinary mortals do. They know this is going to cost them something, and they are ready and willing to pay in order to save time and get results. And if for any reason they cannot make direct contact with the member of Congress whose influence they need, they hire someone who can. They hire a lobbyist.

The upshot of all this is that the government of the United States, which is supposed to be of the people, by the people, and for the people, has become a government of the rich and the powerful. This may not be news. But unless something is done about it, unless a serious effort is made to return to the spirit of Lincoln's dictum, it seems questionable to me that the country can long endure.

The biggest business in the world is the United States government, and part of every Congressman's job is to try to get some of that business into his district. This means jobs for the people back home, better living standards and, presumably, higher profits for local companies. If the Congressman is personally successful, his constituents are happy and he gets re-elected. All this is normal and proper. What is improper—and far too often the case—is the methods by which Congressmen get the government's business into their districts. They use back-scratching: you vote for my bill, and I'll vote for yours. They use political debts. They use political pressure. And if they are powerful enough, they use self-help.

In most cases, the political skullduggery is not that obvious. Punishable crimes are committed, sometimes involving the underworld, sometimes bordering on treason, always violating the codes of ethics which both the Senate and the House have composed for themselves but have very rarely enforced. Only the greenest members of Congress are unaware of the wheeling and dealing going on around them. And they tend to become enlightened as soon as they have a little influence. As long as they can keep their noses clean and their names out of the gossip columns, they are safe. The real crime in Washington, then, is not doing something wrong; it is getting caught.

There is a group in Washington for whom friendship is a tool of their business. They are the lobbyists. In one area, lobbying is a good thing. Across the country there are numerous special-interest groups—in business, in industry, in unions, in farm organizations, in the sciences—and often the ground rules by which these groups operate are determined by federal legislation. When legislation affecting any of these organizations comes before a Congressional committee, the organization can and should be represented by an expert who can express its views and wishes. This is lobbying in its purest form. It is also lobbying in its rarest form. At its best, lobbying is the voice of the people, aimed directly at elected representatives. Proper lobbying helps to accomplish the following:

1. Inform the public and the Congress on various issues so that both are well aware of the facts before legislative action is taken.

2. Ventilate sore spots in legislation.

3. Stimulate public debate.

4. Forecast how a particular piece of legislation will probably work in practice.

The First Amendment to the Constitution guarantees the right of the people to petition the government for redress of grievances—which includes the right to lobby. If you have ever written a letter to your Congressman expressing your opinion on any given subject, you have lobbied. Sometimes a group of people of similar mind may decide they can get a better hearing in Washington if they hire an expert to speak for them to Congressional hearings, and this too is good and proper lobbying. It is important for a Congressman to know how his constituents feel about a specific issue; and if their feelings are strong enough, he may find the courage to stand up against his party if its policy and his constituents' feelings differ. For example, both Democrats and Republicans in the Congress finally found the courage to stand up against first a Democratic and then a Republican administration on the handling of the Vietnam War—after enough of their constituents voiced their opinion on the matter. This has never happened before in the history of the country. It shows that power can truly be the people's when they demand it.

Unfortunately, this form of lobbying is the exception rather than the rule in Washington. For the most part, Washington lobbying today is on a man-to-man basis— the lobbyist on the one hand and the Representative or the Senator or the appointed functionary on the other. The lobbyist is the only one without any responsibility

to the general public. The Senate would never think of
approving a Presidential appointment without a thorough investigation of that person's background. And yet
the Secretary of the Senate and the Clerk of the House
will register a lobbyist without the slightest check into
his background or connections. Moreover, the lobbyist
need not register at all these days, as long as he can
operate under the protective cloak of some political
bigwig, such as Nathan Voloshen and others did out of
Speaker McCormack's office, as Eddie Adams did out
of President Johnson's office, or as Waller Taylor is
doing out of Richard Nixon's office. In such cases, it
isn't really lobbying but influence peddling. The distinc-
tion is more than a matter of semantics.

Influence peddling generally occurs when some matter is too pressing to proceed through so-called normal
channels. If the Congressman concerned cuts through
red tape and acts on the matter, there is usually a
payoff, whatever its disguise. It may be a donation to
the Congressman's campaign fund or a donation in his
name to his national committee; it may also be stock in
a corporation, often issued in the name of a relative. Or
perhaps a relative gets a good job in the company involved; perhaps the Congressman's house gets a new
paint job or a new car in the garage. Maybe his family
gets an unexpected trip to Europe, or the Congressman
happily finds himself booked on a lucrative speaking
tour. But in one form or another, there is a payoff.

On September 8, 1970, Mrs. Helen Delich Bentley,
chairman of the Federal Maritime Commission, attended a conference in the Manhattan offices of the late
Spyros Skouras, who was then board chairman of the
Prudential-Grace Lines, Inc. The purpose of the meeting was to raise funds for the campaign of Republican

C. Stanley Blair for the governorship of Maryland. The meeting had been suggested by Vice-President Spiro Agnew. Blair had been an aide to Agnew. No shipping executive with any sense would have turned down an appeal from her for a political contribution. Even so, Blair lost to Democrat Marvin Mandel.

What was significant about the episode was the fact that men and women in public office, including the Vice President, deliberately set out to get political contributions from a highly specialized area of business which depends greatly on the federal government for subsidies.

In 1970, the chairman of the House Committee on Merchant Marine and Fisheries was Representative Edward A. Garmatz of Maryland. Although a Democrat, Garmatz was an old crony of both Agnew and Mrs. Bentley, and he had been playing both sides of the political fence in Maryland and Washington for years. In January of that year Garmatz hired as special counsel to the committee Ralph E. Casey, completely ignoring the fact that Casey had been a registered lobbyist for the American Institute of Merchant Shipping only a year before, and had also been its executive vice president. This was like inviting the Trojan horse into your home. It certainly limited the chances of the American people for a fair shake on how their tax money is used. Not surprisingly, Congressman Garmatz turned out to be one of a number of Congressmen who had accepted illegal campaign contributions from shipping companies. In September 1970, Justice Department files showed that Garmatz had received $1,500 of the $6,000 which the American President Lines, Ltd. and the Pacific Far East Line had made in illegal campaign contributions during the previous year. Named as the-recipient of $1,000 was Senator Warren G. Magnuson, Washington Democrat and chairman of the Senate Commerce Committee. The Garmatz and Magnuson committees approved subsidy programs for these companies, but the vote that actually issued the money for the two companies was taken by the House Appropriations Subcommittee, headed by John Rooney of Brooklyn. Further checks from the shippers went not only to the top four members of this committee, but also to other Congressional leaders such as House Minority Leader Gerald Ford and House Majority Leader Hale Boggs.

Over the years, I came to the conclusion that the votes of members of Congress are influenced by six different pressure groups, in the following order of importance:

1. Special-interest groups back home.
2. Executive Department persuasions—the President, the Pentagon, State Department, Agriculture, etc.
3. Washington's paid lobbyists.
4. The simple desire to remain in office.
5. Personal economic interests.
6. Dictates of their own conscience.

Ralph Nader has said that if power is to be exercised responsibly, it has to be insecure, that those exercising it have to have something to lose. To paraphrase this, fewer Congressmen would engage in crooked deals with lobbyists if they knew there were a chance the news might leak back to their constituents. Since there is little risk of exposure by their peers and cohorts, many Congressmen feel secure and act irresponsibly. Exposure, then, is essential to reform. Voters have a right to know what their Congressmen are up to. They have a right to know who visited him during the day, and for what. They have a right to know how their Congressman voted on the hundreds of minor bills that are rushed through Congress every session in a daily atmosphere of a tobacco auction. Many of these bills are lobbyist-instigated, giving tax breaks, contracts, or a wide variety of other possible privileges to special interests. These are the bills which the Congressmen back-scratch into law. Any Congressman who has a source of income other than his salary as a Congressman would have difficulty acting as a free man when faced with legislation which might be detrimental to him personally or to the source of his income. Voters therefore have a right to know all the sources of income of their Congressman so that they can clearly determine when he has voted in favor of the public good or in favor of his own interests. There is little chance that this information will be volunteered by Congressmen, but voters have the right to demand all of it.

Another possibility, which I had suggested to Congressman Bennett during our meeting, was that members of Congress should divest themselves of *all* sources of outside income as soon as they were elected.

Bennett frowned and said: "If Congressmen could have no outside incomes, what kind of man do you think we would have in Congress? We would have men from the bottom of the ladder."

Reflecting on his words, I wondered why practically every member of Congress requires a pay-off from a lobbyist before doing what he is already being well paid to do. The Congressman will tell you that he needs money for his campaign funds, and everybody agrees that campaign costs are out of control. The Ninety-first

Congress, controlled by Democrats, passed a bill limiting campaign spending, but President Nixon vetoed it. The general assumption around Washington was that since Republicans have less trouble raising money than Democrats, there was no point in giving the Democrats that kind of break. But since I already knew that my own clients had to make donations to the campaign funds of Republicans as well as Democrats, I couldn't go along with that.

But I could and do go along with Nixon's recommendation to the Ninety-second Congress that the members clean up their houses. I fear, however, that it will never be an inside job. The clean up will come only when an aroused people demand it—and before the people can make the demand they must have some idea of what has really been going on.

Here is a basis for such a clean up.

1. There should be no fund-raising by cabinet members or commission heads, so that they will not owe anyone any allegiance in return for a campaign contribution.

2. Former lobbyists, with long-time industry ties, should not be appointed, as a reward for party loyalty, to goverment posts controlling industries for which they have lobbied in the past.

3. Corporations and unions should not make campaign contributions. All existing loopholes should be plugged and penalties for circumventing the law as it is rewritten should include jail penalties rather than merely a fine and censure. The giver and the receiver should be equally responsible. Ignorance should be no defense as it ludicrously is now. No one is going to contribute without letting the candidate know what he is doing.

This has never happened, and it never will. The law should provide for the recall of an erring legislator and the calling of a new election.

4. In no way should campaign contributions be treated as a tax deduction.

5. The support of the rich should be limited to one party only. Campaign contributions should not be hedged, under penalty of law.

6. The backgrounds of lobbyists should be checked and their actions regulated. There should be no unregistered lobbyists in Washington.

7. Campaign contributions and expenditures should be limited.

8. Under penalty of law, no money in excess of a certain limit should be given or lent to a campaign committee. Ignorance of a contribution should not absolve the candidate. The 1925 Corrupt Practices Act, and the 1946 Legislative Reorganization Act, must be merged and rewritten completely to strengthen and give meaning to the law.

9. The electorate should be taxed from 50 cents to $1 a year for campaign expenses which would be put into a campaign kitty. There must be a campaign financing law which will help all and not just a few, the ceiling being commensurate with the office. But it must be remembered that even if the American people are eventually taxed per capita for a campaign kitty, the money that each candidate derives from this fund *must* be his only source of campaign income. To allow him to go to outside sources for extra income for a campaign would simply be giving the wealthy and well-connected politician the upper hand, thus reopening the loopholes.

And, most importantly, no matter what campaign reform laws are enacted by the Congress for their public funding of campaigns, they must all include a provision that puts a ceiling on total campaign spending in each category. Unless these two overall limits on total campaign spending are included, the legislation enacted would have little effect on all of the existing abuses.

10. Successful candidates for Congress should, like appointed government officials, divest themselves of all outside business interests, including stockholdings and money-earning real estate.

11. Campaign contributions to any one party and any one candidate should be limited and should, under penalty of law, be strictly enforced. There should be no dodges. "Dummy" fund-raising committees for a candidate must be outlawed.

12. Free television time and advertising space should be made available to all candidates on an equal basis.

13. There should be full disclosure of all political contributions. Stringent laws must insure that all money collected or contributed for a political campaign actually goes to the campaign and does not find its way into a politician's pocket.

14. All government contracts must be made public. No provision for waivers or private funds should remain secret.

15. The decision of all waiver review boards must be made public, together with the reason for the waiver.

16. Limits on expenditures for primary campaigns should be instituted.

Nathan Voloshen was indicted, but the entire system

of political influence peddling was also indictable. It was the system that spawned him. Voloshen's misfortune was that he got caught. But he was just a small example of what has been going on in Washington: he was the 1969-70 scapegoat. I would prefer to think that this was not the case. I would prefer to think that Voloshen's indictment was only the beginning of a new era of housecleaning. That is what I am sure Robert Morgenthau intended. He wasn't allowed to go as far as he wanted or planned, but it is encouraging that he was able to go as far as he did. Let us hope that the forces of political reform will continue to prevail, as they did in this case, and not end with the smug satisfaction that "right has been done." It has, but in only this one case. The death of Voloshen in the fall of 1971 should not be the end of it.

I became a lobbyist in 1964 because it seemed to me to be a natural extension of the public-relations work that I was doing in New York, and I quit lobbying in 1969.

In 1970, Jack Anderson, journalistic heir to Drew Pearson, published an account of Voloshen's Washington machinations, involving me in them. Similar accounts appeared in *Life* magazine and *The New York Times*. But, I knew that only a small part of the full story had been told; only the surface had been scratched. There was too much to tell, too much that people had a right to know about in full and candid detail. So, after long and careful thought, I decided to write this book—in the hope that it would bring about substantial changes in our electoral laws.

I still believe in this country. I still believe that the people can save it. But in order to do so they have to be made aware. The cloak of secrecy which shrouds so much of government must be lifted. "Secrecy," once noted former FTC Commissioner Philip Elman, "is the bane, not the lifeblood, of the administrative process." This element of secrecy can be eliminated. But it will not be done until the people demand it. In my opinion, the hour is getting late. It's five minutes to midnight and we don't have much time left . . .